The Official Student Doctor Network MCAT Pearls

A high-yield review of the pre-medical sciences

Alfa Omar Diallo, M.D., M.P.H.

mcatpearls@mac.com

F.E.P. International
Coralville, Iowa

The Official Student Doctor Network MCAT Pearls
A high-yield review of the pre-medical sciences

By Alfa Omar Diallo, M.D., M.P.H.
mcatpearls@mac.com
www.mcatpearls.com

Copyright© 2007
www.medrounds.org/mcat-pearls/

ISBN: 0-9769689-9-1

Cover Design by Daniel Hunt at www.sidekick-design.com

Published and distributed by MedRounds Publications, an imprint of F.E.P. International

www.medrounds.org

F.E.P. International
941 25th Avenue, #101
Coralville, Iowa 52241
United States of America

Contents

List of Figures

List of Tables

Preface

What?

The Student Doctor Network MCAT Pearls will provide aspiring physicians with an affordable alternative to prepare for the MCAT. With the free, online version (*www.mcatpearls.com*) attracting over 160,000 visitors since 2005, the print version of MCAT Pearls will provide students with a portable version of the successful online content. Written using the AAMC MCAT curriculum as its main foundation, SDN's MCAT Pearls will function as the ultimate companion guide because it can follow pre-medical students from the beginning of their studies and evolve into the ultimate, personalized resource and go-to study guide. The structure of the book was specifically designed for busy pre-meds: a question and answer format that allows for high-yield review - alone or in groups. With ample margins for note-taking, the study guide will invariably evolve into your personalized resource. With a comprehensive table of contents, locating information is simple. With 300+ images and 100+ tables, information is crystallized into the pertinent concepts. Unique also to SDN's MCAT Pearls is the emphasis on providing students with a flexible platform to pull together the voluminous amount of information represented on the MCAT: one which can be used early in their studies and grow into custom tailored study guide, or, one that can be used in last minute review sessions.

Why?

Based on my experience mentoring and teaching pre-meds while at the University of Virginia, I was frustrated to find many aspiring doctors unable to afford expensive commercial products to help them excel on the MCAT. This coupled with volunteerism and public service as activities and personal standards that I've been raised with, the impetus to create a comprehensive study aid that anyone can access was realized.

Who?

I wrote and illustrated the manuscript over the past 3 years. Some background on me... I am a first generation American who is an army-brat raised in a tri-lingual household. I went to undergrad and medical school at the University of Virginia, obtained a Masters in Public Health at Johns Hopkins School of Public Health and now I'm a senior resident in the Department of Emergency Medicine at Johns Hopkins Hospital.

Along the way, several instrumental people have given a significant amount of their time to help develop the text and provide their counsel:

Sally Hanson
North Carolina

Dr. W. Craig Carter
Massachusetts Institute of Technology

Dr. Angel Marti
Columbia University

Dr. Machunis-Masuoka
University of Virginia

Sundar Srinivasan
Johns Hopkins University

Mariana Ruiz
Hamburg, Germany

The Student Doctor Network has also played a critical part in preparing the manuscript and its current state could not be possible without these individuals:

Dr. Lee Burnett, D.O.

Dr. Andrew Doan, MD, PhD

Biology

Anna Peck
Olympia, WA

Feng Zhang
Ithaca, NY

Brandon Luk
Tulane University School of Medicine

Organic Chemistry

Megan Hansell, MBA
University of Delaware

Ai Mukai
Chicago, IL

Olivia Dziadek
University of Houston

Inorganic Chemistry

Jin Jung
Binghamton University

Physics

Brett Batchelor
Louisville, KY

Part I

Biology

Chapter 1

Prokaryotes & Eukaryotes

1.1 Prokaryotes

What are prokaryotes?

Prokaryotes are surrounded by a plasma membrane, and are unicellular living organisms which lack membrane-bound organelles and a nuclear membrane. All prokaryotes have a cell wall surrounding the plasma membrane that protects the organism from drying out (desiccation) and other challenging environmental conditions. Prokaryotes are similar to eukaryotes because they both contain DNA, RNA, proteins and small molecules in their cytoplasm.

What prokaryotes are found in the environment?

1. **Bacteria**, found ubiquitously

2. Eubacteria, found in the soil

3. Archeabacteria, found in bogs and hot acid springs (i.e. extreme environments)

What are three morphologic classifications of bacteria?

The three main morphologic classes of bacteria are *bacilli* (rod-shaped), *spirilli* (spiral-shaped) and *cocci* (spherical-shaped). See Figure 1.1 on page 6.

What are three unique characteristics of bacterial genetics?

1. Bacterial chromosome is circular and is located in the membrane-lacing nucleiod region.

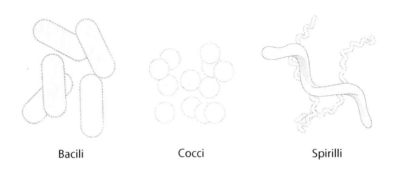

Bacili   Cocci   Spirilli

Figure 1.1: Three morphologic classes of bacteria: Bacilli (left), spirilli (middle), cocci (right). *Public domain image illustrated by Mariana Ruiz.*

2. Some bacteria contain extragenomic information called **plasmids** which are smaller, circular genetic elements. Plasmids help the bacteria survive in adverse environments (e.g. by conferring antibiotic resistance), and replicate independently of the bacterial chromosome.

   - Bacteriophages are viruses that infect only bacteria; they can transmit plasmids or bacterial DNA from one bacteria to another via a process called transduction.

3. Bacteria can incorporate DNA fragments from the external environment into their genomes, i.e. transformation.

How do bacteria reproduce?

By **binary fission**. This simple form of reproduction allows bacteria - given enough food and absence of environmental threats - to replicate quickly and with a particular growth pattern (see Figure 1.2 on page 7):

- Lag phase (a): Bacteria adapt to a new environment

- Log (Exponential) phase (b): Constant rate of cell doubling results in an exponential population growth

- Stationary phase (c): Balance of bacterial growth and death

- Death phase (d): Accumulation of toxic metabolites or lack of nutrients resulting in bacterial cell death and population decline

What four mechanisms do bacteria use to increase genetic variability since binary fission, an asexual process, is used to replicate?

1. **Fast reproduction** - Bacteria reproduce very quickly and, with natural selection of the "fittest" organism, the stronger strain will survive and overcome weaker strains.

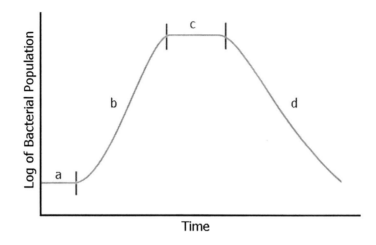

Figure 1.2: Bacterial survival curve: (a) lag phase, (b) log (exponential) phase, (c) stationary phase, and (d) death phase.

2. **Transduction** - The transfer of bacterial genes following phage-mediated lysis of a host cell:

   (a) *Generalized transduction* occurs when a random piece of bacterial DNA is packaged into a phage capsid. After bacterial cell lysis, this phage can transfer the DNA to another bacterium.

   (b) *Specialized transduction* occurs when a phage integrates into a bacterial chromosome. When the lytic cycle takes place, the phage can take nearby bacterial genes with it that can be transferred to a new host when the phage infects a new bacterium.

3. **Transformation** - Incorporation of genetic information into a bacterium by the bacterial uptake of DNA from the environment.

4. **Conjugation** - As close to sex as bacteria can have. A "male" bacteria projects a cytoplasmic extension (a sex pilus) towards a recipient "female" bacteria. DNA is then transferred through the pilus from the male to the female.

Note: These mechanisms can be used by bacteria to obtain or confer antibiotic resistance. Other adaptive mechanisms to environmental stressors can be transferred this way as well.

What is unique about bacterial ribosomes?

Bacterial ribosomes have $30S$ and $50S$ subunits, are not bound to a membrane organelle, are free floating in the cytosol, and generally smaller than eukaryotic ribosomes.

What metabolic pathways do bacteria employ?

Anaerobic (without unbound O_2) metabolic pathways, i.e. glycolysis or fermentation, are found in the oldest strains of bacteria and are an adaptive remnant of having survived in the primordial earth's atmosphere which lacked O_2. With increasing atmospheric concentrations of O_2 over time, strains capable of harnessing O_2 (aerobic) evolved. In addition, bacteria can harness energy from CH_4 and N_2 metabolism.

How do bacteria exist in the environment?

Most bacteria are free-living in the environment outside of other organisms. Still, some bacteria such as *Helicobacter pylori* exist in the stomach as parasites while others live in harmony (symbiotically) with host organisms; e.g. *Escherichia coli* in the large intestine of humans. When bacteria from the environment are introduced into new, favorable environments, e.g. the gastrointestinal tract, colonization takes place and the host gets sick.

1.2 Eukaryotes

What are eukaryotes?

Eukaryotes are unicellular or multicellular living organisms which have membrane-bound organelles and a nucleus enclosed by a double membrane. Eukaryotes, unlike prokaryotes, have chloroplasts and/or mitochondria which are unique energy-producing organelles.

How are mitochondria similar to prokaryotes? What is the implication of this?

They are similar in size/shape, contain DNA and circular chromosomes, synthesize their own proteins, reproduce by binary fission and are susceptible to similar drugs.

These compelling similarities support the *endosymbiotic hypothesis* which states that eukaryotic cells developed a symbiotic relationship with bacteria that have evolved into present-day mitochondria and chloroplasts.

What are four major classifications of eukaryotes?

Protists, plants, fungi, and animals. Of these, animal cells do not contain a cell wall.

How do eukaryotes reproduce?

Sexually, through meiosis which requires two haploid cells (gametes) to fuse to create a complete genome and asexually via processes such as fission or budding.

What is unique about eukaryotic ribosomes?

Eukarotic ribosomes have $40S$ and $60S$ subunits which may be bound to the rough endoplasmic reticulum or may be free floating in the cytosol.

What metabolic pathways do eukaryotes employ?

Depending on the availability of O_2, eukaryotes can use either anaerobic (glycolysis or fermentation) or aerobic (cellular respiration) metabolic pathways.

1.3   Fungi

What type of organisms are fungi?

Nonmotile heterotrophic eukaryotes possessing branched structures (called hyphae) and cell walls composed of chitin which acquire nutrition through absorption from the environment.

How do fungi reproduce?

Asexually (n) or sexually (2n).

- **Asexual reproduction** occurs when conditions are suitable and stable to produce spores. Fungi put great amounts of energy into producing spores (haploid asexual products). Spores are very resistant to unfriendly environments.

- **Sexual reproduction** occurs when spores germinate and grow into mycelia, allowing mating to occur.

What is the difference between molds and yeasts?

Molds are rapidly growing fungi common in colder environments, e.g. bread mold in the fridge, which reproduce asexually.

Yeasts are unicellular fungi common in warmer environments, e.g. baker's yeast, which also reproduce asexually.

"Mold in the cold, yeast in the heat."

Chapter 2

Viruses

What are viruses?

Viruses are obligate intracellular parasites.

What are bacteriophages?

A type of virus that infects bacteria and also is simply known as *a phage*.

The bacteriophages' claim to fame is that they can pick up genes from the bacteria they infect and transfer them to other bacteria (see page 7).

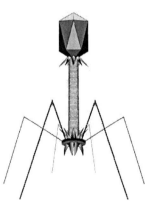

Figure 2.1: Bacteriophage: notice the top portion (icosahedral head), middle section (tail) and bottom portion (plate with tail fibers).

2.1   Viral Structure

Generally speaking, what are two main components of viruses?

A **genome** encased in **proteins**.

- The viral genome can come in the form of DNA or RNA and it can be double stranded or single stranded.

- The proteins that surround viruses are called capsids and can take several forms (helical, icosahedral or complex).

What is an envelope?

Some viruses also have a protective outer covering in addition to the capsid. This envelope is host derived, meaning that by budding from the infected cell, viruses take with them some of the host's envelope - sort of like a vesicle but outside of the cell - which can include host cell membrane glycoproteins, phospholipids, etc.

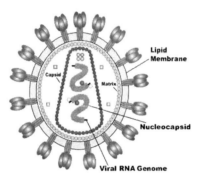

Figure 2.2: The structural elements of a virus: this illustration shows the key components of a virus. For the curious, the virus depicted is HIV (the red dots represent reverse transcriptase, an enzyme unique to the viral family *Retroviridae*, which is capable of converting RNA to DNA). *Public domain image obtained from the US National Insitute of Health.*

2.2   Viral Life Cycle of the Bacteriophage

What are the two life cycles seen in a bacteriophage?

A lytic or lysogenic cycle:

- **Lytic**, coming from the same stem word for lysis, means to cut/split. When a bacteriophage infects a bacterium on a lytic mission, the host cell machinery is used to produce bacteriophage components. Once a critical mass is attained, the bacterial cytosol is filled with bacteriophages and the host cell is sacrificed as it spills open and releases phages into the environment.

- **Lysogenic** cycles are much less barbaric. Here, the bacteriophage integrates itself into the bacterial genome. When this occurs, the bacteriophage is called a provirus and it is replicated with each generation of bacteria. This can occur indefinitely or be triggered by a stress/stimulus to cause the bacteriophage to enter a lytic cycle.

Why are viruses obligate intracellular parasites?

Viruses do not have the machinery to replicate without a host. In the case of bacteriophages, the host is a bacteria, e.g. *E. coli*, and the bacterial ribosomes and machinery are used to generate the parts to produce progeny viruses.

What are the steps of viral infection (on a cellular level)?

1. **A**ttachment onto the cell membrane

2. **I**njection into the cell

3. **R**eplication within the cytoplasm or nucleus

4. **E**xpression of viral proteins

5. **A**ssembly of viral components

6. **R**elease of progeny

What makes the life cycle of retroviruses unique?

Retroviruses have an RNA genome that uses *reverse transcriptase* to turn the genome into DNA (unique among viruses). The DNA genome then integrates into the host's genome (common among viruses).

Chapter 3

The Eukaryotic Cell

Have a working understanding of the cell components listed below. Understand what makes them unique and how they contribute to maintaining normal cell functioning (i.e. homeostasis).

Plasma membrane	Lysosomes
Nucleus	Peroxisomes
Endoplasmic reticulum	Mitochondria
Golgi apparatus	Cytoskeleton

3.1 Plasma Membrane

What is the general function of the plasma membrane?

To serve as a flexible boundary containing embedded proteins that act as transporters and/or channels to allow the passage of specific molecules between the extracellular space and the cytoplasm.

What is the structure of the plasma membrane?

An amphipathic[1], flexible, self-healing bilayer composed of phospholipids with hydrophilic, water-loving heads (phosphates) and hydrophobic, water-fearing tails (lipids).

Hydrophobic lipid tails, aka hydrocarbon tails, are typically fatty acids that have varying lengths and a "kink" from a *cis* double bond. Because of the amphipathic nature of fatty acids, they form *micelles* around hydrophobic substances, isolating them from hydrophilic environments.

Proteins embedded in the plasma membrane function as transporters or channels

---

[1]Containing water loving and fearing moieties.

for specific molecules, serve as adhesion molecules between cells, and function
as receptors to bind extracellular molecules (See Figure 3.1 below).

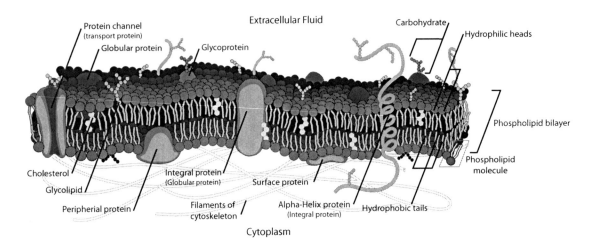

Figure 3.1: The phospholipid bilayer: Schematic three dimensional cross section of
a cell membrane shows a phosholipid bilayer that provides a structure within which
globular proteins are free to diffuse and sugar moieties can be present (as part of
either glycoproteins or glycolipids). A further important component shown is cholesterol which intercalates between lipid molecules and affects membrane fluidity/stability
Public domain image illustrated by Mariana Ruiz..

What is the fluid mosaic model?

An accepted model of cell membrane composition whereby phospholipids and
embedded proteins exist in a two-dimensional fluid plane that constantly glides
over each other.

The fluidity of the cell's membrane is based on several factors:

- *Shorter fatty acid chains* allowing for less steric interaction between fatty
  acid chains, making the cell membrane more fluid

- *Presence of "kinks"* secondary to *cis*-double bonds allowing for less interaction, increasing the fluidity of the cell membrane

- *Presence of cholesterol* decreasing the mobility of CH_2 on surrounding
  fatty acids, thereby making the membrane more rigid and less fluid

	Increased Fluidity	Decreased Fluidity
Fatty acid tail length	Shorter	Longer
Number of *cis* double bonds	Higher	Lower
Concentration of cell membrane cholesterol	Lower	Higher

Table 3.1: Determinants of plasma membrane fluidity.

What are five processes by which substances move across cell membranes?

1. *Simple diffusion*: the movement of dissolved particles from regions of higher concentration to areas of lower concentration (see Figure 3.2 below).

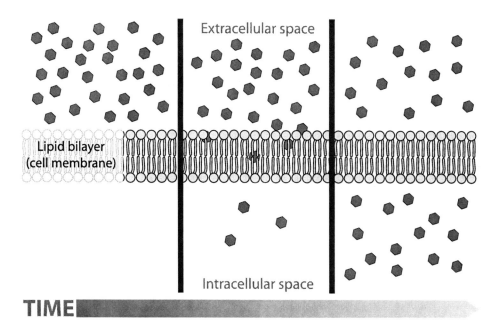

Figure 3.2: Simple diffusion. *Public domain image illustrated by Mariana Ruiz.*

2. *Facilitated diffusion*: the movement of a substance that is coupled with a channel or carrier molecule from a region of higher concentration to an area of lower concentration (see Figure 3.3 below).

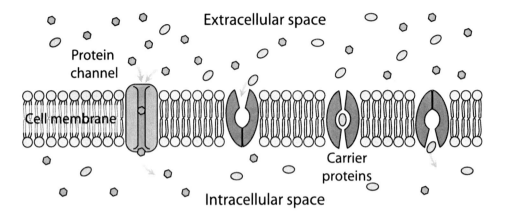

Figure 3.3: Facilitated diffusion. *Public domain image illustrated by Mariana Ruiz.*

3. *Active transport*: the movement of a substance against a concentration gradient, e.g. maintenance of membrane potentials in neurons.

- Energy is required to overcome the concentration gradient. This can be in the form of ATP or from secondary active transport. In secondary active transport, the required energy is derived from energy stored in the concentration differences in a second solute. Typically, the concentration gradient of the second solute was created by primary active transport (i.e. with ATP), and the diffusion of the second solute across the membrane drives the secondary active transport.

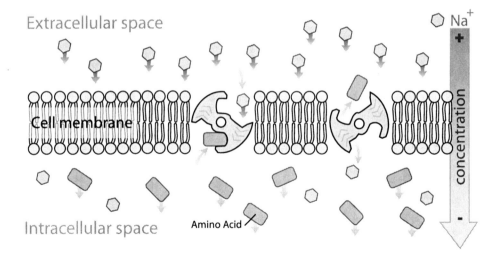

Figure 3.4: Active transport. *Public domain image illustrated by Mariana Ruiz.*

	Particle Movement	Carrier Protein	Energy Required
Simple Diffusion	Down gradient	No	No
Facilitated Diffusion	Down gradient	Yes	No
Active Transport	Up gradient	Yes	Yes
Exocytosis	Intra- to extracellular	No, occurs by fusion of vesicles with cell membrane.	
Endocytosis	Extra- to intracellular	No, occurs by involution of cell membrane.	

Table 3.2: Five processes by which substances move across cell membranes.

4. *Exocytosis*: process by which a cell releases intracellular substances by intracellular vesicle fusion with the cell membrane followed by the subsequent spilling of its contents into the extracellular environment.

5. *Endocytosis*: process by which a cell ingests extracellular substances through cell membrane involutions and vesicle formation. This occurs in two forms:

   - Pinocytosis (ingestion of fluids and small particles like proteins).

   - Phagocytosis (ingestion of large particles like whole cells).

What is osmosis?

The net movement of water from regions of lower solute concentration to areas of higher solute concentration which occurs when:

   - a solute gradient exists across a membrane

   - the solute cannot pass through the membrane

If the membrane is permeable to water, then the movement of water will compensate and rectify the disequilibrium of solute concentrations (see Figure 3.5 below):

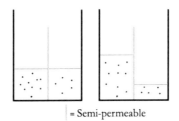

= Semi-permeable

Figure 3.5: Flow of water through a semipermeable membrane to balance solute concentrations: Before (left) and after (right) equilibration.

What is tonicity and how does it effect osmosis?

Tonicity refers to the amount of solute particles in a solution.

Therefore, a hypertonic solution outside of a cell is one in which the extracellular environment has a higher solute concentration than the intracellular environment. Conversely, a hypotonic solution outside of a cell is one in which the extracellular environment has a lower solute concentration than the intracellular environment. In an isotonic solution the extracellular environment has the same solute concentration as the intracellular environment and there is no net water flow.

Based on this and using the rules of osmosis, in a hypertonic environment water will flow out of the cell and in a hypotonic environment, water flow will into the cell (see Figure 3.6 below).

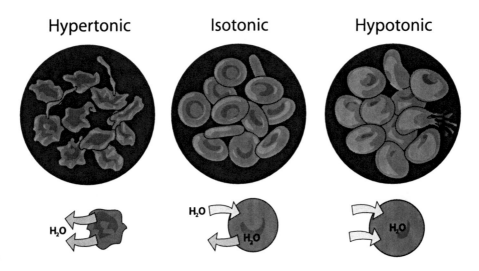

Figure 3.6: In a hyperosmotic environment (top), water will flow out of the cell and the cell will shrink. In a hypoosmotic environment (bottom), water will flow into the cell. *Public domain image illustrated by Mariana Ruiz.*

What are membrane channels?

Proteins which extend across the lipid bilayer with unique polypeptide structures that typically come in two forms:

- Single pass α-helices, responsible for transporting ions and small water soluble molecules

- Multiple pass β-sheets, responsible for β-barrels such as porins

What is the sodium-potassium (Na^+/K^+) pump?

A pump - specifically an ATPase - which swaps 3 Na^+ out of the cell with 2 K^+ into the cell, i.e. an antiport, in the setting of a strong electrochemical gradient for both ions. Think *"Na^+-out my K^+-in"* pronounced *"Nought my kin"*.

As with other pumps that overcome electrochemical gradients, this requires energy by breaking down adenosine triphosphate (ATP) into adenosine diphosphate (ADP). Conversely, if the pump works in reverse, i.e. allows Na^+ into the cell and K^+ out of the cell, ADP is converted into ATP and the pump becomes a energy-currency creating machine.

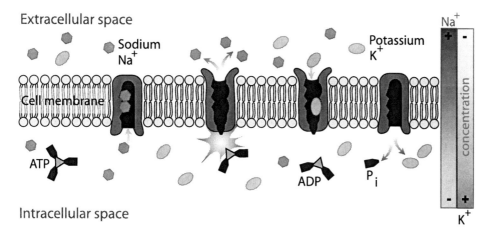

Figure 3.7: Sodium-potassium pump. *Public domain image illustrated by Mariana Ruiz.*

Because there are 3 Na^+ pumped for every 2 K^+, the pump creates an electrical imbalance and contributes to a membrane's electrical charge (membrane potential). More specifically, it generates a negative membrane potential inside the cell.

What is the role of the plasma membrane in maintaining membrane potentials?

Cells which have electrically excitable membranes, including neurons and myocytes, contain voltage-gated ion channels in their plasma membranes which control the flow of cations.

Na^+ and K^+ voltage-gated cation channels are the main ion channels found in neurons. Voltage-gated Ca^{2+} cation channels are also found in myocytes.

What are three plasma membrane structures that allow for cell-cell communication and/or cellular adhesion?

1. *Gap junctions*, a continuous aqueous channel which connects two intracellular compartments and allows for cell-cell communication, e.g. neurotransmitter-gated ion channels (see Figure 3.8 below).

2. *Desmosomes*, button-like points that rivet and anchor cells together (see Figure 3.8 below).

3. *Tight junctions*, a sealing attachment between cells that makes them "water proof" and prevents the passage of almost anything, e.g. the junctions that connect epithelial cells in the intestine to maintain a barrier against the contents of the lumen of the small intestine (see Figure 3.8 below).

Figure 3.8: Three major types of cell junctions: Gap junctions (left), tight junctions (middle), and desmosomes (right). *Public domain image illustrated by Mariana Ruiz.*

3.2 Nucleus

What are notable features of the nucleus?

1. Separated from the cytoplasm by two membranes.

   - This allows a substrate to bind to a plasma membrane receptor, undergo endocytosis, travel through the cytoplasm in a vesicle and bind/fuse with the nuclear membrane without ever coming into direct contact the intracellular cytoplasm.

2. Contains the genetic information of cells in the form of DNA which is packed into chromatin and wrapped around unique proteins (histones).

3. Pores within the nuclear envelope allow for substances to travel between the nucleus and the cytoplasm.

4. Principal coordinator of mitosis, meiosis and protein synthesis.

What is the nucleolus?

A factory for ribosome production and synthesis that is found within the nucleus.

How does the nucleus control protein synthesis?

The nucleus controls protein synthesis by (1) *housing and controlling DNA transcription* to messenger ribonucleic acid (mRNA), and (2) regulating the delivery of mRNA to the cytoplasm through *nuclear pores* for translation into proteins.

3.3 Endoplasmic Reticulum

What is the endoplasmic reticulum (ER)?

A labyrinthine network of membranes that is continuous with the outer nuclear membrane and is located within (*endo-*) the cytoplasm (*-plasmic*).

Individual networks of the membranous tubules and sacs of the ER are called cisternae.

What are the two types of ER?

1. *Rough ER*: ER with ribosomes attached to the cytoplasmic side of the ER; involved in *proteins destined for secretion* and *membrane production (plasma membranes and lysosomes)*.

- Protein synthesis by the rough ER results in proteins destined for secretion within the cisternae of the ER's membranes. Most of the proteins made in the rough ER are covalently bound to carbohydrates to make *glycoproteins*.

- Membrane production occurs by enzymes embedded in the ER which synthesize phospholipid precursors obtained from the cytosol.

2. *Smooth ER*: ER which does not have ribosomes attached to it and is principally involved in *synthesizing* and *detoxification* of molecules.

- Steroid production, e.g. sex hormones by the gonads and cortico-steroids by the adrenal glands

- Hydrolysis of glycogen in liver cells (hepatocytes)

- Detoxification of drugs, e.g. addition of a hydroxyl group to drugs and alcohol to make them more water soluble and able to be excreted

- Ion salvaging, e.g. smooth ER of muscle cells pump Ca^{++} ions from the cytosol and store it in the smooth ER's cisternae for future use

3.4   Golgi Apparatus

What is the role of the Golgi apparatus?

The Golgi apparatus is the organelle responsible for *modifying, packaging, storing* and *shipping cell products*.

The Golgi apparatus looks like a stack of flattened sacs and has a receiving (*cis*) side and a sending (*trans*) side. See Figure 3.9 below on page 25.

Note: Glycosylation of proteins to create glycoproteins occurs in the Golgi appratus

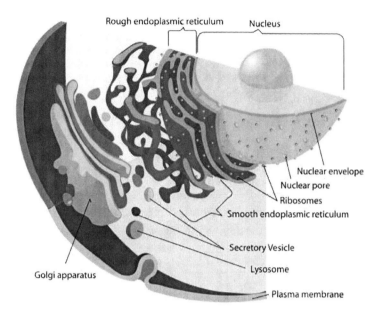

Figure 3.9: The endoplasmic system including the Golgi apparatus *Public domain image illustrated by Mariana Ruiz.*

3.5   Lysosomes and Peroxisomes

What are lysosomes?

Membrane bound vesicles containing hydrolytic enzymes which allow for *intracellular digestion* in an organelle isolated from the cytosol. Macromolecules such as polysaccharides, proteins, fats and nucleic acids are hydrolyzed when lysosomes fuse with phagocytic vesicles.

The lysosomal interior has two notable features:

- It is an acidic environment; the low pH is maintained by a H^+ ion pump

- The low pH allows hydrolytic enzymes to work optimally (hydrolytic enzymes originate from the ER)

Tay-Sachs disease is an example of a lysosomal storage disease whereby patients are missing a lipid-digesting enzyme that leads to intracellular fat accumulation in brain cells.

What are peroxisomes?

Single membrane-bound vesicles which use various substrates to transfer hydrogen *to produce and store hydrogen peroxide* (H_2O_2).

3.6 Mitochondria

What are mitochondria?

Self-replicating organelles which are the *principal site of ATP production.*

Mitochondria contain DNA, synthesize their own proteins and reproduce by binary fission.

Structurally, mitochondria contain an intermembrane space in between an inner and outer membrane. To increase the surface area for cellular respiration, the inner mitochondrial membrane is folded: these folds are called *cristae.* Bathing the cristae, inside the mitochondria, is the mitochondrial matrix.

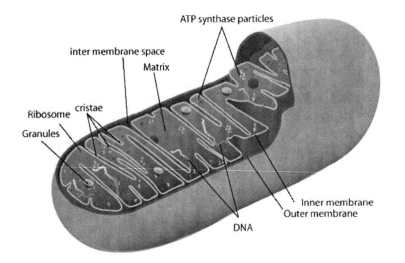

Figure 3.10: Mitochondrion showing its mitochondrial matrix and membrane. *Public domain image illustrated by Mariana Ruiz.*

Figure 3.11: Electron micrograph of a mitochondrion showing its mitochondrial matrix and membrane. *Public domain image obtained from the U.S. Dept. of Health and Human Services/National Institutes of Health.*

3.7   Cytoskeleton

What is the cytoskeleton?

A mesh of protein filaments that provide the cell with a *structural scaffolding*, a *network for organelle transport*, and *a means for cell movement*.

What are the three main kinds of cytoskeleton filaments?

Microtubules (25 nm), intermediate fibers (10 nm) and microfilaments (7 nm):

1. Microtubles (25 nm) are straight, hollow rods composed of α-tubulin and β-tubulin

    (a) Main support filament which serves as scaffolding and a network for organelle transport

    (b) Possess polarity, i.e. they have an orientation in that they grow and shorten only at different ends

    (c) Commonly radiate from a centralized structure called a centrosome (or microtubule organizing center)

    (d) Can serve as a railway for motor molecules, i.e. dyenin and kinesin

    (e) Specialize (only in animal cells) to form centrioles

        i. Appear in pairs that are arranged at 90° angles to each other
        ii. Serve as a template for the 9+2 pattern seen in cilia and flagella (see Figure 3.12 on page 28)

    (f) Specialize to form cilia and flagella

2. Microfilaments (7 nm) are solid rods composed of actin

    (a) Main filament responsible for movement, e.g. muscle contraction

    (b) Elongation/contraction of cellular extensions, i.e. pseudopodia

    (c) Coordinate cell cleavage during cell division

3. Intermediate fibers (10 nm)

    (a) Permanent fixture in the cytoskeleton. Unlike microtubules and microfilaments which assemble and disassemble constantly, these fibers do not change as much. For example, intermediate fibers either provide support in long axon bodies in nerve cells or provide the nucleus with a "cage" of fibers to give it structural support.

    (b) Also found in desmosomes

Cilia and flagella are specialized cytoskeletal structures - what are their function and structure?

Cilia and flagella are specialized extracellular extensions of microtubules which allow organisms to move and/or advance fluids over the cell. See Table 3.3

below on page 28.

The core structure found in both cilia and flagella is a "9+2" microtubule assembly: an arrangement of 9 microtubule doublets surrounding a central microtubule pair. This core structure originates in the basal body (centriole). For a side-by-side comparison of cilia and flagella, see Table 3.3 on page 28.

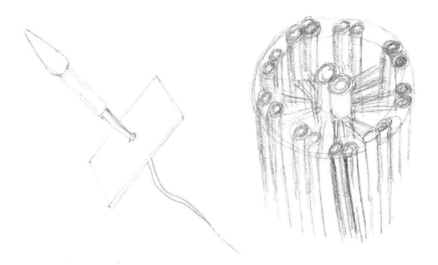

Figure 3.12: Cross-section of sperm flagella: the 9+2 structure.

The 9 doublets surrounding the central pair are attached to each other with side-arms composed of the protein dyenin. With energy provided from ATP, dyenin changes conformation and "walks" up or releases from the adjacent doublet - all these in conjunction allow for the movement of flagella and cilia.

	Cilia	Flagella
Motion pattern	Stroke and recovery, like oars	Undulating motion, like a snake
Human example	Ciliated epithelium lining the trachea	Sperm
Numbers per cell	Thousands	One
Length	Shorter (~10nm)	Longer (~100nm)
Ultrastructure	9+2 pattern	9+2 pattern

Table 3.3: Side-by-side comparison of cilia and flagella.

Chapter 4

Mitosis & Meiosis

Mitosis and meiosis are concepts which should be learned together. Generally speaking, meiosis is the process of cell division used to make sperm or egg cells, while mitosis is the process of cell division used by every other cell in the body. Just some FYI, but when you study mitosis, understand what makes each phase of cell replication unique, and, when you study meiosis, keep track of chromosome numbers during each cycle of replication.

4.1 General

What is a genome?

A cell's genetic library is in the form of DNA. When half the number of chromosomes are present, e.g. sperm or egg cells, the genome is in its haploid form and abbreviated as n; when the whole complement of chromosomes is present, e.g. every other body (somatic) cell, the genome is in its diploid form and is abbreviated as $2n$.

What are the two forms of DNA found in cells?

In inactively replicating cells, DNA takes the form of *heterochromatin*, a dark, densely-appearing substance in the nucleus of cells. In an actively replicating cell, DNA takes the familiar form of chromosomes: highly ordered, organized strings of DNA with an X-like shape that represents two sister chromatids connected at a centromere; called *euchromatin*.

What is mitosis and meiosis?

Mitosis is a $2n$ to $2n$ genome division seen in somatic cells, preserving the parental chromosome number and genetic information in daughter (progeny) cells.

Meiosis is a $2n$ **to** n **genome division** seen in gamete (sperm or ova) production which halves the parental chromosome number and creates genetic diversity in daughter cells.

4.2 Mitosis

What is the purpose of mitosis?

To create identical diploid $(2n)$ progeny (daughter) cells from diploid parent cells $(2n)$

The cell cycle has two general phases, a *growing phase known as interphase* and a *replication/mitotic phase known as M phase*. Although all cells can exist in interphase, some cells never replicate and do not enter the M phase. When this happens, it is called "growth arrest", aka the quiescent stage (G_o).

Interphase has three parts:

1. G_1 Phase

   - Centrosomes have formed

   - Centrioles exist in the centrosomes of animals

   - Increase in cytoplasm and organelles to support daughter cells

2. S Phase

   - Chromosome replication

3. G_2 Phase

   - Continued increase in cytoplasm and organelles to support daughter cells

$$Interphase \begin{cases} G_1 \\ S \\ G_2 \end{cases}$$

Growth arrest occurs in certain types of cells and is called quiesence or the G_0 state. Examples of highly specialized cells that have lost the ability to divide include nerve cells, muscle cells and red blood cells.

The M Phase has four parts:

1. **P**rophase

2. **M**etaphase

3. **A**naphase

4. **T**elophase/Cytokinesis

$$M\ phase \begin{cases} P_{rophase} \\ M_{etaphase} \\ A_{naphase} \\ T_{elophase} \end{cases}$$

Think: "P MAT"

4.2.1 Prophase

What two changes occur in the cytoplasm during prophase?

1. Separation of the centrosomes

2. Formation of the mitotic spindle between the centrosomes

The centrosome is also called the "microtubule organizing center" and is where microtubles are produced that make up the mitotic spindle. The mitotic spindle is an assembly of microtubules and proteins found between the two centrosomes which attaches to and aids in the movement of chromosomes during cell division. See Figure 4.1 below:

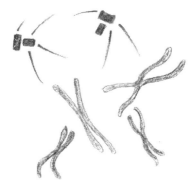

Figure 4.1: Mitosis: Prophase.

Remember, during the G_1 phase of interphase, the centrosome replicates to form two centrosomes, i.e. one for each daughter cell. In the centrosome of animal cells, there is also a pair of centrioles that are arranged perpendicular to each other.

What two changes occur in the nucleus during prophase?

1. Chromosomes become increasingly defined

2. Nucleolus disappears

During mitosis, chromosomes consist of two identical sister chromatids that are attached by a centromere.

Remember, the nucleolus is a specialized structure in the nucleus that is the site of ribosome synthesis.

4.2.2   Prometaphase

What changes occur in the cytoplasm during prometaphase?

Collections of microtubules (spindle fibers) project from mutually opposed centrioles to specific chromosomes, and some simply project into the nucleus/cytoplasm. See Figure 4.2 below:

Figure 4.2: Mitosis: Prometaphase.

When the microtubules attach to chromosomes, they attach to a specialized structure called the kinetochore and are called kinetochore microtubules; those which project into the nucleus/cytoplasm are called non-kinetochore microtubules (*Note: the kinetochores are specialized regions of the centromere*).

What changes occur in the nucleus during prometaphase?

Nuclear envelope fragments and disappears.

4.2.3   Metaphase

What occurs during metaphase?

Individual chromosomes align on the metaphase plate. See Figure 4.3 below:

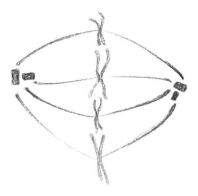

Figure 4.3: Mitosis: Metaphase.

This process is largely mediated by the tugging and pulling of chromosomes - so that they align properly - by kinetochore microtubules. This serves as a checkpoint for cells prior to moving on to anaphase.

4.2.4 Anaphase

What occurs during anaphase?

Previously paired sister chromatids of chromosomes separate towards continually separating, opposite poles. See Figure 4.4 below:

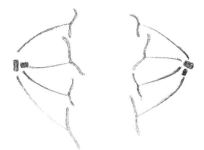

Figure 4.4: Mitosis: Anaphase.

What structures actively separate chromosomes?

The mitotic spindle, i.e. the kinetochore and non-kinetochore microtubules

4.2.5   Telophase

What occurs during telophase?

The nuclear envelope of daughter cells begins to form around each of the aggregated individual cells, chromosomes become less defined and the nucleoli reappear. See Figure 4.5 below:

Figure 4.5: Mitosis: Telophase.

4.2.6   Cytokinesis

What occurs during cytokinesis?

Division of the parent cells cytoplasm for the two daughter cells, also called cleavage. See Figure 4.6 below:

Figure 4.6: Mitosis: Cytokinesis.

What structure is seen in a cell actively undergoing cytokinesis?

Cleavage furrow.

What cytoskeletal fiber is involved in this contractile cell activity?

Actin aka microfilaments.

4.3   Meiosis I & II

What is the purpose of meiosis?

To create haploid (n) daughter cells from diploid parent cells. These haploid daughter cells are also referred to as sex cells or gametes. In humans, there are two types of gametes, sperm (n) and ova (n), and their production occurs in the testes and ovaries, collectively referred to as the gonads. When a sperm (n) and ova (n) fuse, a $2n$ zygote is formed which subsequently undergoes successive cycles of mitosis to form a blastocyte and eventually the human fetus.

How is meiosis similar and dissimilar to mitosis?

Meiosis is similar to mitosis because ...

1. Prior to cell division, the genome is replicated

2. Chromosomes line up at a metaphase plate

3. Chromosomes separate during anaphase

Meiosis is dissimilar to mitosis because ...

1. Complete meiosis takes place in two parts and occurs without genome duplication between meiosis I and II:

Meiosis I		*Meiosis II*	
$\mathbf{P}_{rophase}$ I	2 daughter cells	$\mathbf{P}_{rophase}$ II	4 daughter cells
$\mathbf{M}_{etaphase}$ I $\rightarrow$	each with $\rightarrow$	$\mathbf{M}_{etaphase}$ II $\rightarrow$	each with
$\mathbf{A}_{naphase}$ I	$2n$ chromosomes	$\mathbf{A}_{naphase}$ II	n chromosomes
$\mathbf{T}_{elophase}$ I		$\mathbf{T}_{elophase}$ II	

Table 4.1: Meiosis at a glance.

2. Meiosis has two homologous chromosomes (Remember: each chromosome has two sister chromatids) that each separate in meiosis I. Then, in meiosis II, the two sister chromatids of each chromosome separate into the daughter cells.

3. **Meiosis creates four daughter cells**, each with a ploidy of n, while mitosis creates two daughter cells, each with a ploidy of $2n$. Another way of thinking about this is that meiosis makes haploid cells (n) while mitosis makes diploid cells ($2n$).

You may want to refer to the general flow of "P.M.A.T." from mitosis to compare/contrast the chromosome number changes and distribution in the schematic illustrations of meiosis I and II on pages 36 to 38.

Figure 4.7: Meiosis I: Prophase - Note that in this stage chromosomes "pair-up", allowing for opportunities for chiasma to form and for crossing over to occur.

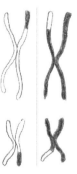

Figure 4.8: Meiosis I: Metaphase - Note that homologous pairs of chromosomes surround the metaphase plate.

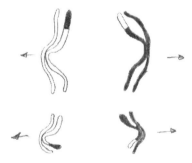

Figure 4.9: Meiosis I: Anaphase - Note that sister chromatids stay together as the homologous chromosomes move towards opposite poles.

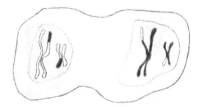

Figure 4.10: Meiosis I: Telophase.

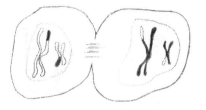

Figure 4.11: Meiosis I: Cytokinesis.

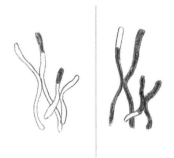

Figure 4.12: Meiosis II: Prophase.

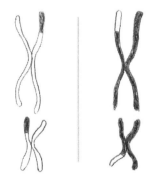

Figure 4.13: Meiosis II: Metaphase - Note that sister chromatids surround the metaphase plate.

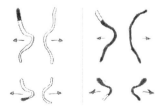

Figure 4.14: Meiosis II: Anaphase - Sister chromatids move towards opposite poles.

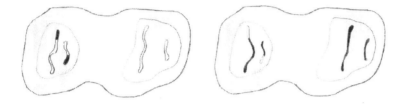

Figure 4.15: Meiosis II: Telophase.

Figure 4.16: Meiosis II: Cytokinesis.

Chapter 5

Genetics

Genetics topics have gotten increased attention on the MCAT because of the human genome project and other advances in genetic engineering. We will go over the various AAMC recommended genetic concepts in this section starting with the fundamental Mendelian framework, a discussion of genome organization, a review of the control of gene expression in eukaryotes, an explanation of sex-linked traits, defining genetic analytic methods and, yes again, a review of mutations (check the Protein Synthesis chapter for another review of DNA-protein errors).

5.1 Mendelian Terminology and Concepts

Understand and be able to explain the following vocab:

Gene

- An "instruction manual" for a particular protein written in a genetic code (DNA) and located on chromosomes, e.g. the gene which codes for the hemoglobin protein.

Allele

- One or more forms of expression of a particular gene at a given location (aka locus).

    - Single alleles exist and normally have only one form of expression, e.g. the allele which makes red blood cells.

    - Multiple alleles exist and have several forms of expression, e.g. blood type: O, A, B or AB.

- Alleles are also known as a "traits." So, for example, in Figure 5.1 below, the alleles are R or r.

Phenotype

- The physical, metabolic, or behavioral manifestation of a gene product. For example, in Figure 5.1 below, the phenotypes are red or white.

Genotype

- The genetic information obtained from the organism's parents which results in a specific allelic combination. For example, in Figure 5.1 below, the genotypes are RR, Rr, or rr.

Monohybrid cross

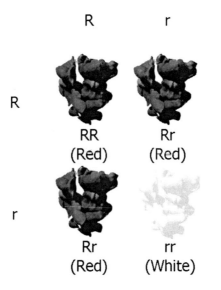

Figure 5.1: Monohybrid cross: In this example, the alleles are R and r, the genotypes are represented by the *RR, Rr rr* and the phenotypes are either the *red* or *white* of the flower (*Note the 3:1 phenotypic distribution*).

Locus

- The physical location on a chromosome where a gene is found. The plural form is *loci*.

Homozygosity

- Presence of an identical pair of alleles, e.g. RR or rr in Figure 5.1 above.

Heterozygosity

- Presence of two different alleles, e.g. Rr in Figure 5.1 above.

Dominant and Recessive alleles

- Dominant alleles are traits which will definitely be expressed in the homozygous form (RR) and will preferentially be expressed in the heterozygous form (Rr).

- Recessive alleles are traits which will only be expressed in the homozygous form (rr).

Codominance

- Codominace exists when the heterozygous genotype expresses both phenotypes simultaneously. This is readily seen in the ABO blood groups were recessive alleles A and B can be expressed on the same red blood cell.

Wild-type

- The natural phenotype or commonly found form, i.e. the "norm".

Incomplete dominance

- When alleles can not dominate each other. In the case of a red allele and a white allele, incomplete dominance will be seen in the heterozygote genotype and will result in a pink phenotype (red + white = pink). *Note the 1:2:1 phenotypic distribution.*

F_1 and F_2 cross

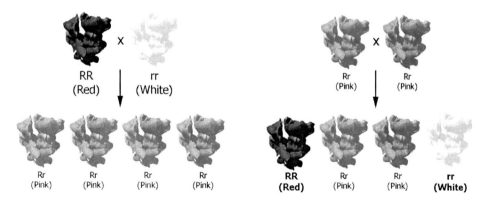

Figure 5.2: F_1 and F_2 cross: In this cross we see the first cross (left) which creates the heterozygote genotype and the second cross (right) which "proves" the heterogeneity because of the 1:2:1 genotypic (and phenotypic) distribution.

Leakage

- Decrease in one gene pool because of "dilution" from another gene pool.

Penetrance

- The amount of people who have a defective gene and express the disease, i.e. how much a defective gene has penetrated the population. The key to **p**enetrance is **p**enetration in a **p**opulation.

Expressivity

- The degree to which a genotype is expressed in the organism's phenotype. The key to expressivity is expression in **one** organism.

Gene pool

- The gene pool includes all the alleles for all the individuals in a given population, e.g. the human gene pool.

Karyotype

- Organization of an organism's genes, commonly by size or type.

Test cross

- A technique used to determine what the genotype of an organism is by crossing it with a a homozygote recessive genotype as in Figure 5.3 below:

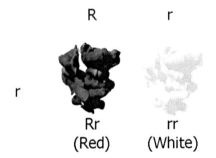

Figure 5.3: Test cross. In this example, the known homozygote recessive genotype (rr) is represented simply as an "r" which allows one to *draw out* what the original genotype was because of the phenotypic products.

What is the law of segregation?

Mendel's first law which states that allele pairs will separate when a gamete is formed (i.e. an ova or sperm) and randomly pair up to become diploid again during fertilization.

What is the law of independent assortment of genes?

Mendel's second law which states that allele pairs will separate independently of each other during meiosis I and meiosis II. For example, two genes such as pea shape and pea color will sort themselves independently of each other.

5.2   Chromosome organization

Chromosome organization is a huge, complicated topic but for the MCAT understanding the following topics should be enough:

What is the main protein that is involved in chromosome packing?

Histones; of which there are five types in eukaryotes. Of all five types, if you want to know one, remember H_1 - its known as the "linker" protein. When histones assemble and have DNA wrapped around themselves, they are called *nucleosomes* and appear as "beads on a string".

What property do histones have that makes them able to bind tightly with DNA?

Histones are very alkaline proteins giving them a positive charges. Because DNA *has an innate negative charge*, this makes for a good union.

What is another name for the histone/DNA packing format?

Chromatin.

What are the two forms of chromatin?

1. *Heterochromatin*: found during interphase that is highly compacted and visible with a microscope.

2. *Euchromatin*: found during an actively replicating cell and is "very loose".

5.3   Control of gene expression in eukaryotes

Control of gene expression is critical to maintaining normal functioning in organisms. As we will see below, control is maintained at different levels. It is important to understand transcriptional regulation, post-transcriptional control, the effects of hormones, and oncogenes/tumor-suppressor genes.

5.3.1   Transcriptional regulation

What are enchancers?

Regions of DNA that are thousands of base pairs away (downstream or upstream) of a particular gene. Enhancers bind transcription factors and increase the rate of transcription of the gene.

Often, an alteration in the shape of the DNA occurs to narrow the spatial gap between the enhancer sequence and the gene in question, e.g. a DNA loop.

What are promoters?

Regions of DNA that are only a few base pairs away (upstream) of a particular gene which bind RNA polymerase and are found upstream from all protein encoding genes.

Promoters contain a sequence of seven bases (TATAAAA) called the TATA box that binds 50+ proteins/transcription factors.

What are transcription factors?

An all purpose term for proteins that regulate gene transcription and facilitate the interaction between enhancers, promoters and particular genes.

There are three types or groups that are commonly found on transcription factors:

1. Helix-turn-helix domain

2. Leucine zipper

3. Zinc-finger domain

5.3.2   Post-transcriptional regulation

You will notice some overlap with concepts that came up in the DNA chapter but the repetition will help underscore important concepts.

What are four post-transcriptional processes that affect mRNA?

1. 5' cap

2. 3' poly-adenine tail, i.e. poly-A tail

3. Intron excision, also known as splicing

4. Quantity of mRNA in the cytoplasm

    - This is more of a conceptual post-transcriptional process and is controlled by signal triggers, the enzymatic degradation of mRNA, etc.

5.3.3 Steroid Hormones

What type of macromolecules are steroids?

Steroids are soluble lipids. Be sure to be able to recognize the basic structure of steroid hormones - i.e. four carbon ring structure:

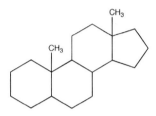

Figure 5.4: The general structure of steroids.

Where do steroids mediate their effects?

The nucleus.

How?

By mediating protein synthesis.

5.3.4 Proto-oncogenes, oncogenes, and tumor-suppressor genes

What are proto-oncogenes?

Proto-oncogenes are normal genes that code mainly for proteins that control normal cell growth. If mutated, these "pre-" cancer genes (proto-) become cancer (onco-) genes.

What are oncogenes?

Oncogenes are abnormal genes that lead to the development of cancer by instructing cells to grow and divide excessively. Think of it as "stepping on a cell's gas pedal."

Note: Oncogenes are mutant forms of proto-oncogenes.

What are tumor-suppressor genes?

Tumor-suppressor genes are normal genes found in cells that prevent or inhibit cancerous processes. When mutated or deleted they can lead to cancer, i.e. tumor-suppressor genes are the "cell's brake pedals."

What is the most studied tumor-suppressor gene?

p53

What does p53 do in normal, non-cancerous cells?

Triggers cell death (apoptosis).

Note: Tumor-suppressor cells are GOOD. They "suppress" uncontrollable growth by triggering cell death. Therefore, if p53, for example, is damaged, it will not be able to trigger cell death and the cell will continue to grow on, and on, and on.

5.4   Sex-linked characteristics and Abnormalities in Sex Chromosome Number

What determines sex in humans?

Sperm, which carry either an X or a Y chromosome, determine the ultimate sex in humans. This happens when a sperm cell fertilizes an egg which carries only X chromosomes: an XX genotype results in a female; an XY genotype results in a male.

What does sex-linked mean?

"Sex-linked" refers to traits (aka alleles) that are found on the X chromosome that follow a predictable pattern of inheritance:

- Fathers pass all X-linked genes to their daughters[1].

- Mothers can pass X-linked genes to both sons or daughters because mothers can only pass an X to her offspring.

---

[1]Because a father's X-chromosome-sperm (as opposed to a Y-chromosome-sperm) must have fertilized an ova for the zygote to develop into a female).

Why are males affected more often by sex-linked diseases than females?

Males only have one X-chromosome while women have two. Therefore, in the case of recessive diseases, even if the male gets the recessive X-linked gene, there is no "offset" from the Y gene and the male will express the gene. Females, on the other hand, will have to have inherited two copies of the X-linked recessive gene (one from each parent) to express the disease. Invariably, most sex-linked disease are recessive.

Duchennes muscular dystrophy and hemophilia are two examples of sex-linked diseases.

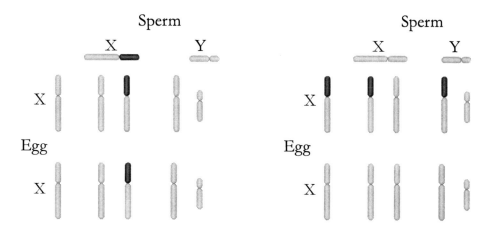

Figure 5.5: X-linked transmission: fathers (left) give the defective allele on the X chromosome to all their daughters (XX) and give an unaffected Y chromosome to their sons (XY); and mothers (right) can give the defective allele on one of the X chromosomes to both daughters (XX) and sons (XY).

What is meant by cytoplasmic inheritance?

A pattern of inheritance that originates from the cytoplasm and organelles found in the ova (sperm basically contain only DNA and a means to get it to the ova, including a flagella, fructose, etc).

Therefore, diseases associated with organelles containing extra-nuclear DNA, e.g. mitochondria, come from the maternal lineage rather than the paternal line.

What are four classic abnormalities in sex chromosome number?

X	Turner syndrome
XXY	Klinfelter syndrome
XXX	Metafemale
XYY	Normal male

5.5 Analytic Methods in Genetics

What is the Hardy-Weinberg principle?

The equation used to determine the gene frequency within a population. Memorize this formula:

$$p^2 + 2pq + q^2 = 1$$

Where, p and q represent the allelic frequencies, p^2 and q^2 represent dominant and recessive frequencies (e.g. YY and yy), and $2pq$ determine the heterozygote frequencies (e.g. Yy).

What five conditions need to be met for Hardy-Weinberg equilibrium to be maintained?

1. Large population size (a small population will be affected by chance variations in allelic frequency)

2. No migrations out of the population (migrations change the allelic composition of the population's gene pool)

3. No mutations (mutations change the allelic frequency within of the population's gene pool)

4. Random mating (inbreeding violates the principle of random mating)

5. No natural selection (the selection of a set of characteristics within a population will alter the allelic frequency of the population's gene pool)

5.6 Segregation of Genes

What is the segregation of genes?

A general term for how genes get distributed during meiosis. There are many ways in which segregation of genes occurs. Four you should be familiar with for the MCAT include:

1. Recombination

2. Linkage

3. Independent assortment

4. Single and Double Crossovers

Recombination

The movement of a section of DNA between paired chromosomes. For example, crossing over of genes which results in the recombination of genes on the same chromosome, i.e. linked genes.

Linkage

Linkage refers to the tendency of genes in close proximity to "travel" together during meiosis. By default, linked genes are on the same chromosome

Independent assortment

How different chromosomes are distributed to daughter cells.

- This can best be seen in how chromosomes align themselves along the metaphase plate. Take for example a homologous pair of chromosomes during metaphase I of meiosis. There is a fifty-fifty chance for how they arrange themselves on either side of the metaphase plate and assort themselves. This process is independent of the other chromosomes at the metaphase plate:

Taking it back to Mendel's experiments with peas for two traits, e.g. color and shape, independent assortment of genes is a direct consequence of how two genes (on different chromosomes) align themselves along the metaphase plate. For two genes on two different chromosomes, i.e. unlinked, there is a predictable result of 1:1:1:1 that can be expected:

Single and Double Crossovers

How genes on the same chromosome distribute themselves in the daughter cells.

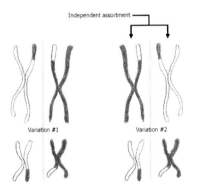

Figure 5.6: Scenario for independent assortment of genes across the metaphase plate.

- Remember that during prophase I, there is a pair of homologous chromosomes, each with two sister chromatids. During metaphase I, the homologous pair of chromosomes aligns itself around the metaphase plate by independent assortment (see above). Sometimes, chiasma form between non-sister chromatids during prophase I or across the metaphase plate. This allows for genes to be swapped:

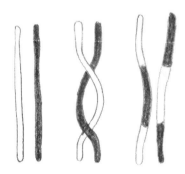

Figure 5.7: Crossing over.

- The likelihood of single crossovers, i.e. crossing over of one gene, is random and is dependent on having a chiasma. But the likelihood of double crossovers, i.e. crossing over of two genes together, is based on the distance between the two genes: if two genes are close together, they are more likely to crossover together.

5.7 Telomeres

What are telomeres?

Telomeres are sequences of DNA found at the end of chromosomes.

Remember that during DNA replication, an RNA primer is needed to give DNA polymerase a foot-hold to begin adding nucleotides? Well, on the lagging strand, there would be no room for a primer to get placed at the 3' end of the parent chromosome if it were not for telomeres. Therefore, if it wasn't for telomere "overhang," DNA replication could not occur in its entirety and the chromosome would become shorter and shorter over successive cycles of replications.

Take home message: Telomeres are single-stranded extensions which allow for repeated cycles of replication and prevent the "shortening" of chromosomes after each replication.

5.8 Mutations

Sick of mutations yet? OK, this will be brief:

- Understand that mutations can be advantageous (e.g. in bacteria in the setting of antibiotics, the strain that mutates to live in the hostile environment will win) or deleterious (e.g. a mutation in p53 that leads to the cell that won't die and cancer).

- Understand that mutations may lead to inborn errors of metabolism, a fancy expression for a great number of diseases such as sickle cell anemia, hemochromatosis, glyogen storage diseases, etc.

- Understand that **mutagens** alter the sequence of DNA and are **muta**tion **gen**erators. When these mutations lead to cancer, mutagens are also known as carcinogens.

Chapter 6

Evolution

6.1 Natural Selection

What is natural selection?

Ground-breaking theory proposed by Dr. Charles Darwin in 1859 which is the mechanism behind the evolution of a population.

Natural selection is the process by which organisms within a population have phenotypical advantages to allow themselves to better adapt to their environment. This in turn allows them to survive and reproduce more effectively than others within that population and increases the frequency of their alleles.

For example, take two rabbits. One white and one brown. Now, let's say it's winter with lots of snow and, in this environment, wolves feed on the rabbits. Because the white rabbit can blend in better with the surroundings, it is less obvious to the wolves and therefore more capable of surviving through the winter. Spring now comes and it's mating time. With more numbers of white rabbits compared to brown rabbits, more white rabbits mate and their population increases.

This example can be applied in any capacity and for any number of variables. The bottom line is that there is a selective advantage conferred to one phenotypical variant which allows it to survive better than the other.

What is group selection?

Natural selection which occurs by groups of members in a society through group-level adaptations. This differs from classic natural selection which looks at the individual as the basic 'unit' in the evolutionary model.

What is fitness?

The ability of one organism to pass on its gene pool to the next generation, i.e. the ability to successfully mate (and have the zygote grow and be born).

What is selection by differential reproduction?

Selection by differential reproduction, also known as artificial selection, is a form of selection within a population that is based on intential breeding choices.

6.2   Speciation

What is a species?

A group or kind of organism that shares distinguishing characteristics with each other, including the ability to successfully mate together and produce viable offspring.

What are polymorphisms?

"Poly-," many; "-morphisms," forms.

For example, types of hair color/structure in humans.

What is adaptation?

The ability of a species to change as a consequence of the environment. Granted, there is only so much that an organism can adapt to within one generation. Natural selection is the process which determines whether or not a species will survive in the changing environment over evolutionary time.

What is specialization?

The consequence of adaption to specific environmental constraints through behavioral or structural means. For example, the beak on a hummingbird has evolved to be especially long and particularly arced to be able to feed on a certain types of nectar-containing orchids.

What is an ecological niche?

The role of an organism within its environment including its relationship to other species (predators, food supply, etc) and abiotic resources (temperatire range, shelter, territory, etc).

What is the role of competition between species?

Based on the work of ecologists in the early third of the 20th century, two species cannot coexist in a niche because one will eventually overcome and monopolize resources, effectively driving off (or killing off) the other species.

What is the effect of inbreeding on a population?

- Decreases heterozygotes within a population while increasing dominant/recessive homozygotes

    - Increases the phenotypical prevalence of "bad" traits by increasing the proportion of homozygotes for deleterious alleles

Inbreeding is "non-random mating" and violates the principles of Hardy-Weinberg equilibrium.

What is the bottleneck effect?

When a population has a drastic reduction in numbers and there is a significant decrease in the gene pool, i.e. a bottlenecking of a population.

What is divergent evolution?

- The evolutionary pattern in which two similar species gradually become increasingly different. The evolution of man and ape from a common ancestor is an example of divergent evolution.

What is convergent evolution?

- The evolutionary pattern in which species of different ancestry develop analogous traits secondary to a similar environment or other selection pressure. For example, dolphins (warm blooded vertebrates) and fish (cold blooded vertebrates) have some similar characteristics since both have evolved to live in water.

What is parallel evolution?

- Another evolutionary pattern in which species of different ancestry and different geographic habitats develop independently of each other but still maintain a similar level of similarity. For example, the similarities between Australian marsupials (mammals) and placental mammals in Europe.

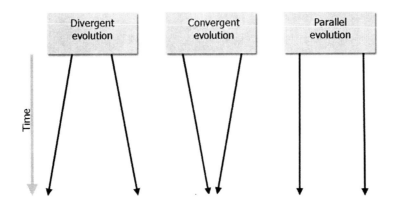

Figure 6.1: Evolutionary trends.

What is parasitism and commensalism?

Both are symbiotic relationships between two organisms, but ...

- In parasitism one of the pair gets hurt, e.g. a tapeworm in your intestines

- In commensalism both benefit, e.g. birds picking off fleas/flies from a rhino's back

Extra, high-yield info ...

What did the bio prof mean by ontology recapitulates phylogeny?

This is an extreme view held by early embryologists which purports that an organism's evolution is seen in how it developed as an embryo.

Present day scientists do not fully adopt this view, but feel that the way an embryo develops leads to clues on comparative evolution among species.

Chapter 7

DNA Synthesis

Deoxyribonucleic acid (DNA) makes up the foundation of molecular biology. To provide you with the foundations for the MCAT, DNA will be covered in five sections:

1. Function

2. Structure

3. Replication

4. Repair

5. Recombinant DNA

7.1   Function

What is the general function of DNA?

DNA contains the genetic code for life. In eukaryotes, it is found in the nucleus of cells and certain cytoplasmic organelles.

Coded in specific sequences of nucleotides, protein-coding regions (**ex**ons) are **ex**pressed, while **non**-coding regions (**intr**ons) serve as filler between exons and are **not** expressed.

What is the role of DNA in the central dogma of biology?

The central dogma states that DNA codes for RNA (transcription) and RNA in turn is translated into protein (translation):

$$DNA \longrightarrow RNA \longrightarrow Protein$$

Note: This "formula" implicitly points out that the "reaction" can only proceed in the forward direction, i.e. you can't make DNA out of protein.

7.2 Structure

What is the accepted, modern-day model of DNA structure?

The double helix first proposed by Watson and Crick in 1953.

1. Each helix is made up of thousands or millions of nucleotides.

2. The helices are held together in the middle of the double helix with hydrogen bonds

What are the components of nucleotides and nucleosides?

	Nucleotide	Nucleoside
Phosphate	√	
Pentose sugar	√	√
Nitrogenous base	√	√

Where are phosphates located in nucleotides and what role do they have?

- Phosphates are located "outside" of the nucleotide and make up the back bone of each helix.

    - The phosphate attaches to the 5' position of the inferior pentose sugar and to the 3' position of the superior sugar

- This is what is meant by 5' to 3' synthesis, and it gives a sense of directionality to DNA strands. In the double helix, one strand will travel in the 5' to 3' direction, while the other strand will be oriented in the 3' to 5' direction (i.e. antiparallel).

Where are pentose sugars located in nucleotides and what do they do?

- Pentose sugars are located in the "middle" of the nucleotide and determine the type of nucleic acid:

    - DNA has a deoxyribose sugar (a sugar with one less hydroxyl group than ribose).
    - RNA has a ribose sugar.

Where are nitrogenous bases located in nucleotides and what is their purpose?

- Nitrogenous bases, or simply DNA bases, are located "inside" the nucleotide and provide the site of attachment between both helices via hydrogen bonds and carry the information or genetic code by having four different flavors of DNA.

    - DNA bases come in two different forms: purines and pyrimidines.

         ∗ **Purines** include adenine and guanine

          · "**Pure** as gold."

         ∗ **Pyrimidines** include cytosine and thymine (The RNA equivalent of thymine is **uracil**)

          · "**Cut** the pie."

– As mentioned above, hydrogen bonds connect the helices to each other. This is a fundamental physical characteristic of DNA that you need to remember. H- bonding will come up over and over again in orgo, e.g. H-bonds can only occur between nitrogen, oxygen and fluorine (N.O.F.), but for the purposes of DNA, remember that A binds to T (or U in the case of RNA) and C binds to G ("AT Carl Goldbergs").

To remember which pair had a double or triple bond, I always wrote out the pairs and extended the horizontal lines of the letters:

Figure 7.1: Nucleotide bonding: the T for thymine is interchangeable for U (for uracil).

Remember that it takes more energy to break a triple bond (C≡G) than a double bond (A=T), so if a question comes up that a DNA-containing solution became less viscous at a higher-than-expected temperature, remember that DNA with more C≡G bonds will have a higher melting point.

7.3 Replication

What model describes how parental DNA unravels and is transferred to replicated DNA?

The semi-conservative model, which states that parental double-stranded DNA unravels completely into two individual single strands and each strand serves as a template for the new, replicated DNA:

What experiment supports this model?

Although the name of the experimenters is not as important (Meselson-Stahl 1957) as the experiment itself, the experiment which confirmed the semi-conservative model suggested by Watson and Crick is known by some as the "most beautiful experiment" ever done.

For the MCAT, take away some core principles:

- Nitrogen is a key component of DNA

- Isotopes have different weights

- E. coli grown in a broth containing a normal nitrogen (^{14}N) will have DNA containing normal nitrogens

    – If this DNA is extracted and centrifuged, it will have one normal band of ^{14}N-^{14}N DNA

- E. coli grown in a broth containing a radioactive isotope of nitrogen (^{15}N) will eventually have all the DNA's nitrogens replaced with the "heavier" ^{15}N isotopes

    – If this DNA is extracted and centrifuged, it will have one "heavy" band composed of ^{15}N-^{15}N DNA

- E. coli grown in the ^{15}N containing broth, if removed and allowed to grow for one generation in normal broth without heavy isotopes of nitrogen, will have new generations of E. coli with one "heavy" strand and one "light" strand

    – If this DNA is extracted and centrifuged, it will have one band located between the lighter ^{14}N-^{14}N DNA and the heavier ^{15}N-^{15}N DNA, i.e. ^{14}N-^{15}N DNA

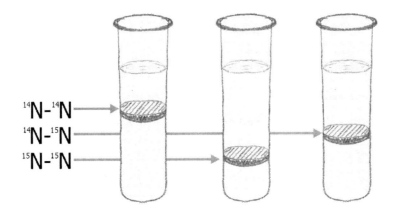

Figure 7.2: Meselson-Stahl experiment.

What is the direction for DNA synthesis?

5' to 3'

Because one strand of DNA is oriented in the 5' to 3' direction and the other strand is oriented in the 3' to 5' direction, synthesis for each occurs slightly differently.

Draw the replication of DNA for each strand.

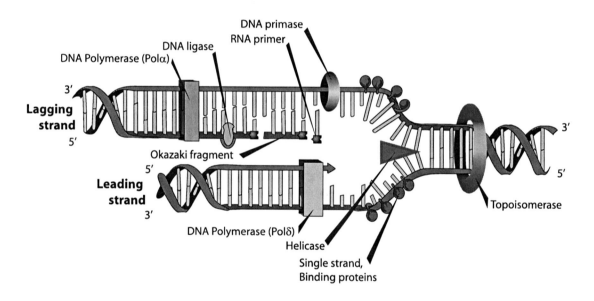

Figure 7.3: DNA replication. *Public domain image illustrated by Mariana Ruiz.*

1. The origin of replication is the site where replication begins

2. The replication fork is the Y-shaped region where DNA elongation/replication takes place

3. DNA polymerase is the enzyme responsible for adding nucleotides and proofreading new strands

4. The leading strand is the strand that is being synthesized in the 5' to 3' direction (Note: this occurs on the parental strand with the 3' end)

5. Lagging strand is the strand that is being synthesized in the 3' to 5' direction (note this occurs on the parental strand with the 5' end)

6. Okazaki fragments are small pieces of newly-synthesized DNA found on the lagging strand that are synthesized in the 5' to 3' direction

7. Primer/primase is the initiator for DNA synthesis and the necessary "starter" for DNA polymerase made of RNA and synthesized by primase

8. Helicase unwinds the DNA double helix

9. Single-strand binding proteins stabilize unwound DNA

10. DNA ligase connects Okazaki fragments

7.4   Repair

What regulates DNA repair during replication?

This process is believed to be under the control of DNA polymerase in eukaryotes

What regulates DNA repair after replication?

Process of excision repair:

1. Nuclease detects "bump" or distorted DNA from incorrectly paired nucleotides and excises it ("nucle" for nucleotide, "ase" for to cut)

2. Polymerase fills the pot hole

3. Ligase seals the end of the new strand

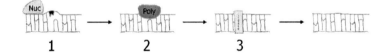

Figure 7.4: DNA repair.

7.5   Recombinant DNA

What is recombinant DNA?

Recombinant DNA (rDNA) is the combined DNA transcript created when two different samples of DNA are treated with restriction enzymes and mixed together

What are restriction enzymes?

Enzymes that are also known as endonucleases[1] which cut DNA at certain sequences to make "sticky" ends.

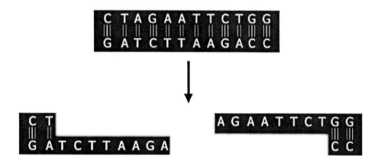

Figure 7.5: Sticky ends: The product of DNA cutting by endonucleases.

How are restriction enzymes used in gene cloning?

If a known gene is located in a certain DNA segment, this segment can be treated with restriction enzymes to create sticky ends. If we then isolate an actively reproducing cell line and treat the cell's DNA with restriction enzymes, a gap or "pot hole" (with two sticky ends) will have been created. Now, if one takes the gene of interest and adds it to the cell line and re-anneals it with the cells/gene solution, one can clone or synthesize the gene.

---

[1] "Endo" for within, "nucle" for nucleotide, "ases" for cutting

Chapter 8

Protein Synthesis

After understanding the concept of DNA synthesis, we will now move on to the second half of the central dogma of biology and discuss protein synthesis. Make sure to take away the main points of protein synthesis. Specifically, be able to follow a given nucleotide (and how it changes) from DNA, to tRNA, to mRNA; and understand the location of each step of protein synthesis.

8.1   General

What is the central dogma of biology?

$$DNA \longrightarrow RNA \longrightarrow Protein$$

What is the role of RNA in this?

RNA is literally the bridge between taking the genetic code locked in chromosomes composed of DNA to the functional polypeptides composed of amino acids.

What is the difference between RNA and DNA?

RNA is unique from DNA for the following reasons:

1. RNA is *single − stranded* in eukaryotes
2. RNA contains the nucleotide *uracil* (instead of DNA's thymine)
3. RNA has a *ribose sugar* (instead of DNA's deoxyribose)

8.2   Codons

What are codons and what is their importance?

Codons are the reading frames that make DNA readable.

How much information can be stored in each codon?

Codons are made up of three nucleotides, and each nucleotide can be one of four types.

Therefore, each of the three spots can be filled with one of the four nucleotides, or a combination of 4 x 4 x 4 possibilities, i.e. 4^3 equaling 64 "words" or bits of information that a triplet code can contain given a four-letter vocabulary.

What is the relationship between codons in DNA, mRNA, tRNA and amino acids?

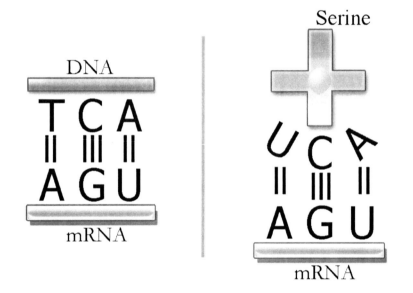

Figure 8.1: Relationship between codons in DNA, mRNA, tRNA and amino acids.

Why are there only 20 amino acids if there are 64 codon combinations - where did the other 44 go?

The 20 amino acids which are found in nature are encoded by more than one codon. Often, two, three or four codons can encode one of the 20 amino acids.

This is known as **wobble** and the variation always occurs in the 3rd position.

Are there any mRNA codons that you should know?

Four codons have two unique functions:

1. Stop codons: "UAA, UGA, UAG!!!" (Repeat as if you were a caveman)

2. Start codon: AUG which also codes for methionine

What are the four steps of protein synthesis?

1. Transcription

2. RNA processing

3. Translation

4. Post-translational protein modification

8.3 Transcription

What is transcription?

Simply put, the conversion of DNA to RNA, or, the process of matching nucleotides to the DNA template and producing a sequence of RNA in the form of mRNA:

$$DNA \longrightarrow mRNA$$

Note: that this process stays within the nucleic acid language.

Where does this occur in eukaryotes?

In the nucleus.

What enzyme makes mRNA?

RNA polymerase II molecules unwind the double-stranded DNA, transcribe the DNA template, and add nucleotides to an elongating mRNA transcript.

What is the directionality of mRNA synthesis?

RNA polymerase adds nucleotides at the 3' end of the mRNA transcript, therefore, the synthesis occurs in a 5' to 3' direction.

What regions on the DNA strand serve as sites which initiate RNA transcription and RNA polymerase binding?

Promoter regions.

What happens to the head and tail of an mRNA after transcription?

Addition of a 5' cap and poly-adenine tail (poly-A tail).

What is RNA splicing?

The process of taking a "raw," freshly transcribed mRNA and removing non-coding segments (Figure 8.2 below).

***Ex**ons are **ex**pressed, **in**trons are **n**ot.*

Introns, or non-coding segments, are "filler" sequences found in DNA but are not needed to make functional proteins. Therefore, these segments are removed by a spliceosome, leaving a tailor-made mRNA with only the exons that will be expressed in the final polypeptide.

The main pearl of splicing was mentioned above, but just to wrap it up, mRNA with introns and exons is called heterogenous nuclear mRNA. As the name implies it is both heterogenous in composition and is also found in the nucleus. So technically, the hnRNA becomes mature after splicing to become mRNA, which is exported into the cytoplasm:

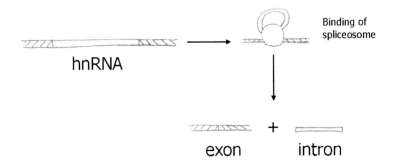

Figure 8.2: RNA splicing.

8.4   Equipment tally

At this point, we have created an mRNA and are in the cytoplasm; what type of equipment is necessary to continue on with translation?

1. rRNA

   • Makes up ribosomes

2. tRNA

   • Carries amino acids on one end and interfaces on the other end with the mRNA

3. aminoacyl-tRNA synthetases

   • Attaches amino acids to tRNAs

What is the function of ribosomes?

Ribosomes, a conglomerate of proteins and rRNA, (1) hold the mRNA and (2) provide a site for tRNAs to interact with the mRNA and make the amino acid polypeptide.

Note: There are two sites for tRNA to fit; one for the incoming tRNA A site and one for the outcoming RNA T site.

How are prokaryotic and eukaryotic ribosomes different?

The main take-home message for the MCAT is that prokaryotes and eukaryotes have different subunits.

• Eukaryotes have 80 S ribosomes made up of 60 and 40 S subunits

• Prokaryotes have 70 S ribosomes made up of 50 and 30 S subunits

Figure 8.3: The ribosome.

8.5   Translation

What is translation?

Simply put, translating RNA to a new molecular language: protein. Or, the
process of matching amino acids via tRNA to the mRNA transcript with the
help of ribosomes to form a polypeptide chain of amino acids:

$$mRNA \longrightarrow Protein$$

Note: This process translates the nucleic acid language to the protein language.

Where does this occur in eukaryotes?

In the cytoplasm.

How does this differ from prokaryotes?

Prokaryotes lack a membrane-bound nucleus, and protein translation occurs as
RNA is being transcribed off of the DNA.

**What are the three general steps to making an amino acid polypep-
tide?**

Initiation, elongation and termination.

What occurs during initiation?

The union of mRNA and tRNA with the first amino acid and a ribosome (with
both subunits).

What occurs during elongation?

1. The codon on the mRNA is recognized by the appropriate amino acid
   carrying tRNA in the A site. *Note: Remember the **A** site as the **a**mino
   acid site.*

2. A peptide bond is formed by a peptidyl transferase between the elongating polypeptide containing tRNA in the P site with the amino acid carrying tRNA in the A site: *Note: Don't confuse peptidyl transferase with
   aminoacyl-tRNA synthetase. The latter connects each of the 20 amino
   acids with the appropriate tRNA.*

3. The peptidyl transferase function conferred by RNA 50S subunit translo-
   cates the P site tRNA and vacates its spot for the A site tRNA

© 2005 - 2007

4. When a stop codon is encoded in the mRNA, translation stops and a
   release factor binds to the A site. Peptidyl transferase then binds a water
   molecule instead of an amino acid and the polypeptide is freed from the
   ribosome complex: *Note: Remember the cave man! "UAA! UGA! UAG!"*

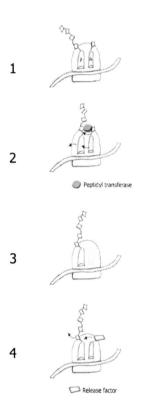

Figure 8.4: mRNA translation.

8.6   Post-translational protein modification

What are two fates of proteins?

Some are destined for secretion outside of the cell and others stay inside the
cell.

What ribosomes preferentially translate these protein fates?

Bound ribosomes usually translate proteins into the endomembrane system
which ultimately places these proteins in the endoplasmic reticulum/Golgi apparatus and are usually destined for secretion, become membrane proteins or

become lysosomes.

Free ribosomes usually translate proteins freely into the cytosol.

What mediates synthesis of secreted proteins.?

Signal sequences on proteins "mark" their destination as secreted proteins.

8.7   Extra pearls

8.7.1   Protein Structure

Primary structure (1°):
The amino acid sequence of a polypeptide chain

- For example, Leucine-Valine-Glutamic acid

Secondary structure (2°):
The local folding pattern of a polypeptide chain

- Two main types:

  1. α-helix
  2. β-pleated sheet

- Mediated by hydrogen bonds

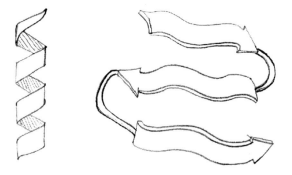

Figure 8.5: Secondary protein structures: α-helix (left) and β-pleated sheet (right).

Tertiary structure (3°):
The interaction between amino acid side chains:

- For example, disulfide bridges, ionic bonds, hydrogen bonds (yes, hydrogen bonds again; but the take-home example is disulfide bridges)

- Hydrophobic amino acids clustering inside a protein while hydrophilic amino acids are exposed to the outside of the protein.

Quaternary structure (4°):
The interaction between two or more polypeptides:

- For example, between the four hemoglobin subunits

Figure 8.6: Quatanery protein structure (4°): Hemoglobin.

8.7.2   Mutations in Protein Synthesis

Mutations, in regard to protein synthesis, will be examined from the perspective of point mutations, i.e. the change or loss of one pair of nucleotides.

- Point mutations can occur in three flavors:

  1. **Insertion**: the insertion of a nucleotide pair

  2. **Deletion**: the removal of a nucleotide pair

  3. **Substitution**: the switching of a nucleotide pair

- Substitutions can affect the protein in three ways:

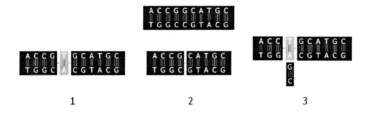

Figure 8.7: Protein point mutations: Insertion (1), deletion (2) and substitution (3).

1. Silent mutation: A change in a nucleotide which still results in the
   same amino acid to be used to make the polypeptide

   – This commonly occurs in the 3rd position of the codon and shows
     the advantage of *wobble*

2. Missense mutations: A change in a nucleotide which results in a
   different amino acid

   – This is seen in sickle-cell anemia where the hemoglobin has a
     polypeptide structure that makes little sense (Valine is incor-
     rectly substituted for glutamic acid)

3. Nonsense mutation: A change in a nucleotide which results in a stop
   codon - this prematurely ends the translation of the protein

• Just to come full circle, when an insertion or deletion occurs, there is a
  shift in the normal reading frame. Therefore, the whole mRNA will be
  translated in a way that is off by one, two or as many nucleotides that
  have been added or removed. In the case of a change of the reading frame
  by a multiple of 3 (i.e. the length of a codon), sometimes the effect may
  not be too detrimental.

The take home message here is that the mutations that are seen in substitution mutations, i.e. silent, missense and nonsense, can also be seen in inser-
tion/deletion mutations.

One more thing, a real-world application of insertion mutations is Huntington's
Disease which is caused by an insertion of too many CAG sequences.

Chapter 9

Cellular Respiration

Cellular respiration is one of those bread and butter concepts that pops up a lot on the MCAT. A good handle on the concepts will allow you to excel on these particular passages.

9.1   Introduction

What is cellular respiration?

A catabolic process (a process which breaks something down; in the case of cellular respiration, glucose is broken down) which uses oxygen and organic compounds (i.e. glucose) to create energy, water and carbon dioxide:

$$C_6H_{12}O_6 + O_2 \longrightarrow CO_2 + H_2O + Energy$$

Glucose ($C_6H_{12}O_6$) is used to learn the general steps of cellular respiration, but other carbohydrates, fats and proteins can all be used at various steps of the process.

The three general steps by which cellular respiration occurs are:

1. Glycolysis

2. The Citric Acid Cycle (Krebs cycle)

3. The Electron Transport Chain

The energy "currency" created by cellular respiration is adenosine triphosphate, i.e. ATP.

What are the two processes by which ATP is made during cellular respiration?

1. Substrate-level phosphorylation

2. Oxidative phosphorylation

Substrate-level phosphorylation is the production of ATP at specific steps of the Krebs cycle and during glycolysis. It may help to remember this by considering the reactants/products of the specific steps of the Krebs cycle or glycolysis as substrates for ATP synthesis. Substrate-level phosphorylation takes place in the *cytoplasm* and *mitochondria*.

Oxidative phosphorylation is the production of ATP by the transfer of electrons to molecules that are coupled with the electron transport chain. Two molecules carry electrons to the electron transport chain: NADH and $FADH_2$. Oxidative phosphorylation produces the overwhelming majority of ATP and only takes place in the *mitochondria*.

How is energy stored in ATP?

Energy is stored in high energy phosphodiester bonds which are hydrolyzed resulting in an energy releasing (exergonic) reaction:

$$ATP + H_2O \longrightarrow ADP + P_I + Energy$$

9.2   Glycolysis

What is glycolysis?

The splitting (-lysis) of glucose ($C_6H_{12}O_6$) producing two three-carbon pyruvate molecules.

Glycolysis takes place in the cytoplasm and ultimately yields 2 NADH and 2 ATP by substrate-level phosphorylation.

Yield for each glucose molecule
2 NADH
2 ATP

Table 9.1: Complete list of products from glycolysis.

How many ATP are produced in glycolysis?

4 ATP.

Although 4 are produced, 2 ATP are utilized to convert glucose into pyruvate and should be subtracted from the total, resulting in a net yield of 2 ATP.

How many ATP are produced from the 2 NADH made in glycolysis?

2 ATP are produced by oxidative phosphorylation per NADH made in glycolysis. Thus, 4 ATP are created from the 2 NADH.

Note: Unlike NADH made in the mitochondria, NADH made from glycolysis enters the electron transport chain at a later point and only 2 ATP are made per NADH.

What are three processes which can follow glycolysis?

1. The Citric Acid Cycle (Krebs Cycle)

2. Lactic acid fermentation

3. Alcohol (ethyl) fermentation

The Citric Acid Cycle (Krebs Cycle) is discussed in depth below and occurs freely in the presence of oxygen (aerobic conditions).

Fermentation is a catabolic process that makes a limited amount of ATP from glucose without the benefit of the electron transport chain. In the absence of oxygen, this produces either lactic acid or ethyl alcohol. Clinically, this occurs after strenous exercise secondary to lactic acid build-up resulting in muscle cramps.

After pyruvate is made from glycolysis in the cytosol and then translocated into the mitochondria, what must each pyruvate be converted in order to begin the Citric Acid Cycle?

Acetyl coenzyme A, or Acetyl CoA

For the conversion of pyruvate to acetyl CoA, decarboxylation must occur, and results in two NADH from pyruvate decarboxylation per glucose molecule.

Pyruvate is converted to acetyl CoA by decarboxylation, releasing one NADH. Therefore, for each glucose molecule, 2 pyruvates are created and 2 NADH are made.

9.3   The Citric Acid Cycle (Krebs Cycle)

What is the citric acid (TCA) cycle?

An eight-step cycle catalyzed by several enzymes which takes place in the mitochondrial matrix using acetyl CoA to yield GTP, NADH, $FADH_2$ and CO_2.

Because one six-carbon glucose molecule yields two three-carbon acetyl CoA molecules, 2 turns of the TCA cycle are required to completely oxidize one molecule of glucose.

What is the yield for each acetyl CoA and glucose that enters the TCA cycle?

	Yield for each acetyl CoA	Yield for each glucose molecule
NADH	3	6
$FADH_2$	1	2
*GTP (ATP)**	1	2
CO_2	2	4

Table 9.2: Complete list of products from the Citric Acid (TCA) cycle: per acetyl CoA and per glucose molecule.

Note: GTP (guanosine triphosphate) is readily converted to ATP (adenosine triphosphate)

What process makes ATP in the TCA cycle?

Substrate-level phosphorylation.

9.4   Electron Transport Chain

What is the electron transport chain (ETC)?

A series of molecules located within the inner mitochondrial membrane which harnesses electrons from NADH and $FADH_2$ to create a pathway for hydrogen to enter the intermembrane space.

This creates a high proton (H^+) gradient (which can also be interpreted as a low pH) and, when ions pass down their concentration gradient through the gatekeepers of the inner mitochondrial membrane, i.e. ATP synthase, ADP is bound to inorganic phosphate to make ATP.

The proton driving force that makes H^+ rush past ATP synthase is called the *proton − motive force* and the synthesis of ATP by ATP synthase from this force is called *chemiosmosis*.

Altogether, this process of making ATP is called *oxidative phosphorylation*.

What is the final electron acceptor in the ETC?

Molecular oxygen, i.e. $\frac{1}{2} O_2$, which through several simple reactions eventually becomes water.

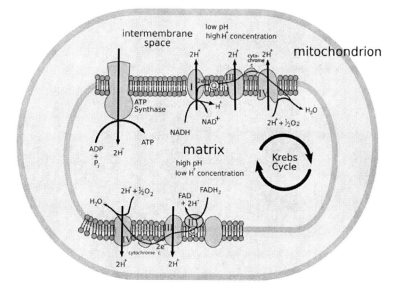

Figure 9.1: The Electron Transport Chain. *Illustration obtained from Wikipedia and used under the Creative Commons license.*

What structure maximizes the surface area of the inner mitochondrial membrane?

Crista

What determines the ATP yield for each NADH and FADH$_2$ which enters the ETC?

The energy level of the electron donating group which enters the ETC.

NADH enters the ETC *earlier* and 3 ATP are produced per NADH, while FADH$_2$ enters the ETC *later* and 2 ATP are produced per FADH$_2$.

What are the first and last electron pair acceptors in the ETC?

Flavin mononucleotide (FMN) and cytochrome a$_3$, respectively. *Note: Cyanide blocks cytochrome a$_3$.*

9.5   The Products of Cellular Respiration

9.5.1   The Products of Glycolysis

What is the complete list of products from glycolysis?

Yield for each glucose molecule
2 NADH
2 ATP

Table 9.3: Complete list of products from glycolysis.

9.5.2   The Products of TCA cycle

What is the complete list of products from the TCA cycle?

	Yield for each acetyl CoA	Yield for each glucose molecule
NADH	3	6
FADH$_2$	1	2
GTP (ATP)*	1	2
CO$_2$	2	4

Table 9.4: Complete list of products from the Citric Acid (TCA) cycle: per acetyl CoA and per glucose molecule.

Note: GTP (guanosine triphosphate) is readily converted to ATP (adenosine triphosphate)

9.5.3   The Processes Used to Produce ATP in Cellular Respiration

What are two processes by which 36 ATP are made during cellular respiration?

1. Substrate-level phosphorylation (4 ATP)

2. Oxidative phosphorylation (32 ATP)

Where do the 4 substrate-level ATP from glucose catabolism come from?

Glycolysis (net)	2 ATP
TCA (2 x 1 ATP/pyruvate)	2 ATP
Total	**4 ATP**

Table 9.5: Origin of substrate-level ATP formation.

What is the complete list of products from the TCA cycle?

	Yield for each acetyl CoA	Yield for each glucose molecule	Total ATP Yield
NADH	3	6	**18 ATP**
FADH$_2$	1	2	**4 ATP**
*GTP (ATP)**	1		**2 ATP**
CO$_2$	2	4	-
Total			**24 ATP**

Table 9.6: Complete list of products from the Citric Acid (TCA) cycle: ATP count.

Where do the 32 oxidative phosphorylation ATPs from glucose catabolism come from?

Process	ATP yield	Notes
Glycolysis (cytosol)	4	The two NADH from glycolysis cannot cross the inner mitochondrial membrane and enter the ETC at a later point, thus 2 NADH from glycolysis per glucose molecule x 2ATP/NADH = 4 ATP
Pyruvate decarboxylation to acetyl CoA (mitochondria)	6	Two NADH from pyruvate decarboxylation per glucose molecule, thus 2 pyruvate/glucose molecules x 3 ATP/NADH = 6 ATP
TCA (mitochondria)	22	6 NADH/glucose x 3 ATP/NADH = 18 ATP; $2FADH_2$/glucose x 2 ATP/$FADH_2$ = 4 ATP; thus 18 + 4 = 22 ATP
	32ATP	

Table 9.7: Origin of oxidative-level ATP formation.

Where do the 4 substrate level phosphorylation ATPs from glucose catabolism come from?

Process	ATP yield	Notes
Glycolysis (cytosol)	2	-
TCA (mitochondria)	2	2 GTP/glucose x 1 ATP/GTP = 2 ATP
	4 ATP	

Table 9.8: Origin of substrate-level ATP: A closer look.

Chapter 10

Enzymes & Metabolism

10.1   Enzyme Structure

What are enzymes?

Proteins that allow biological reactions to occur faster by reducing the energy of activation required for the reaction to take place between a substrate and a product.

For example, carbonic anhydrase catalyzes a key reaction in red blood cells by converting carbon dioxide and water into bicarbonate:

$$CO_2 + H_2O \rightleftharpoons H_2CO_3$$

What is a zymogen?

A secreted enzyme that is inactive and needs to be modified (cleaved) to become active, e.g. pepsinogen.

What is the structure of enzymes?

Most enzymes are globular proteins that can take a variety of structures.

The key structural aspect of an enzyme is the active site, a unique region which binds the substrate.

Another key structural site on enzymes is the allosteric site, a region removed from the active site which allows molecules to bind and affect enzyme function.

Plot the free energy changes (ΔG) over time when the reaction takes place both with and without an enzyme:

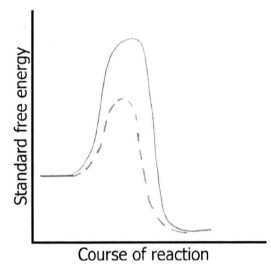

Figure 10.1: ΔG changes in a reaction with (dotted line) and without (solid) an enzyme.

What is the induced fit hypothesis?

Realistic hypothesis that describes the interaction between an enzyme and a substrate. After which, a conformational change occurs bringing together the various components of the enzyme allowing for the enzyme to catalyze the reaction via a stabilized transition state. For example, sucrose which catalyzes the hydrolysis of sucrase into glucose and fructose

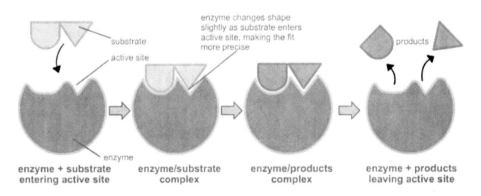

Figure 10.2: The Induced fit hypothysis hypothesis. *Public domain image illustrated by Tim Vickers.*

What is the lock and key hypothesis?

Older hypothesis that describes the interaction between an enzyme and a substrate without a conformational change. For example, acrosomal hydrolytic enzymes which allow for sperm penetration into the egg. This is a very specific "lock" and "key" so that a species can only fertilize its own eggs. Another example is tRNA synthetases which are 20 unique enzymes that bring together specific tRNAs with each of the 20 amino acids. Unlike the induced fit hypothesis, this model does not explain the observed stabilization of a transition state.

10.2   Control of Enzyme Activity

Generally speaking, what are five modulators of enzyme activity?

1. Environmental conditions

2. Cofactors

3. Inhibition

4. Allosteric regulation

5. Cooperativity

What are two environmental conditions which affect enzyme activity?

1. Temperature

   - Most enzymes work at body temperatures (35°C to 40°C), but some bacterial enzymes (e.g. thermophiles in hot springs) can work at higher temperatures. In fact, the DNA polymerase isolated from thermophiles is used in PCR reactions.

2. pH

   - Enzymes change their shapes depending on the pH. For example, pepsin works best at a pH of 2 while trypsin works at a pH of 8.

What are...

Cofactors?

Non-protein molecules which allow enzymes to be active, e.g. vitamins.

These molecules typically bind by weak bonds. In the event that the bond is strong, these cofactors are called prosthetic groups.

Apoenzymes?

An enzyme that does not have its cofactor and is inactive.

Holoenzymes?

An enzyme that has its cofactor and is active.

What are three forms of inhibition?

1. **Feedback inhibition**: when the product of a reaction can bind to the enzyme in the pathway and inhibit it (this is a form of allosteric inhibition, see below).

2. **Irreversible inhibition**: when a molecule interacts with an enzyme using covalent bonds or damages the enzyme's structure and permanently inhibits it.

3. **Reversible inhibition**: when a molecule interacts with an enzyme using noncovalent bonds and decreases the enzyme's activity

What are two types of reversible inhibition?

1. Competitive inhibition, whereby an inhibitor competes with the substrate for the enzyme's active site.

2. Noncompetitive inhibition, whereby an inhibitor binds to an enzyme away from the active site, i.e. an allosteric site.

How is each type of inhibition overcome?

- Competitive inhibition can be overcome by **increasing the concentration of the *substrate*** and thereby increasing the likelihood of enzyme-substrate interactions and decreasing the opportunity for enzyme-inhibitor interactions.

- Noncompetitive inhibition usually results in permanent inhibition of the enzyme and therefore can only be overcome by **increasing the concentration of the *enzyme***.

What is allosteric regulation?

The regulation of enzyme function by the interaction of a molecule at a site other than the active site.

- Noncompetitive inhibition and feedback inhibition are examples of allosteric regulation.

What is an example of cooperativity?

The phenomenon by which the activity of an enzyme with multiple active sites is affected by the concentration of substrates. In positive cooperativity, the more substrate available the more active the enzyme. Negative cooperativity is less common and is seen when the activity of an enzyme is not affected by the concentration of the substrate.

Chapter 11

The Circulatory System

OK, this may go against every teaching paradigm, but we are going to get straight to the chase and first go over the oxygen dissociation curve for hemoglobin. It's an MCAT favorite but also a tricky one. Also, because it's at the beginning of the section, you have to go over it every time you want to cover the circulatory system and it won't end up being one of those "I meant to get to it but..."

If you want the bread and butter, skip this section...

11.1   The oxygen-hemoglobin dissociation curve

The oxygen dissociation curve for hemoglobin - draw it.

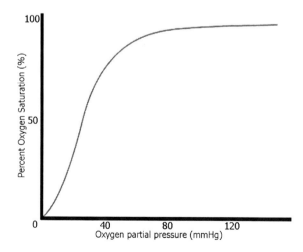

Figure 11.1: Oxygen dissociation curve for hemoglobin.

Basically, what you see in Figure 11.1 on page 89 is the percentage of hemoglobin (Hgb) fully saturated with O_2 (y-axis) and the partial pressure of O_2 (PO_2, in mmHG) in the blood at normal physiologic conditions (x-axis).

Therefore, the extremes of both axes, i.e. close to 100 % O_2 Hgb saturation and close to 100 mmHg PO_2 reflects the arterial blood with a high content of fully saturated Hgb.

What is meant by "shifting the curve"?

"Shifting the curve" is a result of certain conditions, different from normal physiologic conditions, that "move" the curve to the left or right.

What moves the curve to the left and right?

	Increase in Hgb O_2 affinity (Left shift)	Decrease in Hgb O_2 affinity (Right shift)
pH	↑	↓
pCO$_2$	↓	↑
Temperature	↓	↑
*2,3 diphosphoglycerate (DPG)**	Absence	Presence
Carbon monoxide	Presence	Absence
Generic example	Muscle at rest	Muscle at work

Table 11.1: Factors which affect the oxygen-hemoglobin dissociation curve: High pH, low pCO_2, low temperatures and the absence of DPG shift the curve to the left and reflect an increase in O_2 affinity (left column). Contrarily, lower pH, higher pCO_2, higher temperatures and the presence of DPG shift the curve to the right and reflect a decrease in O_2 affinity (right column).

* DPG is the primary organic phosphate in mammals. DPG binds and rearranges hemoglobin into a lower oxygen-affinity state thereby encouraging the release of oxygen and shifting the curve to the right.

How does myoglobin shift the curve?

Myoglobin is found in muscles and binds to oxygen, releasing it when oxygen availability is low (e.g. during exercise): myoglobin has a dissociation curve well to the **left** of that of hemoglobin.

How can this be represented graphically?

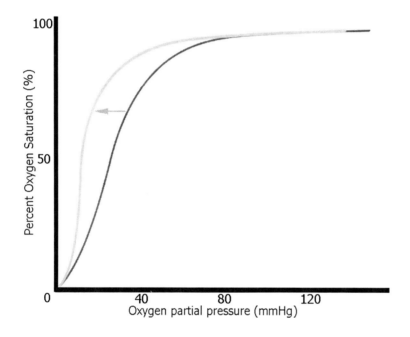

Figure 11.2: The oxygen-myoglobin dissociation curve is illustrated above (light gray) and is shifted to the left compared to the hemoglobin dissociation curve (dark gray).

As we go through the circulatory system, we will first look at the adult circulation. Towards the end of the chapter, we will look at key points of the fetal circulation and how they differ from the newborn.

11.2   Functional considerations of the circulatory system

What are the two general functions of the circulatory system?

1. Mechanism to deliver...

   - Oxygen
   - Fluids
   - Nutrients and ions

2. Mechanism to remove...

   - CO_2
   - Metabolic wastes

What are the main organs of the circulatory system?

1. Heart

2. Lungs

What are the main structures of the circulatory system?

1. Arteries & arterioles

2. Veins/venules

3. Capillary beds

What generalizations can be made about arteries and veins?

Arteries are vessels lined with smooth muscle that carry blood away from the heart, veins are thinner walled vessels that carry blood towards the heart.

What are the exceptions to the generalization of oxygenated and deoxygenated blood being carried by arteries and veins?

After one is born, there are two exceptions:

1. The *pulmonary artery*, which carries deoxygenated blood from the right ventricle to the lungs.

2. The *pulmonary vein*, which carries oxygenated blood from the lung to
   the left atrium.

**What are the structural and functional differences between arterial
and venous systems?**

	Arterial	**Venous**
Vessel thickness	Thicker	Thinner
Blood O_2 *	Higher	Lower
Pressure **	Higher (creating resistance)	Lower (creating capacitance)
Blood flow velocity	High	Low
Valves **	No	Yes

Table 11.2: Structural and functional differences between arterial and venous systems.

* *As mentioned above, the pulmonary arteries and veins carry deoxygenated and oxygenated
blood, respectively.*

** *Arteries contain more smooth muscle than veins, partly to withstand the higher pressures
(arteries are positionally closer to the heart) and partly to regulate blood pressure. For this
reason, arteries are higher pressure vessels and create resistance to blood flow. Veins, on the
other hand, have less smooth muscle, mainly because they do not deal with high pressures
and "store" blood - hence capacitance. Veins also have valves to help keep the blood moving
towards the heart and prevent blood from accumulating in the periphery.*

What is the structure and function of the capillary beds?

Capillaries are only one cell layer thick and allow for the exchange of gases,
heat, ions and solutes.

The principles of Le Châtelier and passive diffusion can be applied here: Because
O_2 tension is relatively lower in tissues and higher in capillary blood, O_2 will
diffuse out of the capillaries and into the tissues. Conversely, because CO_2
tension is relatively higher in tissues and lower in the capillaries, CO_2 will
diffuse into the capillaries.

What is the role of capillaries during shock?

First off, shock is when there is significant blood volume depletion. This can be for various reasons, but capillary beds are important in shunting blood away from various sites when blood volume is low. Take for example someone who just ate lunch and sustained a large gash in her leg and is losing a lot of blood. The gut has a very extensive capillary bed and uses a lot of cardiac output during digestion. Because blood is at a premium, the gut capillary beds will clamp down and allow for blood to be re-routed to more vital structures.

Label the various components of the heart:

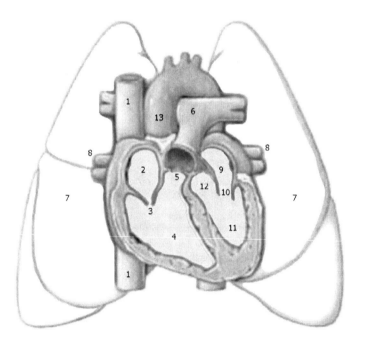

Figure 11.3: The heart: (1) Vena cava, (2) right atrium, (3) tricuspid valve, (4) right ventricle, (5) pulmonary semilunar valve , (6) pulmonary artery, (7) lungs, (8) pulmonary vein, (9) left atrium, (10) mitral valve, (11) left ventricle, (12) aortic valve, (13) aorta.

What is the function of the right and left side of the heart?

The function of the **right** side of the heart is to *collect deoxygenated blood* that is transported from the body to the heart by way of the vena cava and *pump it to the lungs* via the pulmonary artery.

The function of the **left** side of the heart is to *collect oxygenated blood* that is transported from the lungs to the heart by way of the pulmonary vein and *pump it to the body* via the aorta.

What are differences between the systemic and pulmonary circulations after one is born?

The pulmonary circulation is a low pressure system and the systemic circulation is a high pressure system.

What is systolic and diastolic pressure?

Systolic pressure is the pressure of the blood while the heart is squeezing and corresponds with the first documented number (e.g. 130 if the BP is 130/80).

Diastolic pressure is the pressure of the blood while the heart is relaxing and corresponds with the second number (e.g. 80 if the BP is 130/80).

What are the main components of blood?

1. Plasma

   - H_2O, clotting factors

2. Cells

   - Erythrocytes (red blood cells), leukocytes (white blood cells), thrombocytes (platelets)

3. Molecules

   - Electrolytes, Na^+, C, K^+, HCO_3

What regulates intravascular fluid volume (plasma)?

Several things control plasma volume, primarily osmotic tension within the blood which is controlled by hormones. For example, antidiuretic hormone (ADH) and the renin-angiotensin system exquisitively control intravascular volume.

What is the difference between hemoglobin and hematocrit?

Hemoglobin (Hgb) is the oxygen-carrying protein found in erythrocytes. When Hgb is defective such as in sickle cell anemia, erythrocytes have difficulty carrying O_2.

Hematocrit (Hct) is the percentage of erythrocytes in the blood for a given volume of blood. When the erythrocyte count is low, this is called anemia.

It is clear that Hgb and Hct can go hand-in-hand. These intricacies are beyond the scope for the MCAT so take away the one line definitions listed above. You'll learn this in depth in med school, but diseases can affect each differently, e.g. thalassemias will affect the quality of the hemoglobin but not the erythrocyte count, while in leukemia (uncontrolled proliferation of leukocytes) the quality of the hemoglobin is unaffected, but the erythrocyte cell counts can decline.

How is thermoregulation controlled by the circulatory system?

In the event of temperature changes, the skin plays a large part in thermoregulation by allowing blood to fill the capillary beds and allow for heat to escape. Conversely, shunting blood away from the capillary beds when heat is at a premium allows the core organs to stay warm.

11.3   Physiologic considerations of the circulatory system

What affects the affinity to which Hgb binds O_2?

1. The quality of Hgb

   - For example, in sickle cell anemia Hgb is defective and cannot "hold" on to O_2 as well as unaffected Hgb can.

2. Presence of competitive binders

   - Carbon monoxide which binds with greater affinity to Hgb than O_2

What is the oxygen dissociation curve so upright in the middle?

This is an example of *cooperativity*: One O_2 makes another O_2 bind easier and so on. This is an MCAT favorite also. Although Hgb is not an enzyme, review cooperativity in enzymes (see page 87).

11.4   Electrophysiologic considerations of the circulatory system: The QRS complex

What is the pacemaker of the heart?

The *sinoatrial (SA) node*. There are several other components to the electrical conduction system (AV node, bundle of HIS and Purkinje fibers), but the SA node is the fastest and supreme commander of the heart.

If you think about it, it makes sense that the fastest source is the ultimate pacer. Kind of like a track event: In long-distance events, a pacer will go out and pull the rest of the team along. Just an aside, and probably beyond the scope of the exam, but if the fastest pacer is sick, the next fastest pacer steps in.

Draw the electrocardiogram tracing for one heart cycle and label its parts?

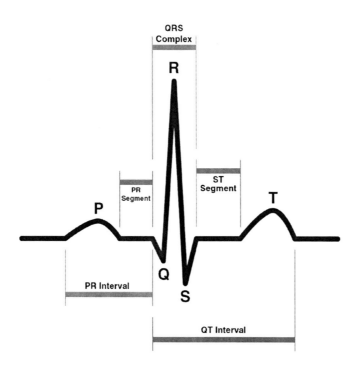

Figure 11.4: The QRS complex: the *P wave* represents atrial depolarization (contraction), the *PR interval* represents completion of atrial contraction and transmission of the electrical signal between the SA and AV node, the *QRS complex* represents ventricular depolarization (contraction), the *ST segment* represents completion of ventricular contraction and the *T wave* represents ventricular repolarization (relaxation). *Public domain image illustrated by Anthony Atkielski.*

11.5 Fetal Circulation

At what point does the fetal circulation switch to the newborn/adult circulation?

After the first breath of air.

What organ is not used by the fetus and what three mechanisms are used to bypass blood away from it?

The lungs are not actively used by the fetus until birth. Three shunts or "bypasses" direct flow away from the lungs (see illustration 11.5 on page 100):

1. Ductus arteriosus

   - Shunts blood from the pulmonary artery to the aorta and away from the developing lungs

2. Ductus venosus

   - Shunts blood from the umbilical vein to the inferior vena cava and away from the developing liver

3. Foramen ovale

   - Shunts blood from the right atrium to the left atrium and also away from the developing lungs

Note: The lungs are not fully developed until late in the third trimester. Additionally, surfactant (a fluid which helps keep alveoli open) is not produced until the third trimester. For these two reasons, premature babies have difficulty breathing and are considered high risk.

Besides these three mechanisms, what intrinsic characteristic of the pulmonary circulation is seen in the fetus and prevents blood flow to the lungs?

The pulmonary circulation is a HIGH pressure system, making it unfavorable for blood to flow there.

After birth and after the first breath, the pulmonary circulation becomes a LOW pressure system and becomes favorable for blood to flow there.

Briefly describe the sequence of events that occurs when a newborn takes her first breath and how blood flow to the lungs increases after birth.

1. The fetus relies on the above-mentioned shunting mechanisms to divert blood away from the pulmonary circulation: a high pressure circuit with lots of resistence to blood flow.

2. The instinctual reflex to breathe occurs and the newborn takes her first breath and the lungs expand.

3. The pressure drops significantly in the lungs.

4. The favorable pressure drop results in an increase in blood flow to the lungs.

5. Now, the pulmonary circulation is the *low* pressure system and the systemic circulation is the *high* pressure system.

6. This causes the three shunts to close.

See Figure 11.5 on page 100.

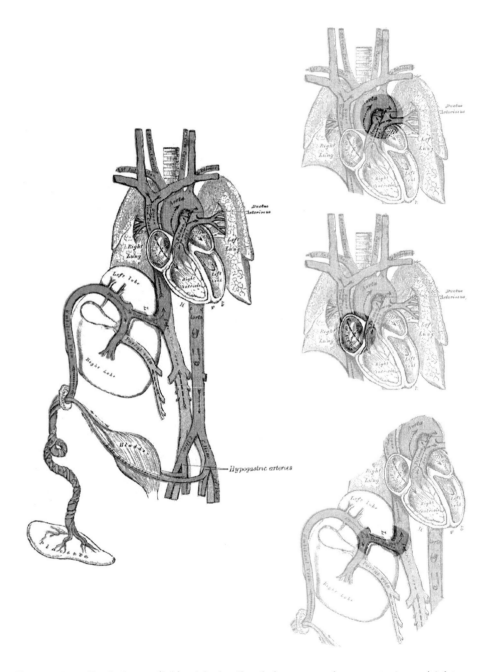

Figure 11.5: Fetal shunts (left) with details of the patent ductus arteriosus (right, top), foramen ovale (right, middle) and ductus venosus (right, bottom). *Public domain image modified from original lithograph plate from Gray's Anatomy.*

Chapter 12

The Respiratory System

12.1 Functional considerations of the respiratory system

What are the different functions of the respiratory system?

- Allow for gas exchange

- Maintain the body's acid-base balance

  - Through CO_2 (from bicarbonate, HCO_3^-) exchange

- Temperature control, including warming air through the nasal passages

- Removing environmental particles and preventing disease

  - Through nasal hairs, mucous membranes and mucociliary movement of phlegm out of the lungs and into the esophagus

What is the basic functional unit of the lung?

Alveoli.

What is the role of surfactant in the alveoli?

Surfactant decreases the surface tension within the alveoli and prevents the alveoli from collapsing onto themselves during exhalation.

Note: In premature newborns, the lack of sufficient surfactant results in significant breathing difficulties for the newborn because surfactant is not produced until the third trimester.

What causes air to enter and leave the lung?

Pressure changes between the lung and the outside environment, see Figure 12.1 below:

- During inspiration, the diaphragm contracts/flattens, increasing the intrathoracic volume and thereby decreasing the pressure in the lungs with air rushing in, see Figure 12.1 below:

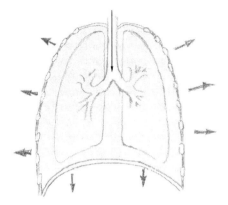

Figure 12.1: Inhalation: Dynamic factors that affect air flow.

- During expiration, the diaphragm relaxes, decreasing the intrathoracic volume and thereby increasing the pressure in the lungs with air rushing out, see Figure 12.2 below:

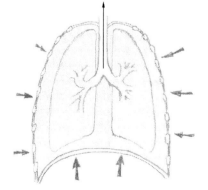

Figure 12.2: Expiration: Dynamic factors that affect air flow.

What is the role of the rib cage during breathing?

The elastic recoil of the ribs allows expiration to be a passive process requiring little effort.

How can Boyle's law be applied to the changes in volume and pressure associated with breathing?

If you treat being at rest as the "equilibrium point," then during inspiration, as the volume increases, pressure has to decrease and air rushes in:.

$$P_{REST}V_{REST} = P_{INSPIRATION}V_{INSPIRATION}$$

Conversely, if during expiration, volume decreases, then the pressure has to increase and air rushes out:

$$P_{REST}V_{REST} = P_{INSPIRATION}V_{INSPIRATION}$$

12.2   Lung Volumes and Capacities

Just like the circulatory system's oxygen dissociation curve, the respiratory system has an MCAT favorite also. It may or may not come up in your version of the test, but it will definitely come up in your 1st year medical school physiology class: lung capacities and volumes.

Tidal volume (TV)?

The amount of air breathed in or out during normal respiration at rest (about 450 to 500 mL). See Figure 12.3 on page 105.

Inspiratory reserve volume?

The additional air that can be inhaled after a normal tidal breath in. About 2.5 more litres can be inhaled. See Figure 12.3 on page 105.

Expiratory reserve volume (ERV)?

The amount of additional air that can be breathed out after normal exhalation (about 1.5 L). See Figure 12.3 on page 105.

Residual volume (RV)?

The amount of air in the lungs after a maximal exhalation (about 1.5 L). See Figure 12.3 on page 105.

Total lung capacity (TC)?

All the air the lungs can hold (about 6 liters). See Figure 12.3 on page 105.

Vital capacity (VC)?

The maximum volume of air that can be exhaled after a maximum inspiration. See Figure 12.3 on page 105.

Inspiratory capacity (IC)?

The volume that can be inhaled after a tidal breath out. See Figure 12.3 on page 105.

Functional residual capacity (ERV + RV)?

The amount of air left in the lungs after a tidal breath out. See Figure 12.3 on page 105.

Anatomical dead space?

The volume that is contained within the airways. See Figure 12.3 on page 105.

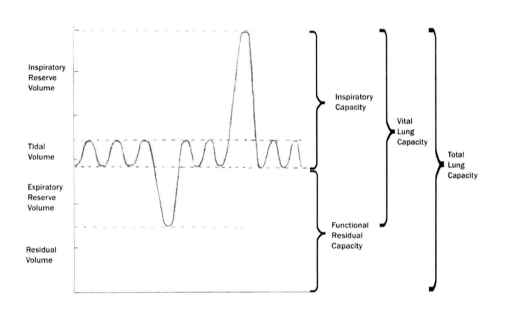

Figure 12.3: Lung volumes and capacities.

Chapter 13

The Digestive System

The digestive system will be covered from two angles: anatomical considerations and enzymatic considerations - here we go...

13.1 Anatomical Considerations

What are the two general types of digestion which take place?

Chemical and mechanical.

13.1.1 Mouth

What type of digestion takes place in the mouth?

Chemical digestion from amylase and mechanical digestion from teeth.

What is the function of saliva?

Saliva *lubricates* the food bolus (bolus - a technical term for a distinct, organized mass) and provides a *vehicle for amylase* to get distributed into the bolus.

What propels the bolus towards the pharynx?

The tongue.

13.1.2   Pharynx

What makes the mouth and pharynx unique from the other structural components of the digestive system?

They are used by both the digestive and respiratory systems.

What critical structure divides both systems?

The epiglottis.

13.1.3   Esophagus

What process begins in the esophagus and continues throughout the digestive tract?

Persistalsis, a rhythmic set of involuntary contractions which carries the bolus along the digestive tract.

What sphincter is the gateway for the stomach?

The lower esophageal sphincter (LES).

The LES also prevents food from regurgitating into the esophagus during stomach digestion. Conversely, during vomiting, the LES relaxes to allow for food evacuation.

13.1.4   Stomach

What are the main functions of the stomach?

1. Continue mechanical digestion through muscular contractions

2. Provide a contained, acidic enviroment for chemical digestion

   - This provides the right pH for pepsin to degrade proteins
   - Also provides a milieu to kill off pathogens

3. Allow for food storage

What are the main regions of the stomach?

Cardiac, body and fundus.

What creates the acidic environment in the stomach?

Parietal cells, which secrete hydrochloric acid.

- pH 2

- Activates enzymes

- Regulated by histamine, acetylcholine and gastrin

What sphincter controls passage out of the stomach?

The pyloric sphincter, the gatekeeper between the fundus and the first part of the small intestine (duodenum).

13.1.5   Small Intestine

What are the main functions of the small intestine?

1. Neutralize acidity from stomach

2. Reabsorb nutrients

3. Produce of enzymes

What are the parts of the small intestine?

1. Duodenum

2. Jejunum

3. Ileum

Note: The channel or space in hollow organs is called the lumen.

What is the unique microstructure found in the small intestine (and not in the large intestine)?

Villi. These also have mini-villi on them called microvilli. With magnification, this looks like a brush and hence this creates the *brush borders*.

The main purpose of villi and microvilli is to *increase the surface area for absorption.* Destruction of villi is seen in absorptive diseases such as Crohn's disease and celiac sprue.

Each villi have a dedicated capillary and a lacteal (which absorbs fats).

What nutrient-enriched blood supply drains the small intestine?

The portal blood supply, which takes nutrient-rich blood from the small intestine and channels it to the liver.

What is the name given to the bolus which has been digested in the stomach, passed through the pyloric sphincter, and has entered the duodenum?

Chyme.

13.1.6   Large Intestine

What are the main functions of the large intestine?

1. Reabsorb water

2. Maintain a population of bacteria (*E. coli*) which produce vitamin K

Note: Chyme now becomes stool as water is reabsorbed and dead local flora (E. coli) contributing to the bulk of fecal matter.

What are the parts of the large intestine?

1. Cecum

    • Including the appendix

2. Colon (ascending, transverse and descending)

3. Rectum

What is the role of the rectum?

To store stool prior to defecation through the anus.

What is the role of the anus?

A sphincter for stool passage which is under both voluntary and involuntary control.

13.1.7   Liver, Gall Bladder & Pancreas

What is unique about the liver compared to most other organs?

Incredible capacity to regenerate itself.

This is probably beyond the scope of the MCAT, but what is the functional unit of the liver?

Portal triad.

Nevertheless, try to remember that the liver is grossly divided into lobes.

What is the function of the liver?

1. Port of entry for nutrient-enriched blood supply draining the small intestine (portal blood system).

2. To detoxify toxins

3. To store vitamins and glycogen

4. To modifiy and eliminate absorbed fats

5. To produce bile

What is glycogen and what is its role?

Glycogen is a storage form of glucose. During times of duress, the body can use this form of sugar.

What is the function of the gall bladder?

To store bile.

What is bile?

A green substance made by the liver which emulsifies lipids in the chyme by separating lipid into droplets (aka *micelles*).

Incidentally, bile is the body's way of eliminating cholesterol and gives stool its brown color.

What is the function of the pancreas?

The pancreas has endocrine (ductless secretions) and exocrine (duct secretions) functions.

The exocrine functions will be discussed below and the endocrine functions will be discussed in the endocrine chapter.

13.2 Enzymatic Considerations

There are a host of enzymes which are used in digestion. Their origin, stimulus and functions are varied and daunting to learn. To get started, learn the enzyme names and where they are secreted. Then, try to memorize the reactions they catalyze. As you will quickly see, the carbohydrate enzymes have specific products, while the others are pretty obvious. For this section, we will look at the three major nutrients separately - see Tables 13.1, 13.2 and 13.3 below.

Remember:

- Enzymes are not consumed in a reaction

- Enzymes decrease the energy of activation and increase the rate of the reaction

- Zymogens are inactive, enzyme pre-cursors

13.2.1 Carbohydrates

Origin	Enzyme	Catalyzes	Destination
Salivary glands Stomach	Salivary amylase	Starch → Maltose	Oral cavity
Pancreas	Pancreatic amylase	Starch → Maltose	Small intestine
Brush border of the small intestine	Lactase	Lactose → Glucose + Galactose	Small intestine
	Maltase	Maltose → 2 x Glucose	Small intestine
	Sucrase	Sucrose → Glucose + Fructose	Small intestine

Table 13.1: Enzymes involved in carbohydrate catabolism.

13.2.2 Proteins

Origin	Enzyme	Catalyzes	Destination
Stomach	Pepsin*	Protein → Polypeptides	Small intestine
Pancreas	Trypsin* Chymotrypsin* Carboxypeptidase	Polypeptides → Amino acids Polypeptides → Amino acids Polypeptides → Amino acids	Small intestine
Brush border of the small intestine	Aminopeptidase Dipeptidase	Polypeptides → Amino acids Polypeptides → Amino acids	Small intestine

Table 13.2: Enzymes involved in protein catabolism.

Pepsin, trypsin and chymotrypsin are secreted in their zymogen forms as pepsinogen, trypsinogen and chymotrypsinogen, respectively. For more info on zymogens, see the enzyme chapter.

13.2.3 Lipids

Origin	Enzyme	Catalyzes	Destination
Pancreas	Lipase	Fats → Glycerol + Fatty Acids	Small intestine
Liver	Bile	Because bile is not a real enzyme it doesn't really catalyze a reaction. Instead, it isolates fat droplets into micelles).	Small intestine

Table 13.3: Enzymes involved in lipid catabolism.

Chapter 14

The Excretory System

14.1 Anatomical considerations of the excretory system

What are the main roles of the excretory system?

1. Control blood pressure

2. Control osmolarity of blood

3. Maintain acid-base balance

4. Excretion of nitrogenous waste

What are the main organs of the excretory system?

1. Kidney (produces urine)

2. Ureters (transport urine)

3. Bladder (stores urine)

4. Urethra (the urethra throws out the urine)

What is the functional unit of the kidney?

The nephron.

What are the two levels of the kidney?

The cortex and medulla. The medulla is in the middle.

Label the parts of the nephron below:

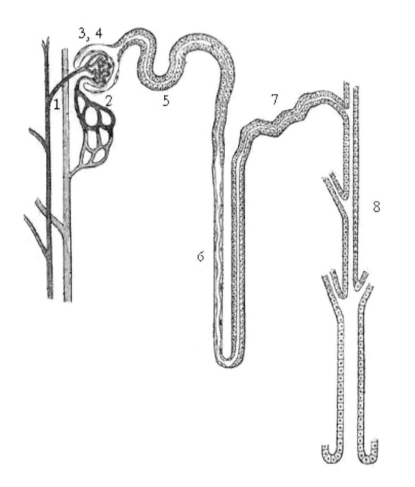

Figure 14.1: The nephron: (1) Afferent capillary, (2) efferent capillary, (3) glomerulus within (4) Bowman's capsule, (5) proximal tubule, (6) loop of Henle, (7) distal tubule, (8) collecting duct. *Public domain image modified from original lithograph plate from Gray's Anatomy.*

Note: The loop of Henle passes through the medulla of the kidney. The increased osmolarity of the renal medulla causes the filtrate in the lumen to be reabsorbed, thereby increasing the concentration of the urine. When the filtrate leaves the loop of Henle through the ascending limb, water is prevented from re-entering the lumen to dilute the filtrate. This is called **counter current multiplication** *and is a very important process to concentrate urine.*

14.2 Functional considerations of the excretory system

What three processes in the nephron are used to create urine?

1. Filtration

   - This occurs across the glomerulus/Bowman's capsule interface
   - Filtration is like a sieve which keeps out the "peas" (aka cells, glucose, proteins) but lets smaller molecules through.

2. Reabsorption

   - This occurs along the length of the nephron, but most of the action occurs in the proximal tubule.
   - Reabsoprtion allows the body to reabsorb many precious ions that are in the filtrate.

3. Secretion

   - This also occurs along the length of the nephron
   - Secretion allows the body to secrete substances that are intended to be excreted into the filtrate.

How is urine concentrated?

1. Passage of the filtrate through the highly osmolar medulla draws water out of the Loop of Henle's lumen (**counter current multiplication**).

2. Passage of the filtrate through the collecting duct also occurs through the concentrated medulla and can produce concentrated urine.

3. Anti-diuretic hormone (ADH) is pivotal in drawing off water to concentrate the filtrate and will be discussed in greater detail in the endocrine chapter on page 131.

Explain how the kidney controls the following:

Blood pressure?

The are several ways that the kidney controls blood pressure:

1. Solute regulation. Remember that water follows solutes to maintain osmotic balance. So, if Na^+ is absorbed (which the body loves to do), water will follow and cause an increase in intravascular volume and therefore blood pressure. More on this later with aldosterone in the endocrine chapter.

2. Renin-angiotensin system. The kidney sees and filters all the blood; so do most organs with extensive capaillary beds, but the kidney sees the greatest percentage of cardiac output. With that said, the kidneys are excellent monitors of blood volume. When blood pressure is low, the kidneys respond by secreting renin. More on this later with the renin-angiotensin system.

Osmoregulation?

Solute control is another one of the kidney's main functions. The main one being Na^+, which is usually reabsorbed because it is such a valuable ion.

Acid-base balance?

Bicarbonate, HCO_3^-, plays a big role in acid-base balance in the blood. The kidney is involved in *excreting* it.

$$CO_2 + H_2O \rightleftharpoons H_2CO_3 \rightleftharpoons H^+ + HCO_3^-$$

Also, remember that carbonic anhydrase catalyzes the reaction which converts bicarbonate back to water and carbon dioxide. This enzyme is located in the proximal tubule. Take-home message: HCO_3^- excretion is regulated by the kidney and this in turn controls the acid-base balance of the body.

Excretion of nitrogenous wastes?

Nitrogenous wastes, aka the break down products of proteins, are excreted by the body through the kidneys in the form of urea.

Chapter 15

The Nervous System

15.1 Microscopic Considerations

What is the function of:

Dendrites?

- "Power lines" which transport signals *toward* the cell body; receive signals from axons

Cell body?

- Houses the nucleus and organelles. Consider it as the brain or power station of the cell

Axons?

- "Power lines" which transport signals *away* from the cell body.

- These are long extensions that can be up 1 meter long!

Schwann cells?

- Schwann cells insulate the axon by creating a myelin sheath. Myelin is a fatty substance that is analogous to the rubber sheath around an electrical cable.

- Outside of the central nervous system (CNS), Schwann cells produce myelin. Within the CNS, oligodendrocytes produce myelin.

Nodes of Ranvier?

- The "gaps" between the Schwann cells and concentration of voltage-gated ion channels

- Provide sites for electrical signals to jump from node to node. This is called *saltatory conduction* and increases the electrical transmission rate significantly.

Synapse?

- "Buds" between the axon of one cell and the dendrites of another that allow for the propagation of signals between neurons.

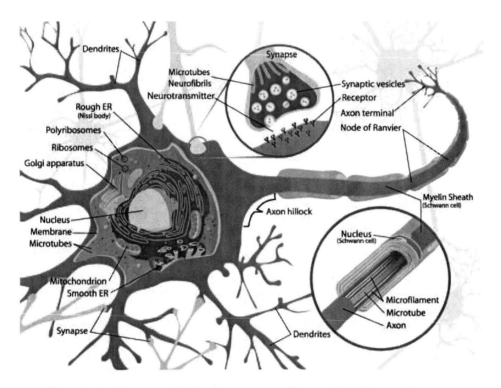

Figure 15.1: The nerve. *Public domain image illustrated by Mariana Ruiz..*

What mediates the communications between neurons?

Neurotransmitters. A chemical transmitter such as acetylcholine binds to a post-synaptic receptor that causes changes in ion conduction.

What ensures that the synapse is cleared of all neurotransmitters to prevent continuous activation of the post-synaptic receptors?

1. Enzymes. For example, *acetylcholinesterase* which breaks down acetylcholine.

2. Reuptake of neurotransmitters

15.2   Action Potentials

What are action potentials?

Electrical impulses carried by neurons.

What is a "potential"?

The difference between electrical charges on either side of a membrane, also called an electric potential.

At rest in a neuron, there is a potential: the *resting membrane potential* typically -70 mV.

What maintains the resting potential of the neuron?

Largely leakage from potassium channels and also from the sodium-potassium pump. This pump places 3 Na^+ extracellularly for every 2 K^+ that are pumped intracellularly. ATP drives this process and by differentially placing cations into and out of the cell, an electrochemical gradient is made.

What is the threshold potential?

The electrical charge required to propogate an action potential. It's the minimum amount of electrical "force" required to get the process going. It may help to think about it as static force, i.e. the initial amount of force to get an object to move across a surface.

This is why it is termed *"all or none."* It either goes or does not. When it is in fact overcome, depolarization is said to have occurred.

What two channels propagate an action potential?

- Voltage-gated Na^+ channels
- Voltage-gated K^+ channels

Note: "Voltage-gated" channels are a key principle. Voltage-gated means that a channel will only operate at certain voltages; outside this window, the channel becomes inactive and closes.

What sequence of events takes place to conduct an action potential along the length of a neuron?

- Voltage-gated Na^+ channels open
  - Fast channel opening
  - $\mathbf{Na}^+$ rushes i**N**to the neuron
- Voltage-gated Na^+ channels close
- Voltage-gated K^+ channels open
  - Slower channel opening
  - K^+ rushes out the neuron to "keep away from the Na^+"
  - There may be too much efflux causing an overshoot of ions. This is called *hyperpolarization.*
- Voltage-gated K^+ channels close

15.2.1 Wrapping Up Synapses and Neural Signals

Based on this system for action potential propagation, is there a potential for signal fade?

No. Because of the *"all or none"* principle, signals continue until they reach their target. Further, with synapses interspersed between the origin of the action potential and its destination, chemical intermediaries (neurotransmitters) also help to perpetuate the signals.

When will a neuron be less likely to initiate an action potential?

During the *refractory period*: the period right after an action potential that is characterized by an inability to be stimulated.

What are EPSPs and IPSPs?

A neuron can receive two types of signals: (1) excitatory post-synaptic potentials (EPSPs) and (2) inhibitory post-synpatic potentials (IPSPs). EPSPs will depolarize the cell and IPSPs will hyperpolarize the cell. The sum of these two will determine the overall potential. If it's above the threshold for stimulation, an action potential will be created.

15.3 Macroscopic Considerations

What are four major functions of the nervous system?

1. Control and integrate body systems

2. Adapt the body's processes and actions to the enviroment

3. Integrate sensory input

4. To allow us to think and have consciousness

What are the main regional divisions of the nervous system?

The central nervous system (CNS) and peripheral nervous system (PNS). The CNS is composed of the brain and spinal cord. Everything else belongs in the PNS, including the cranial nerves.

15.3.1   Central Nervous System

What are the components of the CNS?

The brain and spinal cord, both of which are wrapped in a three-layered membrane called the *meninges*.

What are the three main parts of the brain?

- Hindbrain

    - Most primitive
    - Key structures:
        * Brain stem (inc. medulla oblongata and pons): Allows for basic functions of life (e.g. breathing) and a line in the movie *Water Boy* - the Prof says, "Boy, is there something wrong with your medulla oblongata?"
        * Cerebellum: Coordination of fine motor movements.

- Midbrain

    - Integrates visual and auditory signals

- Forebrain

    - Most advanced part of brain
    - Allows for consciousness
    - Key structures:
        * Thalamus: Relay center for the brain
        * Hypthalamus: Controls endocrine system, e.g. makes ADH and stores it in the post. pituitary

© 2005 - 2007

* Cerebral cortex aka gray matter: Information processor which gives us intelligence, creativity, memory, emotion, etc.

What are the lobes of the cerebral cortex?

Frontal, temporal, parietal and occiptal lobes.

Label the parts below of the spinal cord cross section:

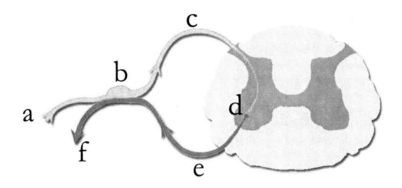

Figure 15.2: The spinal cord cross section: (a) Sensory neuron, (b) dorsal root ganglion, (c) sensory root, (d) synapse, (e) motor root, (f) motor neuron. Sensory information (input) enters the spinal cord segment dorsally; motor information (output) enters ventrally. *Note: In reverse from the brain, gray matter in the spinal cord is on the inside, while white matter is on the outside.*

What are the divisions of the spinal cord?

Cervical, thoracic, lumbar and sacral.

15.3.2   Peripheral nervous system

What are the roles of the...

Cranial nerves and spinal nerves?

The part of the peripheral nervous system originating from the brain (cranial nerves) and spinal cord (spinal nerves) that have a sensory or motor component. This allows them to relay incoming and outcoming signals.

Autonomic nervous system?

The part of the peripheral nervous system in charge of unconscious processes, e.g. regulating how fast the heart beats or activating the digestive tract. There are two sections of the autonomic nervous system: (1) the sympathetic nervous system and (2) the parasympathetic nervous system.

Somatic nervous system?

The part of the peripheral nervous system that is under voluntary control and includes skeletal muscles.

Reflexes?

Reflexes are simple, stereotyped movements intended to protect the organism from harm. These automated actions such as the knee-jerk reflex or withdrawal reflex synapse are mediated at their corresponding spinal segments, commonly bypassing conscious and cerebral input.

15.4   Autonomic Nervous System

What are the roles of the autonomic nervous system (ANS)?

Similar to the volume dial on a stereo, the ANS controls the organism's "volume" by speeding things up (sympathetics) and slowing things down (parasympathetics).

What are the stereotyped functions of the ANS?

Sympathetic nervous system	Parasympathetic nervous system
"Fight or flight"	"Rest and digest"

Table 15.1: Stereotyped functions of the ANS.

What are the neurotransmitters used by the ANS?

Sympathetic nervous system	Parasympathetic nervous system
Norepinephrine	Acetylcholine

Table 15.2: Neurotransmitters of the ANS.

What spinal nerves (divisions) are dedicated to the ANS?

Sympathetic nervous system	Parasympathetic nervous system
Thoraco-lumbar areas	Cervico-sacral areas

Table 15.3: Dedicated spinal divisions of the ANS.

*Note: Think of the **para**sympathetic nervous system as the **par**entheses around sympathetic nervous system*

What are the differences in post-synaptic neuron length in the sympathetic nervous system and parasympathetic nervous system?

Sympathetic nervous system	Parasympathetic nervous system
Long	Short

Table 15.4: Variations in post-synaptic neuron length in the ANS.

Note: Nerves of the autonomic nervous system synapse in the ganglia corresponding to their respective spinal segments. But, in the case of the parasympathetic nervous system the "post synapse" neurons are shorter than the longer sympathetic nervous system "post synapse" neurons. The opposite is true of pre-synaptic neurons.

What mediates an organ's response to the two competing branches of the ANS?

The sum total of the opposing signals - they are in a "tug of war" with each other - which is also known as antagonistic control. Kind of like your biceps and triceps - both are adjusted against each other to effect a desired result.

Still, some organs receive predominant input from one branch. For example, the heart, at baseline, is controlled by the vagus nerve (a cranial nerve) which mediates much of the parasympathetic tone in the thorax and abdomen (i.e. the *rest and digest functions*). So, in a heart transplant recipient, what will his heart rate be compared to that of a normal heart? Well, during heart harvesting, the vagus nerves are cut and the recipient of the heart transplant will have a higher resting heart rate because of the lack of vagal nerve stimulation.

What is the size of the pupil with sympathetic nerve stimulation?

Large. Whether from pursuit of a bear or from hot, passionate flirting, when your heart rate rises (an indicator of sympathetic nerve stimulation), the pupils will enlarge to aid in fleeing a dangerous situation or checking out one's significant other. Although completely beyond the scope, this may help drive this concept home. It has been proven by studies that lovers looking into each other's eyes will have larger pupils. The ancient Greeks felt the same way about beautiful women - bella donnas - and gave women *belladonna alkaloids* to dilate their pupils and enhance the beauty of their women. In medicine, the parasympathetic effects of atropine are used by physicians to dilate the pupils so that the retina can be better visualized.

15.5 Reflexes

Just to drive home some concepts:

- The spinal cord takes care of the quick response to save time by foregoing signals to the brain.

- Reflexes are a feedback loop consisting of three components:

    - Sensory neuron (enters spinal segment)
    - Synapse (within the spinal segment)
    - Motor neuron (exits spinal segment)

15.6   Senses

What are the five special senses?

Hearing, vision, taste, touch, and smell.

These senses rely on mechanical energy (vibration) or chemical (smell) interactions that are converted to an electrical signal that is conveyed to the brain by nerves.

15.6.1   Ear

Label the parts below of the ear:

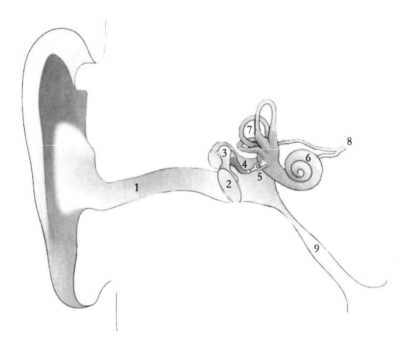

Figure 15.3: The Ear: (1) Auditory canal, (2) tympanic membrane, (3) malleus, (4) incus, (5) stapes, (6) cochlea, (7) semicircular canals, (8) cranial nerve VIII (Vestibulocochlear n.), (9) eustachian tube. *Public domain image modified from an illustration by Dan Pickard*

What is the mechanism behind hearing?

Sound waves enter the auditory canal (1), move the tympanic membrane (2) and cause motion in the bones of the middle ear (3, 4, 5) that is transmitted to the attached cochlea (6). This mechanical movement reverberates within the fluid-filled cochlea and moves hair cells that line the floor of the cochlea. This hair movement is converted into an electrical impulse and is transmitted to the brain via the vestibulocochlear nerve (8).

What is the function of the semicircular canals?

The semicircular canals (7) are involved in position sense and sensation of acceleration.

15.6.2 Eye

Label the parts of the eye below:

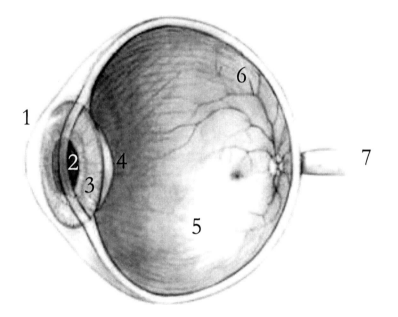

Figure 15.4: The Eye: (1) Cornea, (2) pupil, (3) iris, (4) lens, (5) vitreous humor, (6) retina, (7) optic nerve. *Public domain image obtained from the US National Insitute of Health Eye Institute.*

What is the mechanism behind vision?

Light enters the cornea (1), and, depending on the size of the ANS-regulated pupil* (2), light passes through the lens, becomes inverted, and is projected onto the retina. Light then catalyzes a reaction in photoreceptors lining the retina and this results in an electrical potential that is conveyed through the optic nerves to the occipital lobe of the brain.

* The pupil is a "space" like the hole in a pin-hole camera. It is the iris (3) which is the gate keeper of light for the eye and is dually controlled by the sympathetic (dilation) and parasympathetic (constriction) nervous systems.

What are the two main photoreceptors and what are their roles in visual light processing?

Rods and cones: rods process black and white (low intensity) lights while cones process color (high intensity) lights and discriminate detail.

What pigment is found in the eye that is involved in light transduction and what is its precursor?

Rhodopsin, which is made from vitamin A.

Chapter 16

The Endocrine System

The endocrine system is similar to the nervous system in that it intimately controls the body's overall activities. Both are able to exert local effects, e.g. hypothalamic control of pituitary hormone release, or nerve signals to the eye muscles; and both are able to have more generalized effects on the body such as sympathetic activation or cortisol release. Similarly, the endocrine and nervous systems both use chemicals to mediate their effects: i.e. hormones and neurotransmitters.

In contrast though, the nervous system uses electrical signals to transmit information. Also, the nervous system tends to control things on a more short-term basis while the effects of the endocrine system can range from minutes to hours to weeks and even months.

Ok, here we go...

What are the two main types of glands in the body?

Exocrine and endocrine. **Endo**crine glands put hormones *"endo da blood"* while **ex**ocrine glands *'express their hormones"* into a duct.

Although this is a discussion on the endocrine system, some glands like the pancreas assume both roles. If this is the case, we will go through the exocrine component also.

16.1   The Endo Key Players: The Senders, the Messengers and the Recipients

It can become a "chicken before the egg" type of discussion when you read my anology of using a sender, messenger and recipient, but try to understand the significance of each player in the process... in the end, it's a continuum.

16.1.1   The Sender

What structure in the brain controls the master gland of the body?

The *hypothalamus* sends signals to control the release of hormones from the "master gland of the body" - the *pituitary gland*. These signals are in turn called "blah blah blah" releasing hormones. There are several pituitary hormones and they each have a releasing hormone.

What main type of control is used to regulate the release of hormones?

Negative feedback - the process by which the accumulation of the product effectively "turns off" the start button.

Positive feedback is less commonly seen. A good example of positive feedback is the effect of oxytocin on the placenta when a baby is being born - the contractions encourage the release of more oxytocin that in turn increases the frequency and strength of oncoming contractions.

16.1.2   The Messengers

What are the three general classes of hormones?

Class	Key fact	Example
Steroid hormones	Fat soluble	Sex hormones
Amino acid derivatives	Created from individual amino acids	Epinephrine aka adrenaline
Peptides	Created from chains of amino acids ranging in length from 3 to 200 amino acids long	Insulin

Table 16.1: The three general classes of hormones.

16.1.3   The Recipients

What can respond to the effects of hormones?

Anything can respond to the effects of hormones:

- Cells

  - Hormones can change nuclear transcription of mRNA and subsequent protein expression

- Tissue

  - Hormones can increase the bulk (hypertrophy) of muscles

- Organs

  - Hormones can mobilize the organ to increase synthesis of a particular product

The take-home message is that hormones can affect (and do affect) almost every aspect of the body through potent chemical messengers. In the case of steroids, their fat solubility allows them to easily pass through the plasma membrane and exert their effects on the nucleus by altering protein transcription. IN contrast, peptide hormones bind to cell-surface receptors.

What structure transmits the hormone's "message" when it reaches its destination?

Hormone receptors. Located on the cell membrane or intracellularly, hormone receptors trigger the cell's response to the hormonal signal.

Hormone receptors are very specific structures and provide a *lock and key* fit for the corresponding hormone. See page 85 for a review of the lock and key hypothesis.

How does the hormone get to the recipients?

Blood brings the hormones to the capillaries near the target tissues and diffusion through the interstitial fluid brings the hormone to their target cells.

If a blood test indicates that the stimulating hormone for a particular hormone is low, what does that imply about the hormone level (assume negative feedback)?

Normal or excess hormone:

Because of negative feedback, a hormone will suppress the hypothalamic stimulating hormone. Therefore, if thyroid stimulating hormone is low, that means that there is enough or an excess amount of thyroid hormone present and the hormone will suppress the hypothalamus to secrete thyroid releasing hormone.

What are the seven major endocrine hormone sources - anatomically - from the top down?

1. Pituitary gland

2. Thyroid gland

3. Parathyroid

4. Gastrointestinal hormones

5. Adrenals

6. Pancreas

7. Gonads

16.2   Pituitary Gland

Where is the pituitary gland located?

Right in the middle of the brain. If you put a finger sort of above your ear and one right between your eyes, the pituitary is at the intersection of these two lines. In texts, you may come across this location referred to as the "base of the brain" or "center of the inferior surface of the brain."

The pituitary has two major parts: anterior and posterior.

What is the pituitary's function?

To control the endocrine glands of the body. It is the master gland of the body.

What controls the pituitary gland?

1. Releasing and inhibitory factors from the hypothalamus for each specific hormone the pituitary releases.

2. Negative feedback.

What hormones does the pituitary gland release?

Anterior pituitary (hormone synthesis)

1. Follicle-stimulating hormone (FSH)

2. Luteinizing hormone (LH)

3. Adrenocorticotropic hormone (ACTH)

4. Thyroid stimulating hormone (TSH)

5. Prolactin

6. Growth hormone (GH)

Posterior pituitary (hormone storage for the hypothalamus)

1. Oxytocin

2. Anti-diuretic hormone (ADH or vasopressin)

Note: The anterior pituitary hormones can be remembered with the mnemonic F.L.A.T. P.i.G.

© 2005 - 2007

What is the function of each hormone?

Anterior Pituitary

	Major Action	Target
FSH	Stimulates maturation of ovarian follicles Stimulates sperm production	Ovaries/testes
LH	Stimulates ovulation Stimulates testosterone production (males)	Ovaries/testes
ACTH	Stimulates glucocorticoid production	Adrenals
TSH	Stimulates iodine uptake and thyroid hormone production by the thyroid	Thyroid
Prolactin*	Stimulates milk production and breast development	The breasts directly
GH*	Stimulates overall growth and protein synthesis Stimulates fatty acid catabolism Decreases glucose uptake	The bones and muscles directly

Table 16.2: Anterior pituitary hormones.

* The P.i.G. (prolactin and GH) hormones affect their target organs directly. That is, they both "pig out and get straight to the point."

Posterior Pituitary*

	Major Action	Target
Oxytocin**	Stimulates muscle contractions resulting in milk ejection and uterine contractions:	Breasts and uterus
ADH***	Stimulates water reabsorption to make more concentrated urine Increases intravascular volume and thereby increases blood pressure	Collecting ducts of the nephron

Table 16.3: Posterior pituitary hormones.

Hormones of the posterior pituitary are synthesized in the hypothalamus and only stored in the posterior pituitary.
Oxytocin release is controlled by a positive feedback loop.
**ADH is also known as vasopressin*

16.3 Thyroid Gland

Where is the thyroid gland located?

Above the sternum in the midline of the neck ventral (aka anterior) to the trachea.

What is the thyroid's function?

To control the "ergonomic" aspects of the body, i.e. too much vs. too little thyroid function can result in problems that affect your comfort level: hot vs. cold, hypervigil vs. tired, weight loss vs. weight gain.

Also, in children, the thyroid is involved with the maturation of the nervous system.

What controls the thyroid gland?

1. TSH

2. Negative feedback

What hormones does the thyroid gland release?

T_3 and T_4 (thyroxine and triiodothyronine) and Calcitonin

What is the function of each hormone?

	Major Action	Target
T_3 and T_4	Increases metabolism	Throughout body
Calcitonin*	Decreases plasma Ca^{++}	Bone/plasma

Table 16.4: Thyroid gland hormones.

Calcitonin "tones" down calcium.

16.4   Parathyroid Gland

Where are the parathyroid glands located?

Posterior to the thyroid.

What is the parathyroid's function?

Raises Ca^{++} in the plasma, counters the effects of calcitonin to achieve homeostasis and converts vitamin D into its active form.

What are three substances which control the parathyroid gland?

1. Plasma Ca^{++}

2. Calcitonin

3. Vitamin D

What hormone does the parathyroid gland release?

Parathyroid hormone (PTH)

© 2005 - 2007

What is the function of each hormone?

	Major Action	Target
PTH	Increases Ca^{++}	Bone/plasma
	Makes active form of vitamin D	Blood

Table 16.5: Parathyroid gland hormones.

* *Parathyroid hormone "perks" up calcium.*

16.5 Gastrointestinal Hormones

Where are the gastrointestinal hormones secreted from?

Stomach, small intestine (duodenum and jejunum) and pancreas.

16.5.1 Stomach and Small Intestine Hormones

What three hormones are released by the stomach and small intestine?

1. Gastrin (stomach)

2. CCK (small intestine)

3. Secretin (small intestine)

What is the function of each hormone?

Stomach

	Major Action	Target
Gastrin	Increase H^+ secretion ($\downarrow$ pH) Stimulate growth of gastric mucosa	Stomach

Table 16.6: Gastrointestinal hormones: Stomach.

Small Intestine

	Major Action	Target
CCK	Increase pancreatic HCO_3^- secretion ($\uparrow$ pH) Prevents gastric emptying	Pancreas, stomach
Secretin	Increase pancreatic HCO_3^- secretion ($\uparrow$ pH) Decrease H^+ secretion ($\downarrow$ pH)	Pancreas, stomach

Table 16.7: Gastrointestinal hormones: Small intestine.

* Note: "CCK and secretin are friends - they both tell the pancreas a secret: to raise pH."

16.5.2 Pancreas

Where is the pancreas located?

Inferior to the stomach.

What is the pancreas' function?

Dual. The pancreas has both exocrine and endocrine functions:

Endocrine hormone (cell of origin)

Glucagon (α cells of the Islets of Langerhans)
Insulin (β cells of the Islets of Langerhans)
Somatostatin (δ* cells of the Islets of Langerhans)

Table 16.8: Pancreatic endocrine hormones

* δ = Lower-case delta

Exocrine functions*

Pancreatic amylase
Trypsin
Chymotrypsin
Carboxytrypsin
Lipase

Table 16.9: Pancreatic exocrine hormones

* Refer to the digestive system chapter on page 107 for more detail

What three substances control the secretion of pancreatic endocrine hormones?

1. Glucagon secretion is increased by low glucose levels, and presence of the GI hormones CCK and gastrin

2. Insulin secretion is increased with high blood glucose levels

3. Somatostatin secretion is increased by either high blood glucose or high amino acid levels and the presence of GI hormones CCK and gastrin

What is the function of each hormone?

	Major Action	Target
Glucagon	Stimulates conversion of glycogen to glucose Stimulates fat and protein degradation	Blood
Insulin	Increases glucose uptake by cells, subsequently lowering blood glucose levels	Blood and tissues
Somatostatin	Decreases insulin and glucagon secretion	The gut via the blood

Table 16.10: Pancreatic endocrine hormones.

16.6   Adrenal Glands

What are the adrenals?

Endocrine glands that have an outer layer (adrenal cortex) and an inner layer (adrenal medulla) located on the superior surface of the kidneys.

What is the function of the adrenals?

To produce *glucocorticoid*, *mineralcorticoid* and *sex hormones*.

What two substances control the adrenal gland?

1. ACTH

2. Renin-angiotensin system

What hormones do the adrenals release?

1. Glucocorticoids (cortisol and cortisone)

2. Mineralcorticoids (aldosterone)

   - The renin-angiotensin system controls the secretion of aldosterone. Briefly, renin is secreted by the juxtaglomerular apparatus in the nephron when it senses a decrease in blood flow. Renin converts angiotensinogen to angiotensin I. Angiotensin converting enzyme (ACE) converts angiotensin I to angiotensin II. Angiotensin II in turn stimulates aldosterone secretion by the adrenal gland.

3. Male sex hormones (i.e. androgens, with testosterone being the most well-known)

   - Expression occurs in both men and women

4. Catecholamines

   - Epinephrine (adrenaline)

   - Norepinephrine (noradrenaline)

What is the function of each adrenal cortex hormone?

Adrenal Cortex

	Major Action	Target
Glucocorticoids	Cortisone and cortisol: Reduce immune response and inflammatory response. Raise blood sugar levels	Throughout body
Mineralcorticoids	Aldosterone: Increase Na^+ reabsorption by the nephron, thereby increasing the intravascular volume/blood pressure	Nephron via the blood
Male sex hormones	Testosterone: Males: Little effect because testes make most of testosterone. Females: Increase virility when overexpressed	Throughout body

Table 16.11: Adrenal cortex hormones.

Adrenal Medulla

	Major Action	Target
Catcholamines*	Epinephrine/norepinephrine "Fight or flight" response	Throughout body

Table 16.12: Adrenal medulla hormones.

16.7   Testes & Ovaries

Where are the testes located?

In the scrotum, a temperature regulating organ which is located in the groin.

What are the testes' function?

To produce and maintain a viable environment for sperm as well as to produce testosterone (for a detailed discussion on spermatogenesis refer to the reproductive system on page 147).

Where are the ovaries located?

In the female pelvis, lateral to the uterus.

What are the ovaries' function?

To produce sex hormones, control the menstrual cycle, release eggs and govern pregnancy.

What controls the ovaries?

For the most part FSH and LH, which are secreted by the pituitary gland. Their secretion is in turn controlled by gonadotropic releasing hormone (GnRH) from the hypothalamus.

What hormones do the ovaries release?

- Estrogen

    - The ovarian follicle secretes estrogen. The follicle is a spherical cell which contains and supports the ovum.

- Progesterone

    - The corpus luteum secretes progesterone. The corpus luteum is the remnant follicle after the ovum is released during ovulation.

- Human chorionic gonadotropin (hCG)

    - The placenta secretes hCG during pregenancy.

What is the function of each hormone?

	Major Action	Target
Estrogen	Growth and development of female reproductive organs. Stimulate follicular phase of menstruation.	Throughout body; ovaries and uterus
Progesterone	Stimulate uterine proliferation, specifically the endometrium.	Blood
hCG	Maintains the corpus luteum (c.l.). This in turn ensures that estrogen and progesterone are secreted by the c.l. to prevent induction of menstruation and to maintain the uterus during the pregnancy.	Ovaries and uterus

Table 16.13: Ovarian hormones.

* Remember, catecholamines can also serve as neurotransmitters.

16.8   Menstrual Cycle

Since many 'instruments' are used in this 'symphony,' the menstrual cycle will be presented as a continuum of four stages. Although the cycle is usually idealized to 28 days, ranges between 20 and 40 days are common. Commencement of menstruation (menarche) is seen during puberty, while ending of regular menses (menopause) is seen in the 5th and 6th decades of life.

What are the four stages of the menstrual cycle?

1. Follicular phase

2. Ovulation

3. Luteal phase

4. Menstruation

What makes the four stages unique?

1. Follicular phase (Days 1-14)

   - Begins: End of menstruation from previous cycle

   - Goal: Prepare follicle for ovulation

   - Key hormones: FSH and LH both work together as levels rise, with estrogen also rising precipituously

   - Ends: Follicle is mature and ready for ovum to be released

2. Ovulation (Day 14)

   - Begins: Once the follicle is mature

   - Goal: Release ovum into the Fallopian tube (oviduct)

   - Key hormones: FSH and LH spike secondary to an estrogen peak

   - Ends: Ovum is released

3. Luteal phase (Days 15-28)

   - Begins: After ovum was released

   - Goal: Produce progesterone and estrogen to maintain a pregnancy

     - If hCG is not present to maintain the corpus luteum (c.l.), the c.l. disintegrates and menstruation occurs

   - Key hormones: LH spike/drop off causes the c.l. to form.

     - If hCG is present, the c.l. is maintained and it produces progesterone and estrogen. Progesterone and estrogen in turn inhibit GnRH release and subsequent LH release; thereby preventing the start of the follicular cycle to begin

     - SO: Although LH sparks off the process to create a c.l., it is not necessary to maintain it

   - Ends: Absence of hCG/fertilization

4. Menstruation (Days 1-5)*

   - Begins: Absence of hCG/fertilization

   - Goal: Slough off endometrium

   - Key hormones: Drop in progesterone and estrogen

   - Ends: Once endometrium is gone

Note: Menstrual flow happens concurrently with the early follicular phase so there is a little overlap.

Chapter 17

The Reproductive System

17.1 Structures

Label the various components of the female and male reproductive structures:

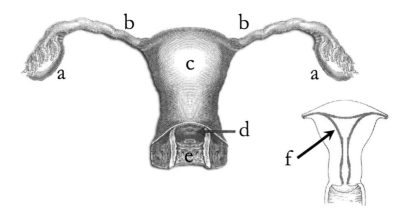

Figure 17.1: Female reproductive anatomy: (a) Ovary, (b) oviduct (Fallopian tube), (c) uterus, (d) cervix, (e) vagina, (f) endometrium. *Public domain image modified from original lithograph plate from Gray's Anatomy.*

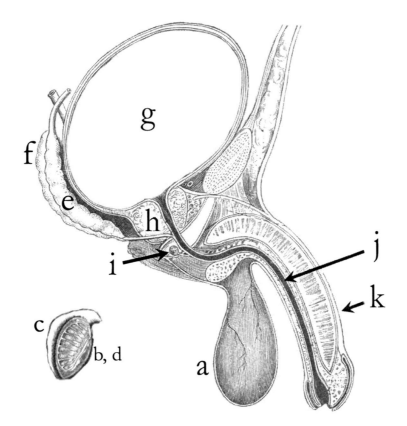

Figure 17.2: Male reproductive anatomy: (a) Scrotum, (b) testes, (c) epididymis, (d) seminiferous tubules, (e) vas deferens, (f) seminal vesicle, (g) bladder, (h) prostate, (i) bulbourethral glands (Cowper's gland), (j) urethra, (k) penis. *Public domain image modified from original lithograph plate from Gray's Anatomy.*

17.2   Gonads

What are the roles of the testes and ovaries?

The testes produce and store sperm. The scrotum regulates temperature by adjusting the proximity of the testicles to the body to achieve a temperature a few degrees lower than the core body temperature.

The ovaries produce estrogen/progesterone, and store approximately 400,000 eggs, 400 of which are ovulated between menarche and menopause (those numbers are just FYI).

What are the steps for spermatogenesis and oogenesis?

The spermatogenesis magic happens in the seminiferous tubules of the testicles and the oogenesis magic happens in the ovarian follicles of the ovary:

Spermatogenesis	
	Spermatogonia (2N) ↓ Primary Spermatocytes (2N) ↓ MEIOSIS I ↓ Secondary Spermatocytes (N) ↓ Spermatids (N) ↓ Spermatozoa (N)

Table 17.1: Spermatogenesis

What are the structural features of sperm and ova?

- Sperm confer the sex of the offspring by providing either an X or a Y chromosome to the ova (the ova always has an X).

    - Head (Acrosome with nucleus)

    - Neck/body (mitochondria "power plant")

    - Tail (flagella for locomotion)

- Ova confer one X chromosome and maternal cytoplasm/organelles

    - Corona radiata (outer layer)

    - Zona pellucida (inner layer)

17.3 Fertilization

What are the two general steps of fertilization?

1. Acrosomal reaction

2. Cortical reaction

What are the four steps of the acrosomal reaction?

1. Sperm encounters ova

2. Acrosome undergoes exocytosis of hydrolytic enzymes

3. Acrosome elongates to form an *acrosomal process* which penetrates through the corona radiata and zona pellucida

4. Sperm nucleus enters the ova

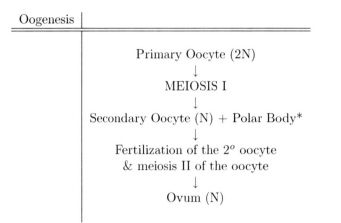

Table 17.2: Oogenesis

Meiosis I in oogenesis is not an equal opportunity employer, and one of the oocytes receives the majority of the cytoplasm while the other (referred to as a polar body) receives much less.

What are two consequences that occur when the sperm nucleus enters the ova?

1. Meiosis II of the ova occurs

2. Cortical reaction occurs

What is the cortical reaction?

Reaction which seals the egg and prevents fertilization by more than one sperm (i.e. polyspermy).

This reaction is mediated by Ca^{++}.

What happens now? See the embryology chapter on page 163 for a discussion on zygote development.

Chapter 18

The Musculoskeletal System

18.1 Muscles

18.1.1 Functional considerations of muscles

What are the functions of the muscles?

Four functions - two obvious, two less-obvious:

1. **Supporting** the organism

2. Allowing for **mobility**

3. Random muscle contractions which allow for **peripheral venous blood return**

4. **Thermoregulation**, e.g. shivering

What are the two roles of the nervous system in controlling the muscles?

The "On-off switch":

- Voluntary muscle control of skeletal muscles (somatic nervous system)

- Involuntary muscle control of smooth muscles (autonomic nervous system)

The "Volume control":

- Sympathetic nervous system, a sub-division of the autonomic nervous system, which speeds up involuntary muscles during the *"fight or flight response."*

- Parasympathetic nervous system, the other sub-division of the autonomic nervous system, which is activated when one *"rests and digests."*

What are the three types of muscles fibers and how many nuclei do each have?

Muscle type	Striated	Number of nuclei
Skeletal	Yes	Many
Cardiac	Yes	1-2
Smooth	No	1

Table 18.1: Characteristics of muscle fibers.

What branch of the nervous system controls each type?

Muscle type	Striated	Number of nuclei	
Skeletal	Yes	Many	Voluntary (Somatic)
Cardiac	Yes	1-2	Involuntary (Automatic)
Smooth	No	1	Involuntary (Automatic)

Table 18.2: Control of muscle types.

What are the two types of skeletal muscle fibers?

1. **Red muscle fibers** have many mitochondria, a high myoglobin content, and are considered *slow-twitch* fibers

   - More mitochondria = greater reliance on aerobic means to create ATP

   - Longer endurance

   - Slow contraction

2. **White muscle fibers** have less mitochondria and are considered *fast-twitch* fibers

   - Less mitochondria = greater reliance on anaerobic means to create ATP

   - Shorter endurance

   - Faster contraction

18.1.2 Steps Involved in Muscle Contraction in Skeletal Muscle

Note: for the purposes of the MCAT you are only responsible for skeletal muscle contraction.

What organelle is found in great abundance in myocytes?

Mitochondria.

What ion makes the magic happen in muscle contraction?

Ca^{++}.

What is the functional unit of muscle cells (myocytes)?

Filaments called myofibrils which are in turn composed of contractile units called sarcomeres.

What makes up the thin and thick filaments?

Thin filaments are composed of actin.

Thick filaments are composed of myosin

Label the various components of the sarcomere:

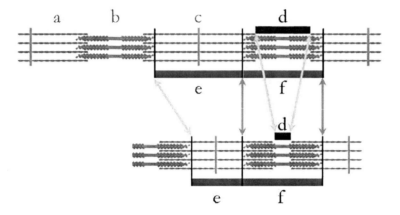

Figure 18.1: Sarcomere microanatomy: Relaxed (above) and contracted (below): (a) actin, (b) myosin, (c) Z-line, (d) H-zone, (e) I-band, (f) A-band, (green, diagonal arrows) H-band and I-band which change in length during contraction, (red, vertical arrows) A-band which does not change in length.

Label the various components of the thin filament.

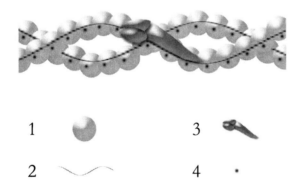

Figure 18.2: (1) Actin, strength and support; (2) tropomyosin, blocks myosin binding sites when the muscle is at rest; (3) troponin, controls tropomyosin's position on the underlying actin; (4)Ca^{++} binding site on troponin which allows Ca^{++} to bind: When Ca^{++} is bound, the tropomyosin/troponin complex shifts allowing myosin to bind.

What is the sliding-filament model?

An accepted model of myosin-actin interaction which results in the shortening of the sarcomere and subsequent muscle contraction.

What are the four steps of the sliding filament model which result in muscle contraction?

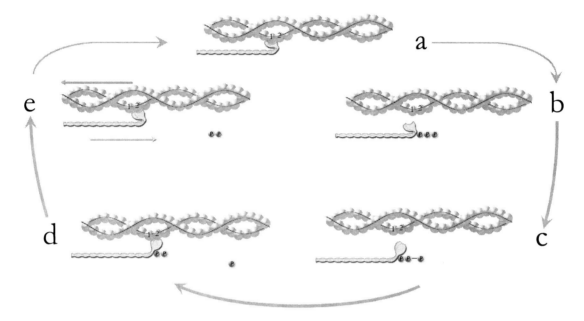

Figure 18.3: (a) Actin-myosin complex at rest with myosin bound at position #1, (b) ATP binding causing myosin to release from actin, (c) Hydrolysis of ATP to ADP + P_I making the myosin head "cock" to the right ($\tilde{5}$ nanometers), (d) Release of P_I and generation of the power stroke at position #2, (e) Release of ADP and completion of power stroke; this configuration is similar to (a). *Note: Ca^{++} binding sites and troponin are not depicted in this illustration; for these thin filament components, refer to Figure 18.2 on page 154.*

What is the difference between tendons and ligaments?

Tendons connect bones to muscles (remember *"tender muscles"*) while ligaments connect bones to other bones.

What is the difference between a simple muscle twitch and muscle tetani?

A *simple twitch* is seen in **a muscle fiber** when an impulse is equal to or exceeds the threshold for contraction. Then, an ensuing brief latent period occurs, followed by a contraction period and a relaxation period.

Muscle tetani or *summation* is seen in **an entire muscle** when an impulse results in multiple simple twitches that cause a summation of contractions. This results in constant contraction until the muscle tires.

18.2   The Skeletal System

18.2.1   Functional considerations

What are three functions of the skeletal system?

1. Ca^{++} storage

2. Physical protection, e.g. skull

3. Structural support and rigidity

What makes up the axial skeleton?

Basically the skull, vertebral column (spine) and associated ribs; everything else is the *appendicular* column.

What is the premise behind an endo- or exoskeleton?

Vertebrates have endoskeletons while arthropods, e.g. insects and crustaceans, have exoskeletons. *Note: The exoskeleton is rigid. If an organism grows, it sheds the old exoskeleton and grows a new one.*

What are the three general types of joints that exist in the human skeleton?

1. Hinge joints, e.g. the elbow

2. Ball and socket, e.g. the femur and pelvis

3. Fixed, e.g. the joints between the bones of the skull, which are immovable

How is bone made (ossification)?

Deposition of a conglomerate of inorganic ions including Ca^{++}, PO_4^+ and OH^- which solidify into hydroxyapatite, also known as the bone matrix:

Two ways:

1. **Endochondral ossification**

    - Replacing existing cartilage with bone which is also known as intracartilaginous ossification

    - This occurs at growth plates (*physis*) which are in between the shaft (*diaphysis*) and bone ends (*epiphysis*):

2. **Intramembranous ossification**

    - Deposition of bone within a collagen matrix

What are the characteristics of the two types of bone?

	Description	Bone marrow?
Cortical bone	Protective Strength Surrounds trabecular bone Haversian systems	Yes
Trabecular bone	Involved in reabsorption and deposition of bone Has a "spongy" look and is also known as spongy or cancellous bone	Yes

Table 18.3: Characteristics of cortical and trabecular bone (see figure 18.4 on page 158).

18.2.2   Functional unit of bone: The Haversian system

Label the various components of the osteons (Haversian systems):

What are the two types of cells involved in bone deposition and reabsorption?

1. Osteoblasts "build" bone.

2. Osteoclasts "cut" down bone.

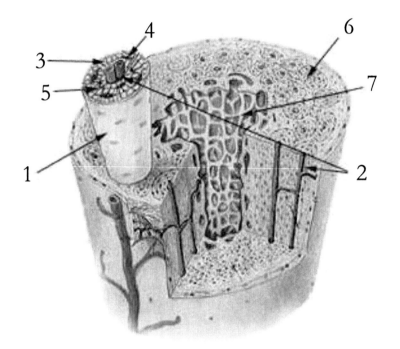

Figure 18.4: The functional unit of bone is the (1)Haversian system or simply, osteon, (2) Haversian canals, the central canal which is a conduit for blood, (3) lamellae, concentric circles around the Haversian canal, (4) lacunae, hollow areas throughout the bony matrix which houses osteocytes and osteoblasts, (5) canaliculi, small canals which radiate away from the lacunae. Note, examples of cortical bone (6) and trabecular bone (7) can also be seen.*Public domain image obtained from the U.S. National Cancer Institute's Surveillance, Epidemiology and End Results (SEER) Program.*

18.2.3   Tendons & Ligaments

What is the difference between tendons and ligaments?

Tendons connect bones to muscles (remember *"tender muscles"*) while ligaments connect bones to other bones.

What six facts should you know about cartilage?

1. Flexible connective tissue

2. Composed of chondrin

3. Made by chondrocytes

4. Cushions bone

5. Makes up certain structures, e.g. ears and nose

6. Babies have more than adults

Chapter 19

The Skin, Connective Tissue & Integumentary System

19.1 The Skin

What are four general functions of the skin?

1. Physical protection

   - Protects against abrasions and takes the brunt of trauma, e.g. hair, nails and callouses.

   - Prevents entry of pathogens.

   - Relatively impermeable to water.

2. Thermoregulation

   - Highly vascularized: Vasodilation vs. vasoconstriction can control blood flow and therefore heat exchange.

   - Fat layer insulates body heat.

   - Hair (pilomoter reflex): a reflex that causes hairs to rise, hypothesized to make small pockets of air.

   - Sweating causes heat loss because the heat of vaporization of water is taken from the organism's body heat. See page 254 for a review on heat of vaporization.

3. Osmoregulation

   - Sweating is a means of controlling fluid loss. Tweaking this system when water is scarce or the environment is hot allows the body to conserve precious minerals and water.

4. Homeostasis

- The potpourri of the above-mentioned all contribute to homeostasis, i.e. *metabolic equilibrium.*

What are some structural characteristics of the skin?

- Made from layers and layers of keratinized epithelium.

- Specialized structures include hair and nails.

- Outer layer (epidermis) is composed of dead skin cells.

- Inner layer (dermis) is alive and is highly vascularized with many nerve endings.

What makes the skin impermeable to water?

The structure of skin is such that there are multiple layers of skin. The epidermis is composed of dead epithelial cells varying from 0.5 mm to 1.5 mm thick - on a molecular level that is pretty significant and allows the skin to be relatively impermeable water.

What is epithelium?

Tissue composed of epithelial cells which can either be layered or one cell thick that serve a variety of roles including *protection, secretion* and *absorption.*

What are the various forms of epithelium?

This is a loaded question because epithelium comes in so many forms, shapes, layers, etc. So, below are different ways to think about epithelium:

- Thickness:
    - Single layer
        * Simple epithelium - each cell rests on a basement membrane
        * Pseudostratified - each cell rests on a basement membrane but at varying levels and appears stratified
    - Multiple layers
        * Stratified epithelium - distinct layers of cells
- Shape:
    - Squamous - stacks of "pancakes"
    - Cuboidal - cube-like
    - Columnar - column-like

© 2005 - 2007

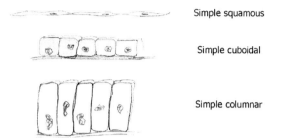

Figure 19.1: Simple epithelium: Squamous, cuboidal and columnar.

19.2 Connective Tissue

What is the role of connective tissue?

Simply to attach and support other cells and tissues. In contrast to epithelial cells which are tightly packed, connective tissue cells are scattered in an extracellular matrix (the matrix is a non-living and non-cellular component of connective tissue and is comprised of different substances).

What are six main types of connective tissue?

What qualifies as a 'connective tissue' depends on what definition you use. Still, below is a list of six generally accepted types of connective tissues, and Table 19.1 on page 162 gives you the salient facts:

1. Loose connective tissue

2. Fibrous connective tissue

3. Adipose tissue

4. Cartilage

5. Bone

6. Blood*

Although blood serves a different function than the other connective tissues, it shares many similarities with the classic connective tissues.

What is the integumentary system?

The "system" includes the skin and associated structures (i.e. hair, nails, sweat glands, and sebaceous glands).

Loose connective tissue	Example	Tissue which keeps organs in place
	Matrix	
	Major fiber type	Collagenous, Elastic and Reticular
	Major cell type	Macrophages
	Misc. info	
Fibrous connective tissue	Example	Tendons (bone to muscle) and ligaments (bone to bone)
	Matrix	
	Major fiber type	Collagenous
	Major cell type	
	Misc. info	*"Tendons attach bones to 'tender' muscles."*
Adipose tissue	Example	Belly fat
	Matrix	Lipid
	Major fiber type	
	Major cell type	Adipocytes
	Misc. info	
Cartilage	Example	Cartilage
	Matrix	Chondrin
	Major fiber type	Collagenous
	Major cell type	Chondrocytes
	Misc. info	
Bone	Example	Femur
	Matrix	$Ca_3(PO_4)_2$ enriched collagen
	Major fiber type	
	Major cell type	Osteoblast (build-up) and osteocytes (break-down)
	Misc. info	*"Osteoblasts 'build' bone, and osteoclasts 'crack' bone."*
Blood	Example	Blood
	Matrix	Plasma
	Major fiber type	
	Major cell type	Erythrocytes, leukocytes and thrombocytes.
	Misc. info	

Table 19.1: Six types of connective tissue at a glance.

Nervous tissue and muscle tissue are considered by some as connective tissue, but these is discussed in greater detail in the nervous system chapter on page 119 and the circulatory system chapter on page 89, respectively.

Chapter 20

Embryology

20.1 Stages of Early Development

20.1.1 Fertilization

What is fertilization?

> The union of sperm and egg.

What is the acrosomal reaction?

The penetration of the sperm's head (acrosome) into the egg facilitated by the release of the acrosome's hydrolytic enzymes.

What is the cortical reaction?

After a successful acrosomal reaction, there is an increase in intracellular Ca^{2+} and the egg's membrane fuses, sealing it to prevent polyspermy.

20.1.2 Cleavage

What is cleavage?

The rapid succession of divisions by the zygote to form a *morula*.

Note: Division occurs so rapidly that G_1 and G_2 phases are skipped, and cells cycle between DNA synthesis (S phase) and mitosis (M phase).

What follows the formation of the morula?

In the center of the morula, a fluid-filled cavity called a blastocoel forms.

At this point, the morula with its blastocoel is called a *blastula*.

20.1.3   Gastrulation

What is gastrulation?

The process by which three germ layers - a gastrula - are created from the blastula through significant cell movements and shape changes.

What are the three germ layers?

1. Ectoderm

2. Mesoderm

3. Endoderm

20.1.4   Neurulation

What is neurulation?

The formation of the embryo's primitive neuronal tissue, including the notochord, neural crest and neural plate.

What is induction?

Process by which a structure can induce under- or over-lying cells to change. This process is used to form the notochord, cornea and many other structures in the embryo.

20.2 Germ Layers and their Ultimate Fates

What are the fates of the three germ layers?

Endoderm	Internal structures	Inner, epithelial lining of respiratory and gastrointestinal tract
Mesoderm	Middle structures	Cardiovascular system, reproductive/ excretory organs, musculoskeletal system
Ectoderm	External structures	Surface ectoderm - epidermis, and other external structures Neuroectoderm - central and peripheral nervous system, neural crest cells and derivatives

20.3 Development of Cells

The bread and butter of this chapter is above. If you have time, learn the information below.

What is cell specialization?

The process by which cells become unique components of a living organism

What is the difference between differentiation and determination?

Differentiation is a general term meaning the specialization of cells within a developing organism. **Determination**, on the other hand, is a predictable cell fate even before there is any sign of differentiation.

How do cells communicate during development?

For the scope of the MCAT, know that *cell adhesion molecules* play an important role in cell communication during development.

What is the role of programmed cell death (apoptosis) in the developing organism?

Apoptosis allows for limb formation and development of the face.

The role of apoptosis is also regulated by gene activation and inactivation.

Chapter 21

The Immune System

The immune system can be quite complicated. Thankfully, for the MCAT a good understanding of the information below should be enough.

What are the four main tissues involved in producing the cells of the immune system?

1. Bone marrow

   - Factory for cells

2. Spleen

   - Surveys the blood for suspicious suspects

3. **T**hymus

   - **T**-cell's **t**urf. In **t**ruth, the **t**hymus is most active during childhood, i.e. little **t**ykes. After puberty, the thymus atrophies and stores some T-cells in adulthood (without trying to stretch the memory aids too much).

4. Lymph nodes

   - "All Along The Watchtower," is not only a great Hendrix song, but also a reasonable analogy for the role of lymph nodes in fending off infections. Each area of the body has its lymphatic drainage with lymph nodes at strategic points - kind of like the catchment area for local storm drains or watch towers along a defensive military line. *Out of the four tissues mentioned above, remember this one because not only do lymph nodes "catch" local infections and become swollen, they can also trap malignant cells if the catchment area includes a tumor.*

What are the two main cells of the immune system?

T-cells and B-cells

T-cells are involved in both the innate and humoral immunity. T-cells involved in innate immunity (killer T-cells) have an immediate, non-specific onset. Contrarily, T-cells involved in humoral immunity (T-helper cells) have a slightly delayed onset that is pathogen-specific.

B-cells are involved in humoral immunity, which is also slightly delayed in onset but results in B-cells that produce pathogen-specific antibodies.

Although not in line with the question, here is a quick recap of the main cells found in blood: erythrocytes (red blood cells), leukocytes (white blood cells) and thrombocytes (platelets). These three cells are clearly identifiable with simple light microscopy while T- and B-cells are indistinguishable with light microscopy.

What are antigens and antibodies?

Antigens are substances which result in the production of antibodies. If the antigen is a pathogen, kudos for the host organism. If not, and the antigen belongs to the host, the organism will have an autoimmune disease.

Antibodies are proteins (specifically called immunoglobulins) produced by B-cells which bind to antigens. This helps fight off infection by producing antigen-antibody complexes as well as helping researchers identify specific substrates, e.g. ELISA or Western blots.

What is the basic structure of an immunoglobin?

Basically, they have a binding site for the antigen. There are five types of immunoglobulins, and Figure 21.1 is a depiction of the most common of the five types.

How are antigens recognized?

Antibodies recognize a certain part of antigens (usually proteins) called an *epitope*. When an epitope is foreign or appears unusual, the antibody will bind and create a complex, signaling an immune response that attracts other cells and causes a clonal expansion of antibodies. Clonal expansion is the process

by which one particular flavor of antibody gets mass-produced to help bind as
much of the antigens as possible (and target them for destruction).

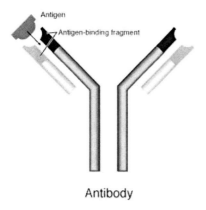

Figure 21.1: Antibodies: Immunoglogluin G (IgG).

Chapter 22

The Lymphatic System

The lymphatic system is pretty amazing - think of its own system of vessels with flow always back towards the heart. For the MCAT, the information you are expected to know is less than most of the other chapters, but be sure to grasp the main concepts outlined below.

22.1 High yield information

What is the function of the lymphatic system?

1. Involved in bringing lipids to the circulation. OK, you may be an uber-nerd and already know this, but it's an amazing and often unexepected factoid. Lipids are collected by lacteals (in the villi of the small intestine) and they feed into the lymphatic circulation, depositing their load in the thoracic duct which leads to the subclavian veins.

2. Highway for lymphocytes to shuttle between lymph nodes and interstitial fluid (fluid between cells) for controlling infections.

3. Helps regulate body fluid distribution, specifically the interstitial fluid.

What is the "blood" of the lymphatic system?

Lymph, a colorless fluid similar to plasma which contains proteins (e.g. albumin) and lymphocytes (a type of white cell).

Where does lymph come from?

Lymph comes from the interstitial fluid. Interstitial fluid in turn comes from the intravascular compartment, i.e. blood, which in this setting is most often in capillaries.

Osmotic pressure drives fluid shifts between the intravascular space (capillaries), extravascular space (interstitial space), and lymphatic system. Key players in controlling osmotic pressure are ions (e.g. Na^+) and proteins (e.g. albumin). Imbalances in fluid distributions in these compartments can result in dehydration, edema (swelling) or other clinical manifestations.

What is the ultimate destination of lymph?

The main thoracic (lymphatic) duct which drains into the subclavian vein

What glands connect the vast network of lymph vessels?

Lymph nodes

Think of them as watch towers which house the local militia. When inflammatory signals from the interstitial space travel through the lymphatics and toward the nearest lymph node, they signal for them to come out and fight. Just like when your roommate can't stop hooking up with people and gets mono - feel their neck, the nodes will be swollen. Joking aside, mono or infectious mononucleosis, is caused by the Epstein-Barr virus and is referred to as the *kissing sickness* because of its apparent transmission mechanism among younger adults through saliva.

Part II

Inorganic Chemistry

Chapter 23

Electronic Structure

23.1   Atoms

What are the three main building blocks of atoms?

1. Protons

   - Positively-charged subatomic particles found in the nucleus that contribute to the weight of the atom.

   - The number of protons for any given element never changes and gives atoms their "uniqueness" - any changes in the number of protons will by default change the atom into a different element.

2. Neutrons

   - Neutrally-charged subatomic particles that also contribute to the weight of the atom, i.e. neutrons have roughly the same mass as protons.

   - The number of neutrons is variable. When atoms of the same element possess different amounts of neutrons, they are called isotopes.

3. Electrons

   - Negatively-charged subatomic particles that move around the nucleus

   - Electrons have a negligible contribution to the mass of an atom (because they have 1,837 times less mass than a proton or a neutron).

   - The number of electrons can change. When atoms of the same element possess different amounts of electrons, they are called ions.

Figure 23.1: Convention for depicting atomic mass (A) and atomic number (Z).

What is the difference between nuclear charge (Z) and effective nuclear charge (Z_{eff})?

Nuclear charge, Z, is simply the amount of charge the nucleus has (and not to be confused with the atomic number designation mentioned above).

Effective nuclear charge, Z_{eff}, is the amount of nuclear charge the electrons actually "feel":

That is, if an atom has many shells of electrons, the positive charge exerted by the nucleus on any given electron will be "blocked" by the layers of intervening electrons that are closer to the nucleus. This makes the "felt" positive charge (Z_{eff}). This effect is often called "shielding."

Conversely, if an atom has no shells between its lone electron and the nucleus (as in the case of hydrogen) then the Z will be very close to the Z_{eff}.

Figure 23.2: Comparison of Z_{eff} for a small atom and a large atom.

What is the Bohr model?

The Bohr model is one of the earliest models used to describe how an electron orbits around the nucleus - similar to a planet orbiting the sun.

What are limitations of the Bohr model?

The Bohr model treats electrons like the rings of Saturn - circular and predictable. Further, the Bohr model is a limited model because it does not apply to atoms possessing more than one electron.

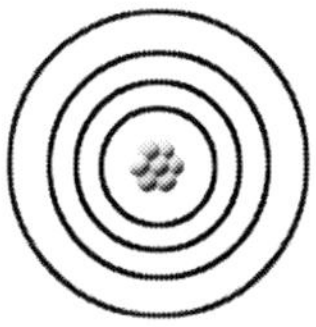

Figure 23.3: The Bohr model: This model suggests that electrons move in circular orbits around nucleus and possess a fixed number of orbits. This makes the Bohr model only empiric and therefore it does not accurately describe the structure of atoms.

What field of study opened up the door to understanding how more than one electron interact with each other around the nucleus?

Quantum mechanics.

What "space" do electrons occupy according to quantum mechanics?

Orbitals.

Note: Orbitals, as we will see, are areas where an electron can be expected to reside and are the accepted description of electron position around a nucleus. Orbits, in contrast, are elliptical, fixed paths that an electron was purported to use to travel around a nucleus.

23.2 Quantum Numbers

What is the role of quantum numbers?

Quantum numbers allow us to "predict" where an electron will be found moving around the nucleus, i.e. a zip code for any given electron.

Can two electrons have all of the same quantum numbers?

No. One zip code, one electron: The unique set of quantum numbers which are assigned to each electron is also known as the *Pauli exclusion principle*. This means that, of the four quantum numbers that an electron can have, two electrons can share up to three similar quantum numbers but not the fourth.

What is the Heisenberg Uncertainty Principle?

The concept which states that one cannot simultaneously predict both the momentum and the location of an electron: as you know more about an electron's location, the less you know about its direction and vice versa.

Why?

Well not only is that definitely beyond the scope of the MCAT but it is hard to visualize in a macroscopic, physical frame of mind. Read on only to see the wonders of science:

Briefly, on such a small scale as with electrons, things do not act as they would in our macroscopic Newtonian world, nor are they "seen" similarily. Quantum mechanics sees the world in two simultaneous ways: waves and particles, while we see one or the other. For example, imagine taking a whole bunch oranges and stringing them onto a rope. Bring along two friends and ask them to hold the rope in between them and oscillate the oranges-on-a-rope up and down between them. Now, to see the world through are "limited" way, you can stand in such a way to see the oranges oscillating between them, or, stand behind one of your friends and, seeing through them, only see a vertical line of oranges going up and down. In quantum mechanics, you would be able to see both at the same time. Cool, right?

What are the four categories of quantum numbers (symbols)?

1. Principle quantum numbers (n)

   - This is the energy level indicator (shells).
   - The difference between lower energy levels is greater than that between the higher energy levels. For example, the difference between n = 1 and n = 2 is greater than n = 4 and n = 5. *Note: This is a logarithmic relationship.*

2. Angular momentum quantum numbers (l)

   - This is the subshell indicator.

3. Magnetic quantum numbers (m_l)

- This indicates the slots for electrons available to be filled in each of the subshells.

- Think of m_l as being a "P.O. Box[1]" with each m_l holding two "letters," or in this case two electrons.

4. Spin quantum numbers (m_s)

- This indicates the spin orientation of the electron

What are the possible values that each quantum number can possess?

Principle quantum numbers (n)	1, 2, 3, 4, 5 …n
Angular momentum quantum numbers (l)	0, 1, 2, 3, 4…n-1
Magnetic quantum numbers (m$_l$)	l to $-l$
Spin quantum numbers (m$_s$)	$+\frac{1}{2}$ and $-\frac{1}{2}$

Table 23.1: Possible values of quantum numbers.

What is the real world corralary of the range of values that each of the four quantum numbers can take?

	Theoretical Value	
Principle quantum numbers (n)	1, 2, 3, 4, 5 …n	Denotes the distance from the nucleus. A log relationship exists between energy values of increasing n's.
Angular momentum quantum numbers (l)	0, 1, 2, 3, 4…n-1	Denotes type of subshell (l): 0 = s subshell 1 = p subshell 2 = d subshell 3 = f subshell

Table 23.2: Principle (n) and angular momentum quantum numbers (l).

---

[1]Note: The zip code analogy on the previous page and the P.O. Box analogy should be seen and used separately, i.e. its only coincidence that they both have postal uses.

	Theoretical Value	
Magnetic quantum numbers (m_l)	l to$-l$	$0 = s = 0$ $1 = p = -1, 0, +1$ $2 = d = -2, -1, 0, +1, +2$ $3 = f =$ $-3, -2, -1, 0, +1, +2, +3$
Spin quantum numbers (m_s)	$+\frac{1}{2}$ and $-\frac{1}{2}$	$+1/2$ $-1/2$

Table 23.3: Magnetic (m_l) and spin quantum numbers (m_s).

What are the numbers of electrons that can fill the different subshells (l)?

s has one P.O. Box, or m_l, therefore it can only hold 2 electrons
(one with $+1/2$ and one with $-1/2$)

p has a total of three m_l, therefore they can hold up to 6 electrons

d has a total of five m_l, therefore they can hold up to 10 electrons

f has a total of seven m_l, therefore they can hold up to 14 electrons

What is Hund's rule?

Subshells with more than one m_l, i.e. p, d and f, will fill so that they are all half-filled before "doubling up".

Half-filled subshells will fill with similar spins, either $+\frac{1}{2}$ or $-\frac{1}{2}$; this is called paramagnetic. When all m_l are filled with two e^- (one $+\frac{1}{2}$ and one $-\frac{1}{2}$), this is termed diamagnetic.

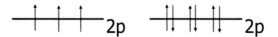

Figure 23.4: Application of Hund's rule: Paramagnetic (left) and diamagnetic (right) e^- filling.

23.3 Orbitals

By which pattern do electrons fill orbitals?

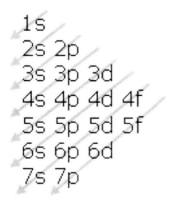

Figure 23.5: The Aufbau principle.

The electrons fill orbitals according to the Aufbau Principle as seen above in Figure 23.5. For example, Na is $1s^2 2s^2 2p^6 3s^1$. Below you will see the usefulness of using Noble Gases to make conventional notation shorter.

What are exceptions to this pattern of filling?

Copper (Cu) and Chromium (Cr) arranged in the middle and end of the transition elements, respectively, which do not fill according to Hund's rule:

	Expected	Observed
Cu	$[Ar]4s^2 3d^9$	$[Ar]4s^1 3d^{10}$
Cr	$[Ar]4s^2 3d^4$	$[Ar]4s^1 3d^5$

Table 23.4: Magnetic (m_l) and spin quantum numbers (m_s).

Note [Ar] is shorthand for the electronic configuration of Argon, which by definition has a "full" complement of e^- and is a useful way of using Noble Gases to document electron configuration.

How do the s, p, d and f orbitals correlate to the periodic table?

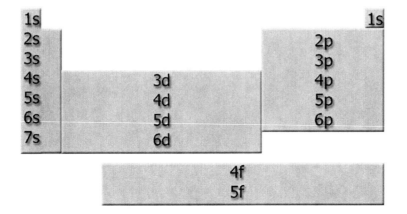

Figure 23.6: s, p, d and f orbital distribution on the periodic table.

What are the general shapes of s and p orbitals?

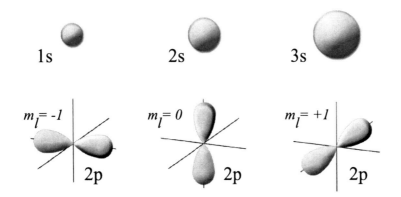

Figure 23.7: Orbital geometries of s and p orbitals.

23.4 Spectroscopy

What is spectroscopy?

The study of how atoms absorb or emit light when subjected to energy changes.

What are two "states" that atoms and molecules are found in?

1. *Ground state* is the baseline, stable state in which atoms and molecules are found most of the time.

2. *Excited state* is the unstable state which is produced when the atom or molecule is subjected to energy. This state is unstable and usually decays to the ground state.

What model describes the changes in light emitted by an excited hydrogen atom?

The Bohr model. The more energy you put in, the higher the frequency of emitted light. At some point, you can put in too much energy and the orbiting electron bounces from a lower energy level to a higher energy level until it is ejected from the hydrogen atom's "orbit," creating a hydrogen cation, i.e. H^+, or simply a lone proton.

Chapter 24

The Periodic Table

Generally speaking, what are two ways that the periodic table is organized?

1. By chemical properties

2. By electronic trends

Chemical properties and electronic trends are two ways to help organize and think about the periodic table. Remember that both are linked to each other, i.e. similar electronic characteristics will be seen in a group of elements, and, similar chemical properties will also be seen in a *group* of elements.

24.1 Organization of the Periodic Table Based on Chemical Properties

What are the nine main groups of elements from left to right?

1. Alkali metals

2. Alkaline earth metals

3. Transition metals

4. Metalloids

5. Non-metals

6. Halogens

7. Noble gases

8. Lanthanides

9. Actinides

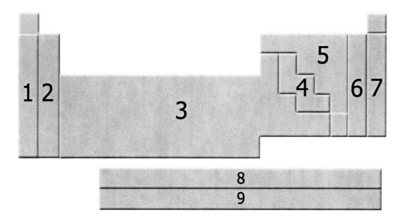

Figure 24.1: Periodic table: Nine main groups of elements: (1) Alkali metals, (2) alkaline earth metals, (3) transition metals, (4) metalloids, (5) non-metals, (6) halogens, (7) noble gases, (8) lanthanides, and (9) actinides.

What are some notable chemical characteristics of the following groups?

1. Alkali metals (Group 1A)

   - Low densities, soft metals.

   - 1 valence e^-.

   - Oxidize very quickly: Potassium actually burns at STP.

   - Rare in element form

2. Alkaline earth metals (Group 2A)

   - 2 valence e^-.

   - Also oxidize quickly.

3. Transition metals

   - Hard metals with high melting point and high boiling points.

   - Relatively loose hold on valence shell electrons allows for electrical conductivity.

   - Compared to Groups 1A and 2A, transition metals oxidize slower (if at all), e.g. Ag tarnishes over months, iron also oxidizes over time (rusts), but Au does not oxidize easily.

4. Metalloids

   - These elements pull away from the classic metals like Cu or Al, but still share metallic and non-metallic properties. For example, Si is a semiconductor of electrical current (a metallic property), while it also is capable of transmitting light (a non-metallic property).

5. Non-metals

  - Wide range of chemical properties and ability to react with other
    atoms. Just think of C or O, they can react with many types of
    atoms.

6. Halogens (Group 7A)

  - Highly reactive non-metals which exist in different forms at room
    temperature, e.g. F_2 is a gas while I_2 is a solid.

7. Noble gases (Group 8A)

  - These are inert gases with a full complement of valence of electrons.

  - Respective noble gases are used for shorthand notation of electronic
    configurations.

8. Lanthanides and actinides

  - These elements are included in this review for the sake of complete-
    ness. Also known as rare earth elements, lanthanides and actinides
    have partly-filled f orbitals with empty outermost p and d orbitals
    (see Figure 24.2 below). Additionally, lanthanides and actinides have
    radioactive elements and some have very short half-lives.

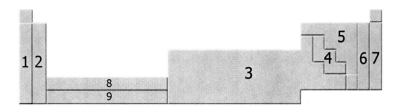

Figure 24.2: Extended periodic table: Note that lanthanides (8) and actinides (9) have
empty p and d orbitals.

What are the representative elements?

The representative elements are the elements in the s and p blocks, i.e. groups
1A, 2A, 3A, 4A, 5A, 6A, 7A and 8A. See Figure 24.3 below.

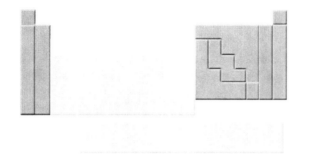

Figure 24.3: Periodic table: The representative elements - Elements in the s and p blocks.

24.2   Organization of the Periodic Table Based on Electronic Trends

What are six key trends of the periodic table?

1. Atomic number

2. Valence electrons

3. Ionization energies

4. Electron affinity

5. Electronegativity

6. Atomic Radii

What is the trend of atomic number in the periodic table?

This is a gimme, but atomic number increases from left to right and from top to bottom:

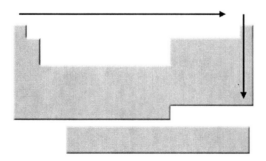

Figure 24.4: Periodic table: Trend of atomic numbers.

What are the valence electrons for the representative elements of the periodic table?

Periodic table group	Number of valence e^-
IA	1
IIA	2
IIIA	3
IVA	4
VA	5
VIA	6
VIIA	7

Table 24.1: Valence electrons for the representative elements.

Note: The general trend of valence e^- number is to increase from left to right. Also, remember that the goal of atoms is to obtain a noble gas configuration, i.e. eight valence electrons. So, for Na, to lose an electron is a good thing, because in its cationic form, i.e. Na^+, sodium assumes the noble gas configuration of Ne.

What is ionization energy?

A general term for the energy required to remove an electron from an orbital in an atom. Think of it also as the energy required to make a cation.

Ionization energies are usually reported as the first ionization energy, second ionization energy, etc., with each subsequent ionization requiring more energy than the one before.

How does the ionization energy relate to the valence electron number?

The amount of energy required to remove an electron depends on if the electron removal (i.e. ionization) will bring the atom closer to or further from its nearest noble gas configuration. So, Na - and all the other group 1A elements for that matter - are one electron away from their noble gas configurations. As mentioned above, Na actually wants to lose that lone electron, so the first ionization energy is low.

What about Na's second ionization energy or Na^+'s first ionization energy?

Intuitively, because Na^+ is at the noble gas configuration, the ionization energy would be extremely high.

In the end, look at the valence electron configuration to determine the ionization energy required to abstract an electron from the atom, with the ultimate goal being to reach the hallowed number of eight valence electrons.

What are the trends of ionization energy across the periodic table?

Again, ionization energy increases from left to right and also increases from bottom to top:

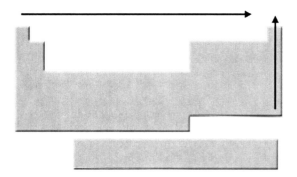

Figure 24.5: Periodic table: Trend of ionization energies.

What is electron affinity?

The desire of an atom to have another electron. Basically the opposite of ionization energy. Cl, for example, would really like having another electron and therefore has very high electron affinity.

Think of it also as the energy required to make a negative ion, aka an anion.

What are the trends of electron affinity across the periodic table?

Again, electron affinity increases from left to right and also increases from bottom to top:

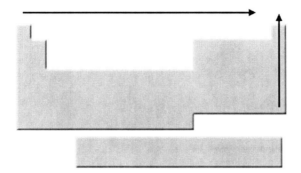

Figure 24.6: Periodic table: Trend of electron affinity.

**Why does the electron affinity trend increase as one goes from bottom
rows to top rows?**

If you think about it, the nucleus has a positive charge (protons) which causes
the attraction and ultimately drives electron affinity. As you go down the rows
of the periodic table the Z_{eff} decreases, decreasing the overall effect the nucleus
has on drawing in the electron.

What is electronegativity?

The attraction an atom has for electrons in a covalent bond.

What is the electronegativity trend of the periodic table?

Again, electronegativity increases from left to right and also increases from
bottom to top:

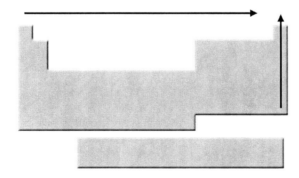

Figure 24.7: Periodic table: Trend of electronegativities.

What is the trend of atomic radii across the periodic table?

Atomic radii get smaller from left to right and also decrease from bottom to top.

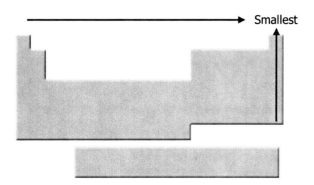

Figure 24.8: Periodic table: Trend of atomic radii.

How can you remember all of these trends?

Remember the cartoon characters Mighty Mouse and Foghorn Leghorn?

Put Mighty Mouse in the top right hand corner of the periodic table and Foghorn Leghorn in the bottom left; now draw the trends and it should make sense. Mighty Mouse, aka fluorine, is strong (electronegative) and small (atomic radii), while Foghorn is bigger (larger radius) and slower (less electron affinity), etc.

Chapter 25

Bonding

What are three important bonds seen in inorganic chemistry?

1. Ionic bonds

2. Covalent bonds

3. Hydrogen bonds

25.1   Ionic Bonds

What are ionic bonds?

Bonds which occur between two atoms with highly different electronegativities such that one atom "pulls" the electron(s) of the other atom towards itself; these bonds commonly involve a metal and a non-metal atom. The difference in charge of the two atoms is the electrostatic force that holds the atoms together. Sodium chloride, NaCl, is a good example of this in Figure 25.1 below:

$$\text{Na} : \overset{\displaystyle ..}{\underset{\displaystyle ..}{\text{Cl}}} :$$

Figure 25.1: The Ionic Bond: In ionic bonds such as NaCl, the difference in charge of the two atoms is the electrostatic force that maintains the bond between the atoms. Note that when NaCl is in an aqueous environment, the electron transfer creates two ions: a cation (Na^+) and an anion (Cl^-).

What is the Octet Rule?

The desire for atoms to share, lose or gain electrons to have the same number of electrons of the nearest noble gas.

All noble gases have eight valence electrons except He, why?

Well, He only has an s orbital and therefore has only two valence electrons. The other noble gases also have a p orbital which are full with six electrons. The six p orbital electrons - plus the two s orbital electrons - equal eight.

What are the exceptions to the octet rule?

As for many rules, the octet rule has exceptions. For example boron, phosphorus, sulfur and xenon. For studying purposes know that they exist. To be sure on the test, calculate formal charges to make sure that you have the right number of electrons (see Formal Charges below on page 198).

What is lattice energy?

The energy released when gaseous ions of opposite charge come together to form a solid.

How is lattice energy calculated?

$$E_{Lattice} = \frac{kQ_1Q_2}{r_2} \tag{25.1}$$

Where k is a constant, Q_1 and Q_2 are the charges on the particles, and r_2 is the distance between their centers squared, aka Coulumb's Law.

Note: this discussion on lattice energy may bring to mind bond dissociation energies, etc. These will be discussed in Chapter 33 Thermochemistry on page 253 and Coulomb's Law will be discussed in Chapter 62 Physics on page 418.

25.2   Covalent Bonds

What are covalent bonds?

Bonds which occur between two atoms with similar electronegativities such that the electrons are shared between both atoms, commonly between two non-metals. Molecular oxygen, O_2, is a good example of this:

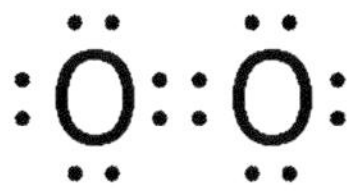

$$:\ddot{O}::\ddot{O}:$$

Figure 25.2: The Covalent Bond: O_2

What is bond order?

Fancy scientific term for the number of electrons shared between two atoms.

What are the three general types of covalent bonds and how do the bond lengths and energies vary with the different types of bonds?

Bond type (e^- number)	Bond Length	Bond Energy
Single bonds (2 e^-)	Short	Low
Double bonds (4 e^-)	Shorter	Medium
Triple bonds (6 e^-)	Shortest	High

Table 25.1: Three general covalent bonds, bond lengths and bond energies.

Bond energy basically means the energy required to break a bond. As we will see later in thermochemistry (and the law of conservation of energy), the energy to create something is equal to the energy required to break it. Therefore, "bond energies" are equivalent to the amount of energy to create or break a respective bond.

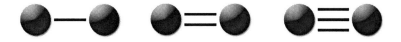

Figure 25.3: Single, double and triple covalent bonds.

What types of bonds can form when s and p orbitals overlap?

Sigma (σ) and pi (π).

What do sigma (σ) and pi (π) bonds look like?

σ- and π-bonds are seen below in Figure 25.4:

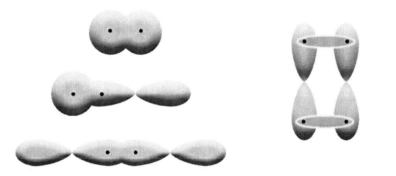

Figure 25.4: σ- and π-bonds. σ- bonds (left) are formed between two s orbitals (left, top), one s and one p (left, middle) or two p_x orbitals (left, bottom). π- bonds (right) are formed between two p_y or two p_z orbitals; each would appear similarly and only one is depicted (right).

What are hybridized orbitals?

Concept that describes the mixing of s and p orbitals.

What are the three most common hybridized orbitals?

sp^3, sp^2 and sp orbitals: see Table 25.2 below:

	# of hybrid orbitals	Used Orbitals	Unused Orbitals
sp	2	s p_x	p_y p_z
sp^2	3	s p_x p_y	p_z
sp^3	4	s p_x p_y p_z	

Table 25.2: sp^3, sp^2 and sp orbitals.

What hybridized orbital creates single bonds?

$$sp^3$$

What theory predicts the spacial configuration assumed by the atoms in a molecule?

Valence shell electron pair repulsion theory (VSEPR).

What are five key arrangements that you should be familiar with?

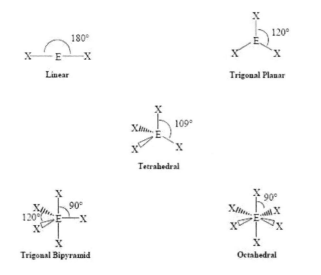

Figure 25.5: Five key bond arrangements: linear (a), trigonal planar (b), tetrahedral (c), trigonal bipyramidal (d), and octahedral (e).

What are the steps involved when predicting a molecule's arrangement given a formula, e.g. CH_4 or H_2O?

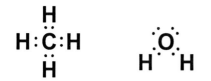

Figure 25.6: VSEPR: Lewis dot structures for CH_4 and H_2O.

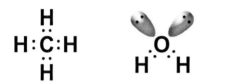

Figure 25.7: VSEPR: lone pairs of electrons for CH_4 and H_2O.

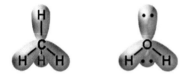

Figure 25.8: VSEPR: most stable arrangement for CH_4 and H_2O.

Note: VSEPR treats bonding and non-bonding electron pairs equally and they can be considered as "spherical objects". Therefore, methane has four "spherical objects" corresponding to its four C-H bonds. Similarly, water also has four "spherical objects" corresponding to two H-O bonds and two pairs of non-bonding electrons. Ultimately, both have tetrahedral structures because of their electrons, but water appears bent because it only has two bonding pairs of electrons.

25.2.1   Resonance Structures

What are resonance structures?

When two or more Lewis dot structures can correctly represent a molecule's electrons. Molecules which have resonance structures, e.g. O_3, never really exist in one form or another. Instead, they are constantly in flux, oscillating between resonance structures:

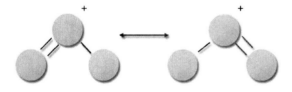

Figure 25.9: Resonance structures of ozone (O_3).

25.2.2   Formal Charges

What are formal charges?

A way of counting electrons that are involved in bonding atoms.

How do you calculate formal charges?

Two simple rules:

1. Non-bonding electrons of a given atom are counted for that atom

2. Bonding electrons are halved between both atoms, i.e. if a pair of electrons are shared between two atoms, one electron is counted for each atom

$Formal\ charge = (Total\ valence\ electrons) - (\#\ of\ non-bonding\ e^-) - (1/2\ \#\ of\ bonding\ e^-)$

25.2.3 Electronegativity and Covalent Bonds

What is the role of electronegativity in the distribution of charge within a covalent bond?

Elements which have high electronegativity (top, right corner of the periodic table - aka Mighty Mouse) will "pull" charge towards them creating a more negative charge towards their end:

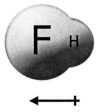

Figure 25.10: e^- charge distribution in HF.

Note, the plus sign has an extended arrow-tipped lines. These indicate the dipole moment of the molecule and show the concentration of positive charge (+) and negative charge (arrow-head).

Figure 25.11: e^- charge distribution in H_2O.

What is the name of a bond (molecule) which exhibits a dipole moment?

Polar bond (molecules).

25.3   Hydrogen Bonds

What is a hydrogen bond?

An intermolecular attractive force in which a positively-polarized hydrogen is attracted to a negatively-polarized atom in a nearby molecule.

What are the three molecules that form hydrogen bonds?

1. Nitrogen

2. Oxygen

3. Flourine

Remember: "Got eN.O.F. of studying yet?"

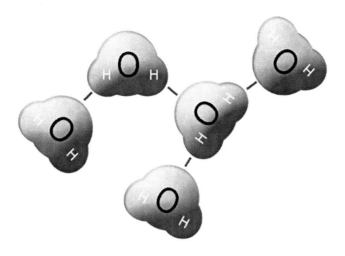

Figure 25.12: Hydrogen bonding in water.

Note: Hydrogen bonds are key to life. For example, hydrogen bonds increase the stability of DNA and direct the shape of the double helix.

Chapter 26

Stoichiometry

What is stoichiometry?

Using chemical equations to calculate quantities of reactants and products using mathematical relationships.

26.1 Chemical Reactions

What are four common chemical reactions seen in inorganic chemistry?

Red-ox	$2Fe + 6HCl \rightarrow 2FeCl_3 + 3H_2$ *Note: The element that is displaced is reduced (H), the element that does the displacing is oxidized (Fe).*
Single displacement (or single replacement)	$AgNO_3 + HCl \rightarrow AgCl + HNO_3$
Decomposition	$2HgO \rightarrow 2Hg + O_2$
Acid-Base (or neutralization)	$2NaOH + H_2SO_4 \rightarrow Na_2SO_4 + 2H_2O$

Table 26.1: Four common chemical reactions

26.2 Mass

What is atomic mass?

Atomic mass is the average of the isotopic masses of an element based on their percentage of abundance in nature. This number is dimensionless and based on the carbon-12 atom, i.e. carbon has an atomic mass of 12 u by definition.

What is molecular mass?

Also known as molecular weight, molecular mass is the weight of one molecule of a substance and can be calculated by summing the atomic mass (u) of the atoms in the molecule.

For example, the molecular mass of water, H_2O, is equal to the atomic mass of two hydrogens (1.007 u per hydrogen) plus the atomic mass of oxygen (15.999 u) or 18.006 u.

What is molar mass?

The mass, in grams, of one mole of an element of atoms, molecules or particles (grams/mol).

What is a mole?

6.022×10^{23} atoms, molecules or any given particle. This number is also known as Avogadro's number.

Therefore, because atomic mass (u) is based on carbon-12 and molar mass (grams/mol) is also based on carbon-12, 1 u = 1 gram/mol.

From our example above, we calculated that H_2O is equal to a molecular mass of 18.006 u, with the conversion explained above, 18.006 u = 18.006 grams/mol H_2O.

26.3   Units

What is the difference between SI units and metric units?

Nothing. SI, or système internationial, is the modern metric system.

What are common SI units used in inorganic chemistry for mass, volume, distance and temperature?

Mass		1 milligram (mg) = 0.001 g
	1 gram (g)	
		1 kilogram (kg) = 1000 g
Volume		1 milliliter (mL) = 0.001 L
		1 decaliter (dL) = 0.10 L
	1 liter (L)	
Distance		1 millimeter (mm) = 0.001 m
		1 centimeter (cm) = 0.01 m
		1 decameter (dm) = 0.1 m
	1 meter (m)	
		1 kilometer (km) = 1000 m
Temperature	1 degree Celsius (^{o}C)	To convert to K, add 273
	1 degree Kelvin (K)	To convert to ^{o}C substract 273

Table 26.2: Four common SI units in inorganic chemistry.

26.4   Empirical and Molecular Formulas

What is the difference between empirical and molecular formulas?

An *empirical formula* gives the simplest *relative* proportion of atoms for a given molecule. A *molecular formula* gives the *exact* number of atoms for a given molecule.

Elaborate using glucose as an example.

The empirical formula of glucose is $C_1H_2O_1$ while the molecular formula of glucose is $C_6H_{12}O_6$.

26.5   Mass Percent Composition

What is mass percent composition?

In the context of compounds, the percent composition of an element in a compound is the percent, by mass, of an element in a compound.

What are the steps to calculating percent composition?

1. Calculate the molar mass of the compound

2. Calculate the molar mass of the element of interest in the compound by multiplying the subscript by the molar mass of the element

3. Divide the molar mass of the element in the compound by the total molar mass of the compound

What is the percent composition of oxygen in water?

Step 1:

Calculate the molar mass of the compound	Molar mass of H_2O = 18 g/mole	18 g/mole

Step 2:

Calculate the molar mass of the element of interest in the compound by multiplying the subscript by the molar mass of the element	Oxygen has a subscript of 1, or one mole of oxygen per mole of water, therefore, 1 mol oxygen times 16 g/mol oxygen equals 16 g oxygen/mol water	16 g/mole

Step 3:

Divide the molar mass of the element in the compound by the total molar mass of the compound	16 g oxygen/mol water divided by 18 g water/mol water = .89 or 89% composition of one mole of water by oxygen.	$\frac{16g}{18g}$ = .89 x 100 = 89%

Table 26.3: Calculating percent composition.

26.6 Density

What is density?

Density (ρ) is equal to the total mass (m) of a substance per unit volume (V):

The less mass per unit volume, the less dense, e.g. "lighter than air" helium (He), which tends to rise. Contrarily, the more mass per unit volume, the more dense or heavier the material. This has implications that will be dealt with later in physics (buoyancy) and gas phase chemistry.

26.7   Conventions for writing equations

What are the conventions for writing equations?

1. Reactants on the left and products on the right, separated by an arrow

2. Physical states are denoted by subscripts following the atom or molecule: (s) for solids, (l) for liquids, (g) for gases, and (aq) for aqueous solutions, i.e. substances dissolved in water.

3. Coefficients are used to balance equations: if none is present, it is assumed to be equal to one. $_{Subscripts}$ after an atom denote the number of atoms within a molecule while ^{superscripts} after a molecule or atom denote charge.

How do you balance equations?

Practice. There is no straightforward way to go through it. I suggest looking at the least-represented atom on either side and starting from there. Red-ox equations require certain steps - refer to the Red-ox chapter on page 257 for an in depth review.

What are limiting reactants and how do you identify them?

The reactant that is completely consumed in a reaction. Or, the reactant, by its limited quantity and inevitable consumption in a reaction, that prevents a reaction from proceeding.

To identify a limiting reactant begin with balancing the equation and convert any given masses to moles. Then, identify how many moles of the reactants are needed for the balanced reaction to proceed. Finally, compare the moles of all the reactants with each other and identify the least represented reactant.

What are theoretical yields and how do you calculate them?

A method for researchers to predict what is the best outcome of a given experiment. The theoretical yield is very difficult to obtain experimentally and responsible for TAs docking points off of your grade and drives industries to find innumerable ways to maximize profits.

To calculate a theoretical yield, identify the amount of reactants and calculate the limiting reactant. With the limiting reactant, you can calculate the maxi-

mum amount of achievable product. Finally, divide your experimental yield by
the theoretical yield and you will see how good you did.

$$Experimental\ Yield = \frac{Actual\ yield}{Theoretical\ yield} \times 100$$

Chapter 27

Acids & Bases

27.1   Definitions

What are two classifications of acids and bases?

Lewis acids/bases
Brønsted-Lowry acids/bases

What are the differences between their definitions?

Lewis acids/bases	Electron-pair acceptors (acids) or donors (bases)
Brønsted-Lowry acids/bases	Proton acceptors (bases) or donors (acids)

Generally speaking, what happens when you mix an acid and a base?

1. Release energy!!!

2. Produce a salt, e.g. NaCl when you add HCl to NaOH

3. Produce water

27.2 K_W, pH, pOH, K_b and K_a

Relate water, acid species and base species in a chemical equation.

$$H_2O_{(l)} \rightleftharpoons H^+_{(aq)} + OH^-_{(aq)} \qquad (27.1)$$

What would the equilibrium constant be for this reaction?

K$_W$ aka the water dissociation constant:

$$K_W = [H^+][OH^-] = 10^{-14} \tag{27.2}$$

where $[H^+]$ is the concentration of hydrogen in moles and $[OH^-]$ is the concentration of the hydroxyl (base) in moles. Note, $[H^+]$ is also sometimes represented as $[H_3O^+]$.

What happens when you take the log of this equation?

$$log([H^+][OH^-]) = log(10^{-14}) \tag{27.3}$$

$$log[H^+] + log[OH^-] = -14 \tag{27.4}$$

or

$$-log[H^+] + -log[OH^-] = 14 \tag{27.5}$$

$$pH + pOH = 14 \tag{27.6}$$

In Equation 27.5, the negative sign is placed before the log because it has been agreed that the quantity for *pH* is positive. The negative sign in front of the log of a decimal ensures that the answer will be positive.

What is the concentration of $[H^+]$ and $[OH^-]$ in pure water?

$1x10^{-7}$ for each. Intuitively, if you multiply $1x10^{-7}$ by $1x10^{-7}$ you get $1x10^{-14}$. Or a pH of 7 and a pOH of 7, which add up to 14.

How do you convert a pH or a pOH to a concentration of H$^+$ or OH$^-$?

Multiply the pH or pOH by negative one, then take the log.

Without a calculator, take the pH or pOH, place a negative in front of it and raise this value above ten. For example, the number of moles of OH in a solution with a pOH of 3 is:

$$pOH = 3$$
$$3 \text{ x -1} = \text{-3}$$
$$10^{-3} = [OH^-]$$

Conversely, if the pH is 11 (pH + pOH = 14: therefore, 14 - pOH = pH. In this example we said that pOH was equal to 3, a very basic solution) we find the moles of H^+ to be:

$$pH = 11$$
$$11 \text{ x } -1 = -11$$
$$10^{-11} = [H^+]$$

Note: Although it seems pretty clear, its an easy mistake to make: 10^{-3} is 100 million times more concentrated than 10^{-11} - don't get tripped up by the exponents.

How are pH and pOH related?

Inversely, i.e. if one goes up the other goes down. The convention is to use pH to measure acidity, but don't get tricked by a question that uses pOH. For example, in a very acidic environment with a pH of 2.0, the pOH is equal to 12 - both represent the same environment.

Another thing to keep in mind is that a low pH is equal to a high concentration of H$^+$ and therefore a very acidic solution. Similarily, a low pOH is also equal to a high concentration of OH$^-$ and therefore is a very basic solution:

Now, if we defined K$_w$ above, what about K$_a$ and K$_b$?

K$_w$ is the water dissociation constant, i.e. the equilibrium constant for the dissociation of water. Therefore, K$_{acid}$ and K$_{base}$ are the acid and base dissociation constants:

$$HA_{(aq)} + H_2O_{(l)} \rightleftharpoons H_3O^+_{(aq)} + A^-_{(aq)}$$

$$K_{Acid} = \frac{[H_3O^+][A]}{[HA]} \quad\quad (27.7)$$

$$BOH_{(aq)} + H_2O_{(l)} \rightleftharpoons B^+_{(aq)} + OH^-_{(aq)}$$

$$K_{Base} = \frac{[B^+][OH^-]}{[BOH]} \qu\quad (27.8)$$

What does it mean for a molecule to have either a high K$_a$ or K$_b$?

The molecule is either a strong acid or a strong base. Since a large K$_a$ or K$_b$ reflects a molecule that is actively moving in the forward direction in the above equations (creating a large numerator in the equations for the equilibrium constants), it is either actively creating large amounts of H_3O^+ or OH^-.

Note: K_a and K_b are inversely related to each other.

27.3 Conjugate Acids and Bases

What does conjugate mean?

For acids and bases, *conjugate* means having features in common but opposite or inverse to each other.

What are conjugate acids and bases?

From the Brønsted-Lowrty acids/bases definition, a conjugate base is formed when *acids donate protons*, and a conjugate acid is formed when *bases accept protons*.

In any given dissociation of an acid (or a hydrogen addition to a base), a new species is created. This species in turn can accept protons (in the case of the acid) called a conjugate base, or a proton can be accepted (in the case of a base) called a conjugate acid. This new species is called a conjugate base (in the case of a dissociated acid) and a conjugate acid (in the case of a dissociated base):

Original form (Acid)	Dissociated/conjugate form
HCl	Cl^-, the conjugate base

Original form (Base)	Dissociated/conjugate form
NaOH	Na^+, the conjugate acid

Table 27.1: Acids and Bases: Examples of the conjugate form.

What is the relationship between the strength of an acid/base and the strength of its conjugate?

Strong Acid	$\Longrightarrow$	Weak conjugate base
Strong Base	$\Longrightarrow$	Weak conjugate acid
Weak acid	$\Longrightarrow$	Strong conjugate base
Weak base	$\Longrightarrow$	Strong conjugate acid

Table 27.2: Relationship between the strength of an acid/base and the strength of its conjugate.

How do amino acids exhibit acid-base properties?

Amino acids have a carboxyl group and an amino group, both of which can serve as weak acids or bases as seen in Figure 48.2 below. The occurrence of either depends on the pH and will be discussed in more depth in the organic chemistry Amines chapter (on page 341) and Amino Acids & Proteins chapter (on page 349).

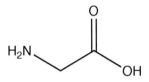

Figure 27.1: Glycine.

27.4   Strong Acids and Bases

What strong acids and bases should you be familier with for the MCAT?

HCl	Hydrochloric acid		NaOH	Sodium hydroxide
HBr	Hydrobromic acid		KOH	Potassium hydroxide
HI	Hydroiodic acid		$Ca(OH)_2$	Calcium hydroxide
HNO_3	Nitric acid			
$HClO_4$	Perchloric acid			
H_2SO_4	Sulfuric acid			

Table 27.3: Strong acids (left) and strong bases (right).

What is the difference between strong acids/bases and weak acids/bases?

Simply put, strong acids/bases dissociate 100%, weak acids/bases do not.

27.5   Weak Acids and Bases

What are weak acids and bases?

Acids and bases which do not dissociate completely. Some examples include: Acetic acids (CH_3COOH), water (H_2O), and hydrofluoric acid (HF).

How can you calculate the amount a weak acid (or base) dissociates?

Take for example the weak acid acetic acid:

$$CH_3COOH_{(aq)} \rightleftharpoons H^+_{(aq)} + CH_3COO^-_{(aq)}$$

If this were a strong acid, the reaction would practically proceed to the right and to completion. In the case of this weak acid, we need to go back to our definition K_{Acid}. With this reaction, this would be:

$$K_{Acid} = \frac{[H^+_{aq}][CH_3COO^-]}{[CH_3COOH_{(aq)}]} \qquad (27.9)$$

Now, one has to be given more information to proceed. OK, lets say the solution was 3.5 M $CH_3COOH_{(aq)}$. What would be $[H^+_{(aq)}]$ given a $K_{Acetic\ acid} = 0.000018$?

$$K_{Acid} = \frac{[x][x]}{[3.5-x]} \quad 0.000018 = \frac{[x^2]}{[3.5-x]}$$

At this point, things seem a little bleak with the possibility of solving a quadratic equation. Luckily, we can drop the x in the denominator under the assumption that it is relatively small. Rewind: Weak acids dissociate poorly, i.e. the amount of conjugate base formed is very small. Well, at least small enough not to impact the "size" of the denominator, and the x can be dropped:

$$0.000018 = \frac{[x^2]}{[3.5-x]} \text{ becomes } 0.000018 = \frac{[x^2]}{[3.5]}$$
$$(3.5)(0.000018) = x^2$$
$$x = 0.00793$$

Note: See intro chapter on MCAT math to solve for square roots without a calculator

How would you calculate the pH of this reaction?

$$pH = -log[H^+]$$

What are two assumptions made in the above weak acid calculation?

1. The weak acid dissociation is small enough that the change from the reactant can be ignored in the equilibrium calculation.

2. The weak acid dissociation is still large enough to ignore the passive dissociation of water.

27.6   Buffers

What are buffers?

A solution of a weak acid and its salt (or a weak base and its salt[1]), which by its presence resists changes in pH.

What classic buffer system is found in the blood?

$$CO_2 + H_2O \rightleftharpoons H_2CO_3 \rightleftharpoons H^+ + HCO_3^- \qquad (27.10)$$

This buffer system plays a big role in the acid-base balance in the blood. The kidney is involved in *excreting* bicarbonate (HCO_3) and also contains the enzyme carbonic anhydrase in the proximal tubule that catalyzes this reaction.

What is the effect of a buffer system on a titration curve?

Buffers increase the amount of acid or base required to change the pH.

----

[1]For example NH_4Cl and NH_3

27.7   Titration

What are titration curves?

A graphical representation of pH changes when an acid or base is added to a solution.

What are indicators?

Molecules that change color depending on specific pH changes.
What is the equivalence point?

The point at which equal amounts of reactants have reacted and neither of them is in excess.

What is the neutral point?

The point at which the pH of a titration solution equals 7.

Label the various parts of the titration curve:

1. pH drop at the start of the titration upon addition of a strong acid to a strong base.

2. Equivalence point.

3. End of titration with the solution pH approaching the pH of the strong acid.

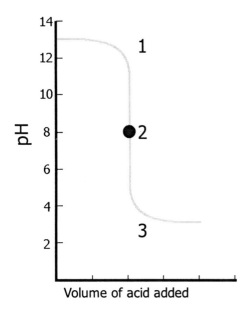

Figure 27.2: Titration curve.

Chapter 28

Electrochemistry

There are two types of electrochemical cells which you should be familiar with:

1. Electrolytic cells

2. Galvanic or voltaic cells

What type of chemical reaction takes place in both types of electro-chemical cells?

A re-dox reaction. You can review this in the red-ox chapter on page 257.

What charges are found at the cathode and anode?

The ca+hode is where positive charges are concentrated and the anode is where negative charges are concentrated.

What red-ox half reaction occurs at the anode and the cathode?

Oxid*a*tion occurs at the *a*node.
Redu*c*tion occurs at the *c*athode.

This can be remembered as "an Ox, red Cat."

What are reduction potentials and cell potentials?

Both are measured in volts but a reduction potential is the energy required to force an atom or molecule to release an electron, while a cell potential is the difference in potential between the two electrodes of a cell.

28.1 Electrolytic Cells

Why are electrolytic cells called electrolytic?

"Lytic" comes from the root word "to split," and electro, well, simply means electricity. So, electrolytic cells use electricity to split molecules, which is also known as electrolysis.

This occurs at the electrodes and can result, in the deposition of an element (electroplating) and the splitting of a molecule to release a gas.

What are electrolytes?

A substance that dissociates into free ions when dissolved in water. These ions in turn facilitate the conduction of electricity.

In organisms, replenishing electrolytes (e.g. Gatorade) is important to maintain homeostasis of key ions (Na^+, K^+).

What is the ΔG of electrolytic cells?

$+\Delta$G, i.e. the reaction is *non − spontaneous*.

What is Faraday's law (aka the first law of electrolysis)?

The mass of a substance produced at an electrode during electrolysis is proportional to the number of moles of electrons transferred at that electrode.

Basically, the amount of electrical current (moles of electrons) in an electrolytic cell is directly related to how much splitting occurs. This is the basis of *Faraday's constant*, which is calculated by multiplying the charge of one electron with the number of electrons in one mole.

How can you relate the effect of one mole of electrons?

$$(1.6x10^{-19}Coulombs)(6.022x10^{23}e/mol) = 96,487C/mole \qquad (28.1)$$

The importance of this calculation is that a connection between moles and electrical charge is made.

How would you calculate the moles of an element that would be deposited at an electrode?

One way would be to calculate the amount of Coulombs that passes through the electrolytic cell. If the electrical charge is represented in amps, convert to Coulombs:

$$Amps = \frac{Coulombs}{seconds} \tag{28.2}$$

The key concept is to understand that Coulumbs are related to moles using Faraday's constant. Importantly, if you are given the amount of time that the current was applied to the system, you can calculate the numbers of moles that were deposited.

Label the various parts of the molten NaCl electrolytic cell:

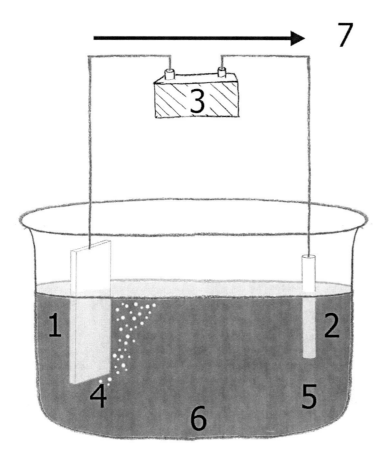

Figure 28.1: The Electrolytic Cell.

1. Anode   5. $Na^+_{(l)}$
2. Cathode   6. Molten NaCl
3. Battery   7. Direction of e^- flow
4. $Cl^-_{2\ (g)}$

Note: In an electrolytic cell, the cathode is negative and the anode is positive but electrons still flow towards the cathode.

28.2   Galvanic Cells (aka Voltaic Cells)

What is the set-up of galvanic cells?

Two half reactions that are connected by a salt bridge.

What is the importance of separating each half reaction?

If the metals were put in the same container the reaction would still occur, but it would be very difficult, if not impossible, to harness the energy of the red-ox reaction.

By putting a metal with a different charge in each half reaction and surrounding the metals with an electrolytic solution connected by a salt bridge, ion exchange can partially occur. The circuit is completed by connecting the metals with a wire. Then, the electron transfer through the wire can in turn be put to work, e.g. interspersing a motor or a light bulb.

What is the ΔG of galvanic cells?

$-\Delta G$, i.e. the reaction is *spontaneous*.

What direction do electrons flow?

From the anode to the cathode.

Label the various parts of the galvanic cell:

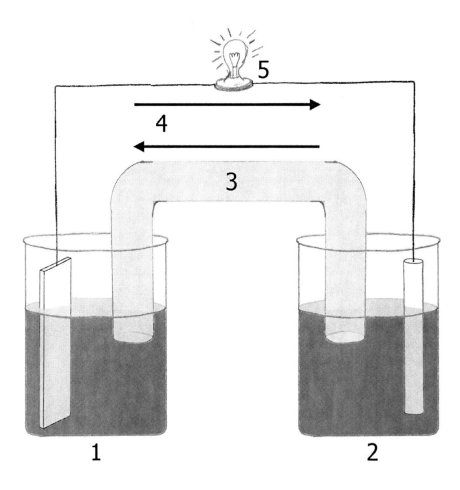

Figure 28.2: The Galvanic Cell.

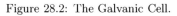

1. Anode side   4. e⁻ flow (in both directions)
2. Cathode side   5. Energy being put to work
3. Salt bridge

28.3   Electrochemical & Galvanic Cells: Side-by-side comparison

	Electrolytic Cell	Galvanic (Voltaic Cell)
Purpose	Use electricity to drive a chemical reaction	Use spontaneous chemical reactions to create energy
Free energy change (ΔG)	$+\Delta G$ (non-spontaneous)	$-\Delta G$ (spontaneous)
Reaction mechanism	Red-ox	Red-ox
System setup	Usually one container	Two containers
Charge of anode	+	-
Charge of cathode	-	+

Table 28.1: Key facts on electrolytic and galvanic cell.

Chapter 29

Phases & Phase Equilibria

For the MCAT, the two key phases which you should be familiar with are the gas phase and the liquid phase. As for phase equilibria, you should have a comfortable understanding of what takes place when an element goes from one phase to another, e.g. solid to liquid.

Before we go into the specifics of phases and phase equilibria, let's touch on the basics:

29.1   The Basics

What is the Kelvin (K) scale?

A temperature scale that is based on true molecular motion. Therefore, 0 K is the temperature at which zero molecular motion occurs, i.e. absolute zero. Kelvins can be converted to Celsius (^oC) by using the formula K $+273 = {}^oC$, e.g. 0 K = -273 ^oC.

What is the connection between pressure and a simple mercury barometer?

Pressure is simply how hard something pushes onto something else and can be measured by a barometer (from Greek *baros* "weight" and *metron* "measure"). Mercury (Hg) is a liquid metal at room temperature that is quite dense. This proves to be a useful combination of properties because a relatively small volume can be used in a barometer to show small changes in pressure. So, when you get your blood pressure measured at the doctor, Hg is used in the barometer to show blood pressure changes by displacing the Hg column for the given pressure. If a less-dense substance were used, then the barometer "column" would have to be much taller to reveal similar pressure changes.

What is the molar volume of a gas at 0°C at 1 atm?

22.4 L/mol

29.2 Gas Phase

What is an ideal gas?

The "perfect gas." Ideal gases are characterized as having the following properties:

- Consisting of identical particles with negligible volume

- Undergoing perfectly elastic collisions

- Exhibt no intermolecular forces

- Store zero intramolecular energy

In reality though, real gases do not have any of these properties, but the assumption of ideal gases is made for day-to-day calculations.

How do real gases differ from ideal gases?

1. Qualitatively, gases change their quality or nature under different conditions, e.g. the attractive forces between gas molecules lower the overall pressure of the gas, and at low temperatures, gases can change phases into liquids or sometimes even solids, resulting in even stronger forces than in ideal gases.

2. Quantitatively, gases have volume and exhibit intermolecular forces: The Van der Waals equation takes into account the realness of gases by adapting the ideal gas law to take into account (i) intermolecular forces and (ii) volume.

3. The collisions are not necessarily elastic.

What is the ideal gas law?

$$PV = nRT \qquad (29.1)$$

Just like the date of the MCAT, this should be scored into your brain. Seriously though, the manipulations of this formula are incredibly powerful and allow you to make some important calculations.

What is Boyle's law?

$$P_1 V_1 = P_2 V_2 \qquad (29.2)$$

One variation of the gas law which states that pressure and volume are inversely related at constant temperature. That is, at a constant temperature, pressure and volume will "compensate" for each. This makes sense: High pressure leads to small volume; conversely, low pressure leads to high volume.

Figure 29.1: Boyle's Law.

What is Charles' law?

$$\frac{V_1}{T_1} = \frac{V_2}{T_2} \qquad (29.3)$$

Another variation of the ideal gas law which states that, at constant pressure, temperature and volume are directly related. This makes sense: Hotter gases will take up a large volume. Conversely, cooler gases are denser and take up less volume. Just an aside, colder air is more efficient in combustion. Because colder air is in fact denser, you get more "bang for your buck" because there are more O_2 molecules per unit volume. Therefore, jets taking off on winter days can create more thrust, get into the air quicker and can get away with using a shorter runway.

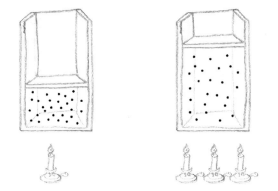

Figure 29.2: Charles' Law.

What is Avogadro's principle?

$$\frac{n_1}{V_1} = \frac{n_2}{V_2} \qquad (29.4)$$

Another variation of the gas law that shows that volume is directly related to the number of moles of gas at constant pressure and temperature. Therefore, the more moles of a gas you have, the more volume the gas takes up.

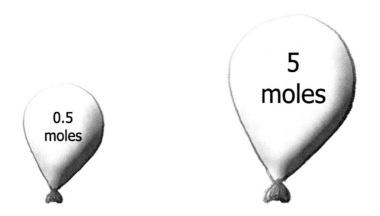

Figure 29.3: Avogadro's Law.

In summary, what are the three gas laws and what is held constant in each?

	Boyle's Law	Charles' Law	Avogadro's Principle
Law:	$P_1V_1 = P_2V_2$	$\frac{V_1}{T_1} = \frac{V_2}{T_2}$	$\frac{n_1}{V_1} = \frac{n_2}{V_2}$
Holding constant:	Temperature	Pressure	Pressure Temperature

Table 29.1: Side-by-side comparison of the gas laws.

What are partial pressures of gases?

The pressure exerted by a particular gas in a vessel containing more than one gas.

How does partial pressure relate to moles?

In a given vessel, the total moles present of all the gases can be correlated to the total pressure of all the gases present. Further, the mole fraction - the moles of one gas over the total moles of all gases - can be correlated to the partial pressure of the gas:

$$Mole\ fraction\ of\ Gas\ A = \frac{Moles\ of\ Gas\ A}{Total\ moles\ of\ all\ gases} \qquad (29.5)$$

$$Partial\ pressure\ of\ Gas\ A = \frac{Pressure\ of\ Gas\ A}{Total\ pressure\ of\ all\ gases} \qquad (29.6)$$

Therefore, since we are dealing with proportions, you can use these proportions to find the individual pressure of a gas when given only moles of the gases and the total pressure of a system:

Take the mole fraction of the gas and multiply it by the total pressure of all the gases:

$$(Mole\ fraction\ of\ Gas\ A)\,(Total\ pressure\ of\ all\ gases) = Pressure\ of\ Gas\ A \qquad (29.7)$$

Again, since we are dealing with proportions, this can be interchanged to find the mole fraction of Gas A given the total moles of a gas and partial pressure of gas A.

What is Dalton's law of partial pressures?

Law 1 *The total pressure of a gas mixture is the sum of the partial pressures of each gas in a given vessel.*

$$P_{Total} = p_1 + p_2 + \ldots + p_n \qquad (29.8)$$

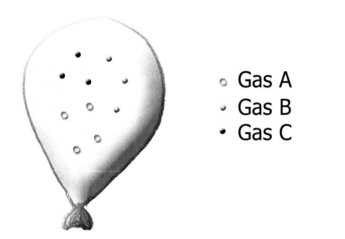

Figure 29.4: Dalton's Law of Partial Pressures: In this example, there is a mixture of three gases. Each gas contributes to the overall mixture in a $4_{Gas\ A}{:}3_{Gas\ B}{:}3_{Gas\ C}$ ratio totaling 10. The number designation is arbitrary and is used to illustrate the point of "parts of a whole." When it comes to doing your own calculations, the same methodology can be applied using the appropriate units.

What main assumption is made with Dalton's law of partial pressure?

Each gas in the vessel does not react with any other gas and can be treated as an independent member of the vessel.

What is the basis of the kinetic theory of gases?

A theory that explains the macroscopic properties of gases based on their microscopic (molecular) properties.

What are four assumptions of the kinetic molecular theory?

1. Gas molecules are in constant, random motion.

2. Collisions between gas molecules are elastic, i.e. there is no loss of kinetic energy due to the collision.

3. The total volume of the gas molecules is negligible compared to the volume of the container.

4. The force of attraction between molecules is negligible.

These assumptions should seem similar to the ideal gas law. Again, memorize these or at least understand them.

29.3   Role of Forces in the Liquid Phase

What are three main intermolecular forces that exist among liquids?

1. *Dipole interactions*: A dipole is formed when an unequal distribution of electrons occurs in a molecule due to the different electronegativities of their individual atoms. When a dipole exists in a liquid, the positive ends of the molecules will align themselves with the negative ends of other molecules.

   • Acetone is a good example of a polar molecule because the very electronegative oxygen 'pulls' the electrons more towards its side, creating a dipole allowing for dipole-dipole interactions.

Figure 29.5: e^- charge distribution in acetone.

2. *Hydrogen bonding*: The strongest of the listed intermolecular forces; which exist between hydrogen and lone pairs of electrons found on N, O, or F (Remember: "E-N.O.F. bonds exist," pronounced "Enough bonds exist."

   • Boiling points (b.p.) are directly related by the number of hydrogen bonds that a molecule can form in its liquid state. For example, water can form up to four bonds, whereas hydrogen fluoride (HF) can only form one. Therefore, water has a higher b.p.[1]

   • Hydrogen bonds are the reason why ice floats: The crystalline lattice of ice is comprised of a regular array of hydrogen bonds which space the water molecules farther apart than they are in liquid water. This in turn causes the density of water to decrease upon freezing.

---

[1]Although hydrogen bonding is significant, appreciate the fact that boiling point also depends on other types of intermolecular forces and properties (e.g. the weight of the molecule).

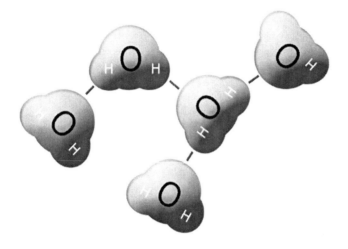

Figure 29.6: Hydrogen bonding in water.

3. *Van der Waals forces (aka London dispersion forces)*: The weakest force among the ones listed. These forces occur when the electron distribution of a molecule momentarily changes when the molecule interacts with other molecules, producing an imbalance of electron distribution around a nucleus. The part where electrons concentrate is more negative while the other part is more positive. Noble gases exhibt this property and the electron cloud is distributed in such a fashion that appears oval. Nevertheless, in theory, all molecules are able to possess Van der Waals forces and they are the weakest force among the ones listed above.

- Van der Waals forces are transient
- This is what allows geckos to stick on glass, leaves, etc.!

29.4   Phase Equilibria

What are the three main states of matter and how do they relate to each other?

$$\begin{array}{ccc} & Solid & \\ \text{Melting} & \downarrow\uparrow & \text{Freezing} \\ & Liquid & \\ \text{Evaporating} & \downarrow\uparrow & \text{Condensing} \\ & Gas & \end{array}$$

By what processes do solids and gases relate to each other?

$$\begin{array}{ccc} & Solid & \\ \text{Sublimation} & \downarrow\uparrow & \text{Deposition} \\ & Gas & \end{array}$$

Dry ice is the classic example of sublimation in which solid carbon dioxide becomes a gas; another is ice in your freezer - over time, the ice cubes "disappear". The formation of frost is an example of deposition.

What is a phase diagram?

A diagram which relates pressure and temperature with corresponding phase states for a given substance. Invariably, a point exists where all three phases coexist in a thermodynamic equilibrium:

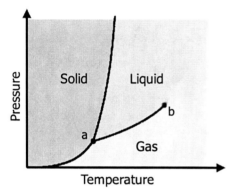

Figure 29.7: Phase diagram: (a) the triple point where all three states coexist, and (b), the critical point: the temperature over which a gas cannot be liquefied by increasing pressure.

What are do you call the temperature transition between solids to liquids, liquids to solids and liquids to gases?

A no-brainer: melting point (solid to liquid), freezing point (liquid to solid) and boiling point (liquid to gas).

What is molality and why is it useful?

Molality (m) indicates the number of moles of a given substance per kilogram of solvent. For example, 3.0 kilograms of solvent, containing 1.0 mole of dissolved particles, constitutes a molality of 0.33 mol/kg or 0.33 molal.

Molality is useful because it's a unit that is constant in regards to physical conditions like pressure and temperature.

What are colligative properties?

Properties that are determined by the concentration of solute in a liquid and not in the identity of the solute.

What are four colligative properties?

1. Vapor pressure

2. Boiling point elevation

3. Freezing point depression

4. Osmotic pressure

What is Raoult's law?

Raoult's law states that the vapor pressure of a liquid is equal to the vapor pressure of the liquid times the molar fraction of the solvent:

$$P = (P_{Pure \ Liquid})(Liquid_{Mole \ fraction}) \tag{29.9}$$

Where P is equal to the vapor pressure of a mixed liquid, $P_{Pure \ Liquid}$ is equal to the vapor pressure of the pure liquid and $Liquid_{Mole \ fraction}$ equals the mole fraction of the liquid. Remember that mole fraction is equal to (moles of substance in question)/(total moles of all substances).

What does Raoult's law show?

Raoult's law shows how a solute affects the vapor pressure of a liquid. Therefore, the changes in vapor pressure are directly related to the molality of the solute in the solution.

Note: Just like Dalton's Law of Partial Pressure, this is an additive formula if there is more than one solute

What is boiling point elevation?

$$\Delta T_b = k_b m_{Solution} \tag{29.10}$$

By adding solute to a liquid, the vapor pressure is lowered and the boiling point is increased, i.e. more energy is needed to expel the solvent into the air. You can think of it as the solute "infiltrating" the surface (i.e. the liquid-gas interface) and thereby decreasing the "concentration" of the surface molecules which ultimately are the ones trying to escape. If there are less molecules available to escape, the vapor pressure is lower. Again, boiling point elevation is directly related to the molality of the solution (for every 1 m increase, boiling point is *elevated* by 0.51 °C).

This is why salt is added to water when you make pasta: The presence of the salt increases the boiling temperature of the water making it hotter than unsalted water. This in turn makes the pasta cook faster (not to mention makes it taste better).

What is freezing point depression?

$$\Delta T_f = k_f m_{Solution} \tag{29.11}$$

By adding solute to a liquid, the ability to form a crystalline lattice is decreased and the freezing point is decreased, i.e. a colder temperature is needed to help organize the liquid into a solid. Again, freezing point depression is directly related to the molality of the solution (for every 1 m increase, freezing point is *decreased* by 1.86 °C).

Automobile cooling systems use anti-freeze (ethylene glycol) to decrease coolant freezing temperatures to prevent freezing in the winter and increase coolant boiling temperatures to prevent boiling in the summer.

What is osmotic pressure (ψ)?

The pressure that a liquid exerts across a semi-permeable membrane when the number of solutes (i.e. concentration) on either side of the membrane is different. This results in a net movement of water from regions of lower solute concentrations to areas of higher solute concentration occuring when two conditions are met:

1. A solute gradient exists across a membrane

2. The solute cannot pass through the membrane

If the membrane is permeable to water, then the movement of water will compensate and rectify the disequilibrium of solute concentrations. The net flux of water will continue until the concentration of solutes is equilibrated on both sides. See figure 29.8 below.

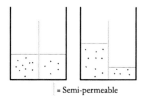

= Semi-permeable

Figure 29.8: Osmotic equilibration: Flow of water through a semipermeable membrane to balance solute concentrations: Before (left) and after (right) equilibration.

What are colloids?

Droplets of a substance that are dispersed into another, forming an apparently homogenous substance. Examples include fog at da club, milk, smoke, and blood.

What is Henry's Law?

Law 2 *The mass of a gas that is dissolved into a liquid is directly proportional to the partial pressure of that gas.*

Chapter 30

Solution Chemistry

30.1 Calculating concentration

What are six methods of representing concentration?

1. Molarity (M)

   - Moles of a substance per liter of solution

2. Molality (m)

   - Moles of a substance per kilogram of solvent
     - m stays constant irrespective to temperature and pressure

3. Normality (N)

   - Moles of equivalents per litre of solution that can donate or accept one mole of protons: That is, one mole of NaOH in one mole of water is not only a 1 M solution, but also a 1 N solution because one mole of NaOH can accept one mole of protons.
   - Normality is often used in red-ox or acid/base calculations

4. Mass percentage (% by mass)

   - Mass of a substance in a mixture as a percentage of the entire mixture's mass

5. Volume percentage (% by volume)

   - Volume of a substance in a mixture as a percentage of the entire mixtures volume

6. Mole fraction (molar fraction)

   - Number of moles of a substance as a proportion of the total number of moles in a mixture

30.2   Ions in Solution

What two forms can ions take in solutions?

Anions (negative charge) and ca+ions (positive charge)

What are three examples of common ions found in solution?

	Formula	Charge
Ammonium	NH_4^+	+1
Phosphate	PO_4^{3-}	-3
Sulfate	SO_4^{2-}	-2

Table 30.1: Three common ions and their charges.

What is hydration?

The process of combining with water. Plaster of Paris is an example of a hydrated reactant. Specifically, water is hydrated to calcium sulfate.

What is the role of hydration in organic chemistry?

The hydronium ca+ion (H_3O^+) is an ion of water that is commonly used in the hydration of organic molecules by way of nucleophilic addition.

30.3   Solution Equilibria

What is K_{sp}?

The product of a reaction's product's concentrations at equilibrium.

What is the equilibrium expression for K_{sp}?

Take for example $AgCl_s \rightleftharpoons Ag_{(aq)}^+ + Cl_{(aq)}^-$, at equilibrium, the solubility constant is equivalent to:

$$K_{sp} = [Ag^+][Cl^-] \tag{30.1}$$

Now, for the dissociation constant of $PbCl_{2\ (s)} \rightleftharpoons Pb^{+2}_{(aq)} + 2Cl^{-}_{(aq)}$, since there are two moles of chloride ions for every mole of lead, this needs to be taken into account - raise each ion to the number of moles that get dissociated. In the AgCl example, you would raise each to one. Since this adds no added value to the calculation (because when there is an absence of a power its assumed to equal one), none are noted above. But for lead chloride, one would write the solubility constant in the following manner:

$$K_{sp} = [Pb^{+}][Cl^{-}]^2 \qquad (30.2)$$

Note: If you are given a K_{sp} and balance the equation, you can calculate the concentrations of the ions.

How is the K_{sp} related to the amount of dissociation that occurs for a given molecule?

They are directly related: The higher the K_{sp}, the more dissociation will occur at equilibrium.

This takes it back to K_{acid} and K_{base} - no? Remember, a higher K_a or K_b reflects an acid or base which actively is dissociating to create H^+ or OH^-.

This makes sense though when you look at how the K_{sp} is calculated: Because the numerator represents the product of the concentrations of each of the products, if more dissociation occurs, then the concentration of the products will be higher and multiplying them in turn will create a larger number.

30.4   Common Ion Effect and Miscellaneous Points of Interest

What is the common ion effect?

A term used to describe the effect that two dissolved solutes have on each other when they both contain the same ion. So, if two solutes contain sodium, the solute that will dissociate more easily (i.e. have a higher K_{sp}) can suppress the other from dissociating. This is an example of Le Chatelier's principle in which the presence of one molecule shifts the equilibrium in the other direction to "balance" out the number of molecules.

For example, say you are at the circus and there's a popcorn vendor. He has two popcorn machines that fill his bin: One can produce 10 bags of popcorn per minute, the other 1 bag per minute. The one that creates more popcorn will "dominate" and "suppress" the other machine because there is enough common ion effect (i.e. the popcorn) produced by the 10-bag machine.

What is the effect of pH on solubility?

pH is a key player in the solubility of proteins (e.g. casein) and other substances. Weak acids and bases are commonly affected by pH in that the availability of H^+ or OH^- changes the charge of the molecule and thereby changes its ability to stay dissolved or precipitate out of solution.

What are complex ions?

We've actually touched on several, but complex ions are molecular aggregates that consist of a metallic component and one or more electron-donating molecules, e.g. sulfate (SO_4^{-2}), chloride (Cl^-) and hydroxide (OH^-).

What does miscible mean?

The ability to mix (versus immiscible). Remembering that *like dissolves like* will get you far: non-polar solvents dissolve non-polar solvents, polar solvents dissolve polar solvents, etc.

Chapter 31

Rate Processes in Chemical Reactions:
Kinetics and Equilibrium

31.1 General

Rate processes can be tricky, re-read this section until things fall into place. As always, doing practice problems never hurts after you understand the theory that's detailed below.

Rate processes can be divided into two general categories:

1. Reaction rates or kinetics

2. Reaction equilibrium

31.2 Reaction Kinetics

What are reaction rates?

Simply, the time per unit volume it takes for a product to form (or for reactants to be consumed):

$$Rate = -\frac{\downarrow in\ available\ reactants}{time} = \frac{\uparrow in\ accumulation\ products}{time}$$

Note: The negative in front of the reactants side of the equation reflects the decrease in reactants that occurs in the formation of a product.

What are six factors that affect reaction rates?

1. Temperature

   - The reaction rate will increase as temperature increases. This is true until extremely high temperatures[1].

2. Concentration

   - Increasing the concentration increases the amount of interactions among reactants.

3. Pressure

   - Increasing the pressure is practically equivalent to increasing the concentration. This is really important for gases; however, reactants that do not involve gases are almost unaffected.

4. Presence of catalyst (more below)

   - Catalysts decrease the energy of activation (E_A) for a substance to change states.

   - Catalysts are not transformed or consumed in a reaction.

5. Order

   - The sum of the exponents of reactant concentrations. This reflects how quickly the reactants are consumed.

What is the rate law?

Because a reaction rate can be expressed as the disappearance of reactants - and assuming the reaction will only proceed in the forward direction - the general rate law for a reaction is equal to (1) the product of the reactant's concentration, (2) each raised to a certain power, and (3) multiplied by a constant (k):

$$aA + bB \rightarrow cC + dD \quad Rate = k[A]^x[B]^y$$

The powers x and y listed in the above rate law are derived by analyzing empirical data as we will see below.

What are the three rate laws that are most commonly observed?

1. Zero-order reaction

2. First-order reaction

3. Second-order reaction

---

[1]The Arrhenius law ($K = Ae^{-E_a/RT}$) tells us that increases in temperature at high temperatures will result in progressively smaller ΔK.

What are the rate constants (and units) for each of the rate laws?

	Rate is equal to:	Units of the rate constant (k)	Description of the rate
Zero-Order Reaction	$rate = k$	$\frac{mole}{L \cdot sec}$	Rate of reaction is constant and independent to the amount of reactants.
First-Order Reaction	$rate = k[A]$	$\frac{1}{sec}$	Rate of reaction is directly proportional to the concentration of one of the reactants.
Second-Order Reaction	$rate = k[A]^2$ $rate = k[A][B]$	$\frac{L}{mole \cdot sec}$	Rate of reaction is directly proportional to the square of the concentration of one of the reactants or to both reactants.

Table 31.1: Zero-, First- and Second- Order Reactions.

Why do the units of the rate constants change?

The units change because the rate constants are different for each order of reactions.

Note: The unit for rate is always moles/(L)(sec) and the unit for concentration is always moles/L. Therefore, to maintain these rigid givens, the constant (k) is the scapegoat for being the flexible one and must adapt itself to have the appropriate units.

What is the rate determining step?

The slowest step in a set of reactions. Because it is the slowest, it sets the whole pace of the reaction. Think about a relay team for the 4x100m relay. If the third runner is the slowest (which actually is commonly the case), the overall time to race completion is dependent on that person's completion of her leg of the race.

How do kinetic and thermodynamic factors affect a reaction rate?

This is more of an organic chemistry topic, but let's talk about it a little. Reaction outcomes are influenced by two factors: (1) the relative stability of the products (aka thermodynamic factors), and (2), the rate of product formation (aka kinetic factors).

If a reaction is governed by thermodynamic factors, then the driving force will be to form the more stable product.

Conversely, if a reaction is governed by kinetic factors, then the driving force will be to form the product with the lowest activation energy.

How do temperature and time spans affect the type of control a reaction will be under?

Generally speaking, kinetic control is more often observed when reactions take place at lower temperatures and over shorter time spans; thermodynamic control is more often observed when reactions take place at higher temperatures and over longer time spans.

What are catalysts?

A substance that accelerates a reaction but is neither consumed nor transformed. Catalysts are added to reactions to facilitate their completion and are not considered reactants or products. This increased reaction rate is a result of a catalyst's ability to reduce activation energies. Consequently, this makes reactions occur at lower temperatures or with less energy required:

Figure 31.1: ΔG changes in a reaction with and without an enzyme: activation energy, over time, in a reaction without an enzyme (upper, solid line) and with an enzyme (lower, dashed line).

31.3 Reaction Equilibrium

What are three applications of reaction equilibrium in reversible reactions?

1. Law of Mass Action

2. The equilibrium constant

3. Le Châtelier's Principle

What is the Law of Mass Action?

The Law of Mass Action states that a reaction rate is proportional to the product of the concentrations of the reactants.

What is the equilibrium constant (K_{eq})?

A number that can determine the concentration of reactants or products when a chemical reaction is at equilibrium.

K_{eq} is an extension of rate constants (k) detailed above but extends those concepts to reversible reactions where the rate of the forward reaction equals the rate of the reverse reaction.

For a given reversible reaction, what is the equilibrium constant?

$$aA + bB \rightleftharpoons cC + dD \therefore K_{eq} = \frac{K_{Forward}}{K_{Reverse}} = \frac{[C]^c[D]^d}{[A]^a[B]^b} \qquad (31.1)$$

Note: Pure solids and liquids do not appear in the equilibrium constant expression.

What does the K_{eq} reveal about the direction a reaction will proceed?

$K_{eq} > 1$ Products favored
$K_{eq} = 1$ Neither products nor reactants favored
$K_{eq} < 1$ Reactants favored

Table 31.2: K_{eq} and the direction of a reaction.

Is temperature at all important for a K_{eq}?

YES!!!! A K_{eq} is specific to a given reaction's environment at a given temperature.

Please don't forget this.

What is Le Châtelier's Principle?

In my humble opinion, probably the most profound principle proposed:

Principle 1 *If a chemical system at equilibrium experiences a change in concentration, temperature, or total the equilibrium will shift in order to minimize that change.*

In chemistry, Le Châtelier's principle could be seen at work the following ways:

Concentration	Increasing the concentration of a substance will shift the equilibrium to the side that would reduce that change in concentration.
Temperature	For an exothermic reaction, if we were to lower the temperature, the equilibrium would shift in such as way as to produce heat. Conversely, for an endothermic reaction, if we were to raise the temperature, the equilibrium would shift to decrease the temperature.
Pressure	For example, in a system where gas exists in the product form (e.g. 4 moles) and reactant form (e.g. 2 moles), if an increase in total pressure occurs, then the equilibrium would shift to the side with the smaller amount of gas (the reactant side, i.e. 2 moles).

Table 31.3: Applications of Le Châtelier's principle.

Chapter 32

Thermodynamics

Thermodynamics is the physics of energy, work, heat, entropy and the spontaneity of processes. The concepts are easily testable points of knowledge that you should be familiar with. OK, so I say that about everything. Still, compared to the other inorganic chapters, this one contains a lot of concepts and definitions so focus on understanding them in addition to getting the math right.

32.1 Thermodynamic System

What are three types of thermodynamic systems?

1. Isolated: No exchange of heat, matter or work with the environment.

2. Closed: Exchange of heat and work, but no exchange of matter.

3. Open: Exchange of heat, work and matter.

	Exchanges with the environment:	Does not exchange with the environment:	Example
Isolated		Heat Matter Work	A very, very good thermos
Closed	Heat Work	Matter	Greenhouse
Open	Heat Matter Work		Ocean

Table 32.1: Thermodynamic systems

© 2005 - 2007

What are four thermodynamic processes?

The four processes are systems going through changes in which a certain property is fixed or controlled:

1. Isobaric - pressure is constant

2. Isothermal - temperature is constant

3. Isochoric - volume is constant

4. Adiabatic - heat does not enter or leave (i.e. similar to isothermal)

What are six state functions seen in thermodynamics?

1. Temperature

2. Pressure

3. Volume

4. Entropy

5. Enthalpy

6. Gibbs free energy

32.2   State functions

State functions are properties of a system that *depend on the current state* of a particular system.

What is temperature?

Temperature is the property that describes the transfer of energy which travels from areas of higher temperature to areas of lower temperature. Higher temperature reflects increased vibration and kinetic movement of atoms in a system. There are many units to measure temperature but familiarity with Celsius, Kelvin and Fahrenheit degrees should be plenty:

$$Kelvin \longrightarrow Celsius$$
$$K - 273 = ^{o}C$$

$$Celsius \longrightarrow Fahrenheit$$
$$^{o}C = (5/9)(^{o}F - 32)$$

What is pressure?

Pressure is how hard one thing pushes on another and reflects the forces within a system. Pressure can be calculated by dividing the exerted force over a defined area:

$$P = \frac{F}{A} \qquad (32.1)$$

Pascals (Pa), atmospheres (atm), and millimeters of mercury ($mmHg$) are common units of pressure, but conversions should be supplied by the MCAT passage. Be sure to understand that the smaller the area for a given force the higher the pressure - remember the classic physics example of someone standing you on your hand wearing a tennis shoe vs. wearing stilettos.

What is entropy?

Entropy, S, is the measure of disorder in a system with the greater the disorder the greater the S.

A more advanced interpretation of entropy shows that entropy can be calculated from heat capacity. Although this is beyond the scope of the MCAT, it does point out how inter-related thermodynamic concepts are.

What is the relationship between entropy and various states of matter?

Gas	Highest entropy
Liquid	"Medium" entropy
Crystal/solids	Lowest entropy

Table 32.2: Relationship between states of matter and entropy.

If this is unclear, think about which one takes more energy to create. To get from crystal to liquid or liquid to gas you need to add energy, which makes the system more disorderd.

What is ΔS at equilibrium?

Zero.

What is enthalpy?

Enthalpy, H, is the measure of internal energy in a system.

What are three ways energy[1] can be transferred?

---

[1] **Heat** is a transient term used for energy that is being *transferred* while the term **energy** is used before or after heat transfer.

1. Conduction

   - No matter exchange.

   - Transfer of heat is accomplished by direct contact, e.g. a stove heating a tea kettle.

2. Convection

   - Matter exhange.

   - Transfer of heat when a hotter (lower density) substance rises to take the place of a colder (higher density) substance, e.g. hot air coming off of asphalt on a road in the desert.

3. Radiation

   - Release of energy from a hot object in the form of electromagnetic radiation, e.g. the heat you feel from a light bulb

   - Only form of energy transfer in a vacuum

What is Gibbs free energy?

Gibbs free energy is a very important function:

$$\Delta G = \Delta H - T \Delta S \qquad (32.2)$$

Note: Temperature is in Kelvins, and is therefore always a positive value.

This function will be revisited in more detail below, but briefly:

$$\Delta G > 0 \quad \text{Non-spontaneous reaction} \ (+\ \Delta G)$$
$$\Delta G = 0 \quad \text{Reaction at equilibrium}$$
$$\Delta G < 0 \quad \text{Spontaneous reaction} \ (-\Delta G)$$

What is the role of ΔH, T and ΔS in determining the outcome of a reaction?

$$\Delta G = \Delta H - T \Delta S$$

ΔH	$T*$	ΔS	
-	+	+	Spontaneous at all temperatures
-	+	-	Spontaneous at low temperatures
+	+	+	Spontaneous at high temperatures
+	+	-	Non-spontaneous at all temperatures

Table 32.3: Role of ΔH, T and ΔS in reaction outcomes.

What is the relationship between the standard free energy of a system (Δ G^o) and the equilibrium constant (K_{eq})?

ΔG^o is the likelihood that a reaction will proceed spontaneously (or not) at *standard conditions* (298.15 K and 1 atm of pressure). The magnitude of ΔG^o indicates how far the system is from equilibrium because when $\Delta G^o = 0$, equilibrium is achieved.

Therefore, the relationship between ΔG^o and K_{eq} is directly related because they both reflect, in their own manner, how far the reaction is from equilibrium.

32.3 Laws of Thermodynamics: Zeroth, 1st, 2nd Laws

What is the Zeroth law?

First off - this law is called "Zeroth" because its felt to be so fundamental that it gets the zero declaration. In fact, they thought of this law way after the first three and because of its purported import, it was made the Zeroth, not the fourth law.

Secondly, the law is pretty obvious, but then again the more obvious something is the more profound it ends up being because it is the ground work for the definition of temperature.

OK the definition: The Zeroth law states that two systems (A and B) are in thermal equilibrium when (1) both systems are at equilibrium, (2) when A meets B they remain in equilibrium. Also, this law states that if another system (C) exists, and A is in equilibrium with B, and B is in equilibrium with C, then A is in equilibrium with C. Pretty intuitive. Don't spend too much time on it, just read it, understand it and move on.

What is the 1st Law of Thermodynamics?

Also known as the Law of Conservation of Energy:

Law 3 *In a closed universe where only System A and B exist, the total energy that enters into A equals the total energy that leaves System B.*

Another way of looking at it: the internal energy of System A can only change if it absorbs or transfers energy by heat and/or work to another System B. The change in internal energy will be of the same magnitude but different signs for the Systems A and B.

Although beyond the scope of the MCAT - but an interesting footnote - Albert Einstein's discovery of special relativity reflects the Law of Conservation of Energy, showing that mass and energy are interchangeable: $E = mc^2$.

In quantum mechanics, conservation of energy is not true because of Heisenbergs uncertainty principle.

How is the change in internal energy calculated?

$$\Delta E = Q - W \qquad\qquad (32.3)$$

Where ΔE is the change of energy in the system, Q is heat transferred into the system from the surroundings, and W is work done by the system.

What are mechanical, electrical, thermal and chemical energy units?

		Conversion
Mechanical	*Joule*	1 J
Electrical	*eV*	$1\text{eV} = 1.60 \times 10^{-19}$ J
Thermal	*cal*∗	1 cal = 4.1855 J
Chemical	*kJ*	1 kJ = 1000 J
	kcal ∗∗	1 kcal = 1000 cal = 4,185 J

Table 32.4: Mechanical, electrical, thermal and chemical energy units

∗ One calorie is the amount of heat necessary to raise the temperature of 1 g of water from 14.5 °C to 15.5 °C; it is equal to 4.1855 J. The nutritional calorie represents 1000 of these 15 °C calories.

∗∗ 1 kcal

What is the 2nd Law of Thermodynamics?

A mathematically complex law that explains entropy and how energy moves about us:

The 2nd law of thermodynamics, briefly, states that energy will flow from more concentrated areas to less concentrated areas.

A good example is a pot of boiling water on the stove. Take the pot off, and the pot/water will transfer their energy into the cooler kitchen air.

Chapter 33

Thermochemistry

Thermochemistry is the application of thermodynamics to chemistry that allows one to better understand chemical reactions, phase changes, and the spontaneity of reactions.

33.1 Can you feel the heat?

What are two classifications of reactions in regards to heat utilization?

1. Endothermic reactions

$$Reactants + Energy \rightarrow Products$$

- Heat is removed from the reactant vessel, e.g. temperature drops in the calorimeter.
- Heat is used to break bonds in the reactants.

2. Exothermic reactions

$$Reactants \rightarrow Products + Energy$$

- Heat is released into the reactant vessel, e.g. temperature increases in the calorimeter.
- Heat released comes from new bond formation in the products.

What thermodynamic state function is used in evaluating heat transfers in chemical reactions?

Enthalpy (H)

What are four various forms of enthalpy used in calculating heat transfers in chemical reactions?

1. ΔH^o_{vap}

   - Heat required to vaporize one mole of a substance (kJ/mol).

2. ΔH^o_{rxn}

   - Amount of heat gained or lost in a chemical reaction (kJ/mol).

3. ΔH^o_f

   - Heat required to form one mole of a pure substance from its elements (kJ/ mol).
   - The heat of formation for pure substances is zero.

4. ΔH^o_{comb}

   - Heat released from the combustion (chemical reaction with O_2) of one mole of a substance (kJ/mol).

Note: "^{o}" refers to standard conditions or 298 K at 1 atm

What is Hess's law?

Hess's law states that enthalpies are additive. In other words, given a reaction it is possible to calculate the ΔH^o_{rxn} by subtracting the $\Delta H^o_{Reactants}$ from the ΔH^o:

$$\Delta H^o_{rxn} = \Delta H^o_{Products} - \Delta H^o_{Reactants} \qquad (33.1)$$

How can Hess's law be used to derive enthalpies for chemical reactions?

1. Balance chemical reactions.

2. If there are several equations, try to cancel out as many common pairs of factors (e.g. a reactant-product common pair or product-reactant common pair).

3. Use the given ΔH^o and add appropriately.

4. If you exchange the positions of the products and the reactants in one of the equations you must change the sign of ΔH.

What is bond dissociation energy?

Bond dissociation energy is the energy released when cleaving a bond.

$$Br - Br + Energy \rightarrow Br + Br \quad \text{- 46 kJ/mol} \quad \text{Bond dissociation energy}$$

$$Br + Br \rightarrow Br - Br + Energy \quad \text{+ 46 kJ/mol} \quad \Delta\text{H}_f$$

Table 33.1: Bond dissociation energy: Br_2

33.2 Calorimetry

What is calorimetry?

The science of measuring heat changes in chemical reactions. This measurement is done using a calorimeter which can be an elaborate set-up or a simple double-Styrofoam cup-thermometer set-up from inorganic lab.

What is heat capacity?

Heat capacity (C) is the ability of matter to store thermal energy and is measured in Joules/Kelvins (J/K).

What is specific heat capacity?

Heat capacity (C) is the heat capacity per unit mass and is measured in Joules/kilograms Kelvins (J/(kg · K)), i.e. the amount of heat required to raise the temperature of 1 kg of a substance by one Kelvin:

$$Q = m \ c\Delta T \qquad (33.2)$$

Where Q is the heat energy placed into or taken out of the substance, m is the mass of the substance, c is the specific heat capacity, and ΔT is the temperature differential.

What is the specific heat capacity of water?

$$c_{water} = \frac{1cal}{^oC \cdot g} = 4186 \ J/(kg \cdot K) = 4.186 \ kJ/(kg \cdot K) \qquad (33.3)$$

Chapter 34

Red-ox

What is an oxidation-reduction reaction?

A reaction where there is a transfer of charge by which a loss of electrons (oxidation) and a gain of electrons (reduction) occurs.

What mnemonic can you use to remember electron flow?

OIL RIG: Oxidation Is Loss, Reduction Is Gain.

34.1   Red-ox Reactions

What are red-ox reactions?

Reactions that involve the transfer of electrons which can be divided into two reactions representing the reactants which are being oxidized and the reactants being reduced:

Complete Reaction:

$$2MnO_4^-{}_{(aq)} + 5H_2C_2O_4{}_{(aq)} + 6H^+_{(aq)} \rightarrow 10CO_2{}_{(g)} + 2Mn^{2+}_{(aq)} + 8H_2O_{(l)}$$

Reactants being oxidized:

$$H_2C_2O_4 \rightarrow CO_2$$

Reactants being reduced:

$$MnO_4 \rightarrow Mn^{2+}$$

What are the oxidizing and reducing agents in the above reaction?

MnO_4 is the oxidizing agent and $H_2C_2O_4$ is the reducing agent.

Think of oxidizing/reducing agents as the mediators that control oxidation and reduction. That is, the "culprit" which causes a reactant to be oxidized.

So, in a red-ox reaction where there is one molecule being oxidized and one molecule being reduced, the molecule undergoing oxidation (losing e^-) serves as the reducing agent (or e^- donor) and the molecule undergoing reduction (gaining e^-) serves as the oxidizing agent (or e^- remover).

What is a disproportionation reaction?

A reaction where a substance is being oxidized and reduced in the same reaction. This commonly occurs with H_2, which can dissociate oxidatively and lose electrons (H_2 to $2H^+$) and also dissociate reductively and gain electrons (H_2 to $2H^-$), all in the same reaction. The reverse is called comproportionation.

34.2   Oxidation Numbers

How do you calculate oxidation numbers?

Oxidation numbers are used to track the charges of atoms in a molecule such that their sum equals the entire charge of the molecule.

What is the role of electronegativities when predicting the oxidation numbers of an atom?

Atoms that are more electronegative, i.e. the upper right corner of the periodic table, will tend to have negative oxidation numbers, while atoms that are less electronegative, i.e. the lower left corner of the periodic table, will have positive oxidation numbers. Intuitively, it makes sense: an atom with a high electronegativity will want electrons and be negative (and therefore serves as an oxidizing agent - an electron remover).

What are the general oxidation numbers for the groups across the periodic table?

First off I use the term "general" because oxidation numbers can vary greatly, but these are the general numbers assigned to the groups across the periodic table:

Secondly, an atom can either donate or receive electrons depending upon if the atom is pairing up with an atom that is more or less electronegative, respectively:

	Group:							
	I	II	III	IV	V	VI	VII	VIII
Oxidation number of the atom if it is gaining e^-				-4	-3	-2	-1	0
Oxidation number of the atom if it is losing e^-	+1	+2	+3	+4	+5	+5	+7	0

Table 34.1: Oxidation numbers for Groups across the periodic table.

What makes for a good oxidizing agent and reducing agent?

Again, electron affinity comes into play. Atoms or molecules with large affinities for electrons (top right-hand corner of the periodic table) are good oxidizing agents (electron removers), while atoms in the lower left-hand corner with lower affinities for electrons are good reducing agents (electron donors).

Therefore, fluorine makes an excellent oxidizing agent as do the oxygen species (O_2 and O_3) and chlorine. In regards to molecules that make good oxidizing agents, common ones are permanganate (MnO_4^-), chromate (CrO_4^{2-}), and dichromate ($Cr_2O_7^{2-}$).

For common reducing agents, look towards Group I atoms such as sodium (Na) and other metals such as zinc (Zn), aluminum (Al) and calcium (Ca).

From the example above (35.1), what are the oxidation numbers of the reactants and products?

Complete Reaction:

$$2MnO_4^-{}_{(aq)} + 5H_2C_2O_4{}_{(aq)} + 6H^+_{(aq)} \rightarrow 10CO_2{}_{(g)} + 2Mn^{2+}_{(aq)} + 8H_2O_{(l)}$$

Reactants being oxidized:

$$H_2C_2O_4 \rightarrow CO_2$$

H_2	C_2	O_4			C	O_2	
+1	+3	-2			+4	-2	
x 2	x 2	x 4	*Net charge:*		x 1	x 2	*Net charge:*
+2	+6	-8	= 0		+4	-4	= 0

Reactants being reduced:

$$MnO_4 \rightarrow Mn^{2+}$$

Mn	O_4			Mn^{2+}	
+7	-2			+2	
x 1	x 4	*Net charge:*		x 1	*Net charge:*
+7	-8	= -1		+2	= 0

34.3   Balancing Red-ox Reactions

What are the steps to balancing a red-ox reaction?

1. Assign oxidation numbers to identify reducing and oxidizing players.

2. Separate oxidizing reactants from reducing reactants into two half reactions and ignore spectator ions, i.e. ions not involved in the oxidation or reduction of the key players.

3. Balance the atoms in each half reaction.

4. Choose between balancing under acidic conditions or basic conditions:

   - Under acidic conditions, use H^+ to balance charges on the necessary side to bring total charges to zero.
   - Under basic conditions, use OH^- to balance charges on the necessary side to bring total charges to zero.

5. Balance each half reaction with water and electrons as necessary.

6. Combine both half reactions and cancel out extra molecules as necessary.

Part III

Organic Chemistry

Chapter 35

Covalent Bonds

The covalent bond is the predominant bond found in organic molecules and was touched upon on page 194. For MCAT purposes, we will go over covalent bonds from the perspective of alkanes.

35.1 Orbital Hybridization

What is orbital hybridization?

The application of quantum mechanics to the simple hydrogen-electron model which allows for the creation of more complex electron distribution models, i.e. hybridized orbitals.

In organic chemistry, the main atom we will look at is carbon. The orbitals that are hybridized are s and p, which 'coalesce' to form new orbitals.

What are three levels of orbital hybridization seen in carbon bonds?

$$
\begin{array}{ll}
sp^3 & \text{Single bonds} \\
sp^2 & \text{Double bonds} \\
sp & \text{Triple bonds}
\end{array}
$$

What are the geometries of these three levels of orbital hybridization?

$$
\begin{array}{lcl}
sp^3 & \text{Tetrahedral} & 4\ e^- \text{ pairs} \\
sp^2 & \text{Triangular planar} & 3\ e^- \text{ pairs} \\
sp & \text{Linear} & 2\ e^- \text{ pairs}
\end{array}
$$

See Figure 35.1 below.

Figure 35.1: Bond geometries: Tetrahedral geometry with 109.5^o angles (left) , triangular planar geometry with 120° angles (center), linear geometry with a 180° angle (right).

What is the valence shell electron repulsion theory (VSEPR)?

A theory which predicts the shape of a molecule by taking into account all pairs of bonding and non-bonding electrons. By considering all pairs of electrons and the fact that electrons repel each other, approximate geometries of molecules can be predicted:

Bond angle geometry (^{o})	# of e^- pairs	Molecular geometry	
Linear (180°)	2	Linear	CO_2
Trigonal planar (120°)	3	Trigonal planar	BH_3
Tetrahedral (109.5^o)	4	Tetrahedral	CH_4
Tetrahedral (107°)	4	Trigonal pyramidal	NH_3
Tetrahedral (105°)	4	Bent	H_2O
Trigonal bipyramidal (120° & 90°)	5	Trigonal bipyramidal	PCl_5
Octahedral (90°)	6	Octahedral	SF_6

Table 35.1: Valence shell electron repulsion theory (VSEPR).

Note: In some molecules, the molecular geometry differs from the bond angle geometry because lone electron pairs are not taken into account for the molecular geometry. Ammonia and water exemplify this well this because the lone electron pairs push the surrounding atoms closer together, making for narrower bond angles (107° or 105°) than what would be expected for a tetrahedral bond arrangement between four bonding atoms (109.5^o).

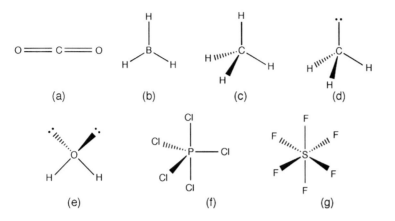

Figure 35.2: Selected molecular geometries: carbon dioxide (a), .

Between non-bonding or bonding pairs of electrons - which occupies more space?

Non-bonding pairs of electrons take up more space.

What are the electron dot structures for H, C, N, O, F, S, P, Si, and Cl?

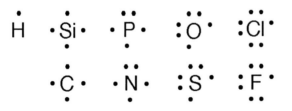

Figure 35.3: Selected electron dot structures: hydrogen (H), silicon (Si), phosphorus (P), oxygen (O), chloride (Cl), carbon (C), nitrogen (N), sulfur (S), fluorine (F).

What are resonance structures?

Two or more structures that can correctly represent the electron distribution of a molecule. Molecules which have resonance structures, e.g. H_2O, never really exist in one form or another. Instead, they are constantly in flux, oscillating between resonance structures, see Figure 35.4 below.

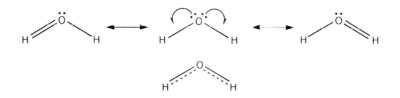

Figure 35.4: Resonance structures of H_2O.

In covalent bonds, what is the relationship between bond length and bond energy?

Bond length and bond energy are inversely related. Meaning, the shorter the bond the greater the bond energy.

35.2   Stereochemistry of Covalent Bonds

What is stereochemistry?

The study of the spatial arrangement of atoms in molecules (including the study of chiral molecules).

What are chiral molecules?

A chiral molecule is a molecule that is not super-imposable onto its mirror image.

What are chiral centers?

A chiral center, also known as a stereocenter, is an sp^3 hybridized carbon that is bonded to four different molecules.

What are meso compounds?

Any compound with a line of symmetry.

35.2.1 Isomers

What are isomers?

Two compounds with the same molecular formula. Given this broad definition, there are many types of isomers:

- **Structural isomers:**
  Two compounds with the same molecular formula but a differing arrangement of atoms. Structural isomers can also be called constitutional isomers.

- **Stereoisomers:**
  Two compounds with the same molecular formula and the same order of atom attachment, but a differing spatial arrangement of atoms.

    - **Enantiomers:**
      Stereoisomers that are mirror images of each other and are identified by R and S nomenclature and are optically active.

    - **Diastereomers:**
      Stereoisomers that are not mirror images of each other.

    - **Geometric isomers:**
      Stereoisomers that differ in the arrangements of atoms in molecules with double bonds and are identified by cis-/trans- designations.

35.2.2 *Cis-/trans-* Designation

How is the *cis-/trans-* designation for alkenes determined[1]?

1. Assign priority to the groups attached to *each end* of the double bond.

   - Priority is assigned on the basis of atomic weight: highest atomic weight has the highest priority.

   - If two groups have the same atomic number, move to the next attached group and then compare the atomic number:

2. If the higher priority group for one end of the C=C is on the same side as the highest priority group for the other end, use cis-. If the converse true, use trans-.

35.2.3 *E* & *Z* Designation

What is *E* & *Z* designation?

Another system to designate the location of substituent groups across a carbon-carbon double bond.

---

[1] *Cis* comes from the Latin root for "on the same side" and *trans* comes from the Latin root for "across."

How do you determine *E* or *Z* nomenclature of alkenes?

1. Assign priority to the groups attached to *each end* of the double bond.

   - Priority is assigned on the basis of atomic weight: high atomic weight, high priority.
   - If two groups have the same atomic number, move outward for each group and then compare the atomic number:

2. If the higher priority group for one end of the C=C is on the same side as the highest priority group for the other end, use *Z*. If the substituent groups on either end are on opposite sides, use E^2.

Figure 35.5: *Cis-/trans-* alkenes: cis- *(Z)* and trans- *(E)* designations

35.2.4   Relative and Absolute Configurations

What is the difference between relative and absolute configurations?

Relative configurations: When the arrangement in an optically active molecule is determined (by experiment) to be "+" or "-" but it is unknown as to what *R* or *S* configuration they are matched to.

Absolute configurations When the arrangement around a stereocenter is precisely determined by experiment, e.g. X-ray crystallography, to be *R* or *S*.

35.2.5   *R* or *S* Nomenclature

How do you determine *R* or *S* nomenclature of enantiomers?

1. Identify a stereocenter.

2. Assign priority # 1, # 2, # 3, and # 4 to each of the four groups attached to the stereocenter.

   - Priority is assigned on the basis of atomic weight: high atomic weight, high priority, i.e. # 1.
   - If two groups have the same atomic number, move outward for each group and then compare the atomic numbers, see Figure 35.6 below:

---

[2]The *Z* and *E* are abbreviations for the German words zusammen and entgegen, which mean together and opposite, respectively.

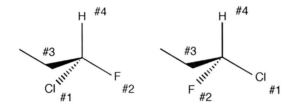

Figure 35.6: Nomenclature of enantiomers: Assigning priority.

3. Rotate the formula - or model - so that the lowest priority group, # 4, is pointing **away** from you:

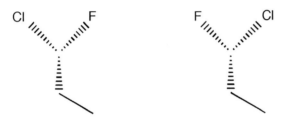

Figure 35.7: Nomenclature of enantiomers: Directing the lowest priority away.

4. Draw an arrow in a circular fashion from highest priority to lowest, i.e. # 1, # 2 and # 3. If the arrow orientation is clockwise the designation is R. Conversely, if the arrow orientation is counterclockwise then the designation is S:

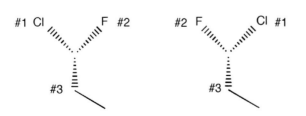

Figure 35.8: Nomenclature of enantiomers: Determining R (left) or S (right) designation.

35.3   Optical Activity

What is polarization of light?

When light passing through a medium is organized into a particular plane, i.e. the creation of plane-polarized light.

What is an optically-active compound?

The ability of a substance to rotate plane-polarized light. When this rotation is quantified by a polarimeter, the specific rotation for a molecule can be determined.

What is a racemic mixture?

A mixture that contains equal quantities of both forms of an enantiomer - *Racemic mixtures are optically-inactive.*

How are racemic mixtures separated?

Liquid chromatography (preferred technique) or gas chromatography.

Chapter 36

Substitution & Elimination Reactions

36.1   Nucleophilic Substitution Reactions

Nucleophilic substitution is a chemical reaction in which a nucleophile is *hungry* for positive charge and therefore substitutes itself on a carbon in place of a leaving group.

This reaction can take place using one of two mechanisms:

1. S_N1, substitution nucleophilic **uni**molecular, which is a two-step process that includes *the formation of a carbocation* and *nucleophilic attack.*

2. S_N2, substitution nucleophilic **bi**molecular, which is a one-step process including *a concurrent nucleophilic attack on the carbon and the detachment of the leaving group.*

36.1.1 S_N1

What main condition favors an S_N1 reaction?

The relative stability of the carbocation. Relative carbocation stabilities are $3^o > 2^o > 1^o > methyl$. As seen in Figure 36.1 below:

Figure 36.1: Relative stabilities of carbocations.

How can the creation of the carbocation be facilitated?

1. The more substituted a carbocation is, the greater the delocalization of charge and the greater the stabilization of the carbocation.

2. Use of polar protic solvents:

   - A "polar" aspect is good to stabilize ions.
   - A "protic" aspect is good for solvation: through hydrogen bonds, solvation stabilizes the transition to (1) the cation (carbocation) and (2) to the anion (halide leaving group).

3. Weak bases make good leaving groups.

What is the mechanism for the reaction between *tert*-butyl bromide and water?

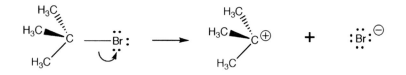

Figure 36.2: $S_N 1$ reaction: Step 1.

- Rate-limiting step: formation of the carbocation

- Keep in mind:

  - Stability of the carbocation is paramount.
  - Carbocations are extremely reactive.
  - The more stable the leaving group, the more likely the carbocation will be formed.
  - Chirality is lost: carbocations have a trigonal planar structure.

Figure 36.3: $S_N 1$ reaction: Step 2.

- Nucleophilic attack - in this example water will be our nucleophile.

- Keep in mind:

  - Charges still need to be equilibrated.

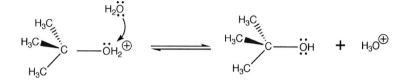

Figure 36.4: S_N1 reaction: Step 3.

- Equilibration of charge.

How does an S_N1 reaction affect the stereochemistry of the product?

The carbocation has a trigonal planar structure that allows a nucleophilic attack to occur from either side. This results in a racemic product with no optical activity as seen in Figure 36.5 below:

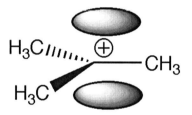

Figure 36.5: Trigonal planar stereochemistry of carbocations.

36.1.2 S_N2

What main conditions favor an S_N2 reaction?

1. Structure of the substrate is paramount in allowing enough room for a nucleophile to attack and a leaving group to depart. Favorable structures are *methyl > 1° > 2° > 3°*:

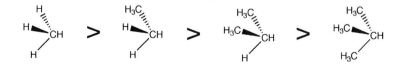

Figure 36.6: Favorable substrates for an S_N2 reaction.

2. The presence of a "strong" nucleophile, i.e. a nucleophile with sufficient negative charge to attack the substrate

How can an S_N2 reaction be facilitated?

1. Use of polar aprotic solvents

   - A "polar" aspect is good to stabilize ions

   - A "aprotic" aspect is good because hydrogen bonds do not get in the way of the anion's (nucleophile) attack of the substrate

What is the mechanism for the reaction between methyl bromide and hydroxide?

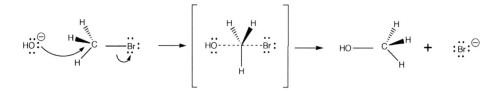

Figure 36.7: S_N2 reaction.

- The rate-limiting step is the formation of the transition state.

- Keep in mind:

  - "Back-side attack" by nucleophile.

  - The transition state is a shifting of bonds and is the reaction's energy barrier.

How does an S_N2 reaction affect the stereochemistry of the product?

The backside attack of the nucleophile inverts the configuration of the substrate in the product:

Figure 36.8: Inversion of stereochemistry in S_N2 reactions: reactant (left) and product (right).

	S_N1	S_N2
# of steps	2	1
Reaction rate order	1	2
Limiting step	Carbocation formation in the substrate	Transition step formation in an unhindered substrate to allow for attack by a strong nucleophile
Ideal substrate	$3^o > 2^o > 1^o > methyl$	$methyl > 1^o > 2^o > 3^o$
Stereochemistry of product	Racemic	Inverted

Table 36.1: Summary of S_N1 & S_N2 Reactions.

36.2   Elimination Reactions

Elimination reactions occur in alkyl halides where a molecule is eliminated, which results in the *formation of an alkene*.

Eliminations can take place via one of two mechanisms:

1. *E*1, elimination unimolecular, which is a two-step process that includes the *formation of a carbocation* and a *nucleophilic attack*.

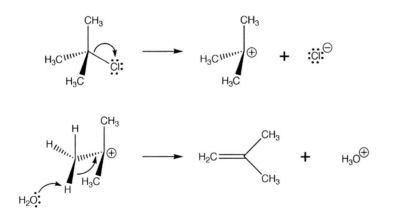

Figure 36.9: *E*1 reaction.

2. *E2*, elimination bimolecular, which is a one step process whereby *a nucleophile attacks a hydrogen and prompts a leaving group to detach from the carbon.*

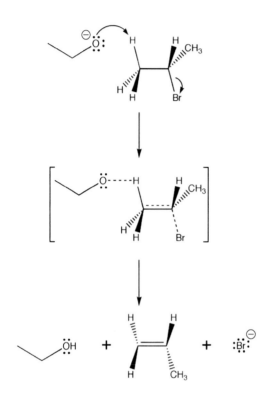

Figure 36.10: *E2* reaction.

36.3 Substitution vs. Elimination Reactions: Which one and why?

What favors an S_N2 reaction vs. an $E2$ reaction?

	S_N2 and $E2$
# of steps	1
Reaction rate order	2
Limiting step	Transition step formation in an unhindered substrate to allow for attack by a strong nucleophile.

Table 36.2: Similarities between S_N2 and $E2$ reactions.

	S_N2	$E2$
Site of nucleophilic attack	On the carbon bearing the leaving group	On the β hydrogen
Substrate	1° halide	2° or 3° halide
Solvent	Weakly basic, highly polarizable	High conc. of a strong, polarizable base that is sterically hindered
Temperature	Lower temperatures	Higher temperatures

Table 36.3: Factors favoring S_N2 vs. $E2$ reactions.

What favors an $S_N 1$ reaction vs. an $E1$ reaction?

The distinctions here are less obvious and less easily controlled. If an elimination product is desired, force the $E2$ elimination using a strong base.

	$S_N 1$ and $E1$
# of steps	2
Reaction rate order	1
Limiting step	Carbocation formation in the substrate
Substrates	Ones that can form stable carbocations, i.e. 3° halide
Nucleophile	Weak bases
Solvent	Polar, aprotic solvents

Table 36.4: Similarities between $S_N 1$ and $E1$ reactions.

	$S_N 1$	$E1$
Temperature*	Lower temperatures	Higher temperatures

Table 36.5: Factor which favors $S_N 1$ vs. $E1$ reactions.

* Elimination reactions have higher free energies of activation because more bonds are broken, therefore, at higher temps, elimination (E1 and E2) will be favored over ($S_N 1$ and $S_N 2$).

Chapter 37

Alkanes

What are alkanes?

The simplest organic molecule that is composed of a single-bonded carbon backbone which is connected to the maximum number of hydrogens. The fact that the maximum number of hydrogens are bonded to the carbons makes alkanes *saturated*. The general molecular formula for alkanes is C_nH_{2n+2} and all the carbons involved in the single bonds are sp^3 hybridized.

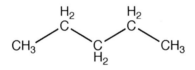

Figure 37.1: An alkane.

37.1   General

What is the IUPAC convention for naming alkanes?

1. Find and name the longest continuous carbon chain.

2. Identify and name substituent groups attached to this chain.

3. Number the chain consecutively, starting at the end nearest the longest (or largest) substituent group.

4. Designate the location of each substituent group by the appropriate number and name. The prefixes di-, tri-, tetra- etc., are used to distinguish similar substituent groups.

5. Finish the name listing groups in alphabetical order.

The suffix for alkanes is *-ane* and the common prefixes for organic molecules such as meth-, eth-, prop-, etc. apply. Unbranched alkanes are denoted with an *n-* - see table 37.1 below.

methane	CH_4	$n-$pentane	$CH_3(CH_2)_3CH_3$
ethane	C_2H_6	$n-$hexane	$CH_3(CH_2)_4CH_3$
propane	C_3H_8	$n-$hepane	$CH_3(CH_2)_5CH_3$
$n-$butane	C_4H_{10}	$n-$octane	$CH_3(CH_2)_6CH_3$

Table 37.1: Common alkanes.

What are some examples of common alkane substituent groups and branched alkanes?

methyl	CH_3-	butyl	$CH_3CH_2CH_2CH_2-$
ethyl	C_2H_5-	isobutyl	$(CH_3)_2CHCH_2-$
propyl	$CH_3CH_2CH_2-$	sec-butyl	$CH_3CH_2CH(CH_3)-$
isopropyl	$(CH_3)_2CH-$	*tert*-butyl	$(CH_3)3C-$

Table 37.2: Common substituent alkane groups.

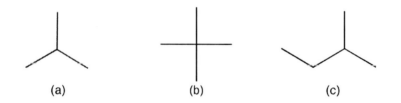

(a)   (b)   (c)

Figure 37.2: Examples of branched alkanes: (a) t-butane (isobutane), (b) neopentane, and (c) isopentane.

37.1.1 Cycloalkanes

What are cycloalkanes?

A single ring of single-bonded carbons to which hydrogens are attached. The formula for cycloalkanes is C_nH_{2n}:

Figure 37.3: Examples cycloalkanes: cyclopropane (left) and cyclopentane (right).

Note: Cycloalkanes can fuse to form bicyclic cycloalkanes.

What stress exists in smaller cycloalkanes?

Ring strain. Ring strain occurs by two mechanisms:

1. Angle strain, which is seen when bond angles depart from the ideal, tetrahedral angle ($\sim 109^o$)

2. Torsional strain, which is seen when bonds are not properly staggered

Cyclohexane has the least strain.

37.2 Physical and Chemical Properties

What are four physical properties of alkanes?

1. Insoluble in water.

2. Less dense than water.

3. Boiling point is directly related to length of chain.

4. At standard conditions:

   - Methane to butane are gases
   - Pentane to heptadecane ($C_{17}H_{36}$) are liquids
   - Octadecane and up are solids

What are the chemical properties of alkanes?

Alkanes are also called paraffins which is derived from the Latin term meaning "lacking affinity." Therefore, alkanes have low levels of reactivity secondary to stable C-H and H-H bonds.

What is the infrared absorption of C-C and C-H bonds?

Bond	Frequency (cm^{-1})
C-H	~1200
C-C	~2900

Table 37.3: Infrared absorption of C-C and C-H bonds.

37.3   Reactions Involving Alkanes

What are three important reactions involving alkanes?

1. Combustion: The chemical reaction of a substance with oxygen.

2. Halogenation: The substitution of hydrogen with a halogen.

   - This occurs in three steps:

     (a) **Initiation**: Splitting of a diatomic halogen, e.g. F_2, creating a free radical (represented with a F^*):

     $$F_2 + energy \rightarrow F^* + F^*$$

     (b) **Propagation**: Propagation of free radicals:

     $$CH_4 + F^* \rightarrow CH_3^* + HF$$
     $$CH_3^* + F_2 \rightarrow CH_3F + F^*$$

     (c) **Termination**: When two radicals form a bond (this can lead to impurities when the pairing up of radicals is not the desired end-product).

     $$F^* + F^* \rightarrow F_2$$
     $$CH_3^* + F^* \rightarrow CH_3F$$
     $$CH_3^* + CH_3^* \rightarrow C_2H_6$$

3. Cracking: Breaking larger hydrocarbons into smaller ones, including alkanes. This is commonly accomplished with heat, pressure and catalysts.

© 2005 - 2007

What pattern exists for the relative stabilities of free radicals?

Methyl < Primary < Secondary < Tertiary

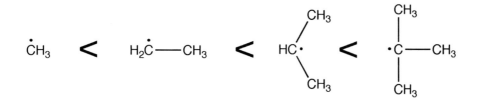

Figure 37.4: Relative stabilities of free radicals.

Chapter 38

Alkenes

What are alkenes?

Alkenes are hydrocarbons containing at least one carbon-carbon double bond, making them "unsaturated." The general molecular formula for alkenes is C_nH_{2n}, and the carbons involved in the double bond are sp^2 hybridized.

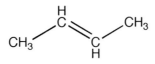

Figure 38.1: An alkene: 2-butene.

38.1 General

What is the IUPAC convention for naming alkenes?

1. Find and name the longest continuous carbon chain, label it as the base name and use the appropriate suffix: "-ene," indicating an alkene or cycloalkene.

   - The base chain must include the carbon atoms involved in the double bond.

2. Number the longest chain from the end that is closest to the double bond.

   - If the double bond is in the center of the chain, begin numbering from an end that has a substituent closest to the end of the root chain.

3. Identify any double bonds using the lowest-numbered carbon, e.g. 2-pentene for a double between the 2nd and 3rd carbon.

   - If there is more than one double bond, use the same numbering approach, i.e. choose the lowest-numbered carbon to identify the location of the double bond.

© 2005 - 2007

- Alkenes with multiple double bonds have special designations: e.g. dienes have 2 C=C bonds, trienes have 3 C=C bonds, etc.

  - Identify their locations by using the lowest-numbered carbons. For example, 2,3-pentadiene is the name for a five carbon diene with double bonds between carbons 2 and 3; and 3 and 4.

Figure 38.2: Alkenes: Ethene (ethylene), left, and butene (butylene), right. *Note: ethene and butene are the IUPAC names and ethylene and butylene are the common names.*

How are cycloalkenes named?

For cycloalkenes, the double bond carbon numbering is similar to that of straight-chained alkenes:

1. Find the carbon which (a) is part of the double bond, and (b) is closest to ring substituents (if there are any)

   - If there is more than one substituent, choose the longest one or the one with heavier atoms (i.e. the higher melecular weight).

What are two types of substituents that contain double bonds?

1. Vinyl groups, $H_2C=CH$

2. Allyl groups, $H_2C=CHCH_2$

Note: The nomenclature for how groups are arranged around the double bond - cis-, and trans-, - will be covered in the Covalent Bond Chapter on page 267.

38.2   Physical and Chemical Properties

How do the physical and chemical properties of alkenes differ from those of alkanes?

Not much: alkenes follow the same rules as alkanes. Nevertheless, double bonds can cause kinking in alkenes, e.g. fatty acids, which can decrease their boiling points.

What is the infrared absorption of a C=C bond?

Bond	Frequency (cm^{-1})
C=C	~1600

Table 38.1: Infrared absorption of C=C.

38.3   Reactions Involving Alkenes

What are three important reactions involving alkenes?

1. Catalytic addition (hydrogenation)

   - Converts alkenes to alkanes.
   - Reactions require a metal catalyst (e.g. platinum) and high pressures.

2. Electrophilic addition

   - Halogenation
     - Elementary bromine or chlorine can be added to alkenes to create *vicinal di*-halogen alkenes:

     $$CH_2 = CH_2 + Br_2 \Longrightarrow BrCH_2 - CH_2Br$$

   - Hydrohalogenation
     - Addition of HCl or HBr in a Markovnikov[1] fashion:

     $$CH_3 - CH = CH_2 + HCl \Longrightarrow CH_3 - CHCl - CH_3$$

3. Combustion

   - Chemical combination with oxygen to yield carbon dioxide and water.

4. Elimination reaction

   - Method to synthesize alkenes.
   - Elimination of H_2O from alcohol will yield alkenes.

5. Cracking

   - Method to synthesize alkenes by breaking larger hydrocarbons into smaller ones. This method is used in the petroleum industry where heat, pressure and catalysts yield a variety of products including alkenes.

---

[1]Markovnikov's rule states that when a hydrogen halide (e.g. HBr) reacts with the carbon-carbon double bond of an unsymmetrical alkene to produce an alkyl halide, the hydrogen adds to the carbon of the alkene functional group that has the greater number of hydrogen substituents, and the halogen adds to the carbon on the other end of the double bond which has a smaller number of hydrogen substituents.

Chapter 39

Alkynes

What are alkynes[1]?

Hydrocarbons containing at least one carbon-carbon triple bond (C≡C) making them *unsaturated*. Moreover, the carbons involved in the triple bond are *sp* hybridized.

$$HC \equiv CH$$

Figure 39.1: An alkyne.

What is the IUPAC convention for naming alkynes?

Similar to alkenes, only that the suffix for alkynes is *-yne*.

What are the two simplest alkynes?

Ethyne[2] and propyne.

Figure 39.2: Ethyne (left) and propyne (right).

---

[1]This chapter is here for completeness sake. Don't dwell too much on this one; read it, understand it, and move on.

[2]Although the term acetylenes is an old expression for all alkynes, acetylene is also used to specifically refer to ethyne.

39.1   Physical and Chemical Properties

How do the physical and chemical properties of alkynes differ from those of alkanes and alkenes?

In contrast to alkanes and alkenes, alkynes are quite unstable.

This property makes alkynes very reactive and they are used in industrial and manufacturing settings, e.g. acetylene torches.

What is the infrared absorption of a carbon-carbon triple bond?

Bond	Frequency (cm^{-1})
C≡C	~2200

Table 39.1: Infrared absorption of C≡C.

39.2   Reactions involving alkynes

What are important reactions involving alkynes?

Similar to alkanes and alkenes, addition, halogenation, reduction, and combustion reactions.

Chapter 40

Alcohols

What are alcohols?

Any organic molecule that has a hydroxyl group $(R-OH)$ attached to a carbon. The carbons bonded to the hydroxyl group are sp^3 hybridized and the general molecular formula for alcohols is $C_nH_{2n+1}OH$.

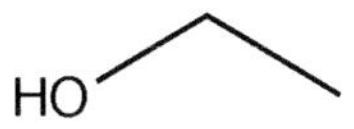

Figure 40.1: An alcohol: ethanol.

40.1 General

What is the IUPAC convention for naming alcohols?

1. Find and name the alkane.

2. Identify the number of the hydroxyl bonding position:

   - As outlined earlier, the goal is to count in such a manner as to derive the lowest number for the substituent group.

3. Drop the terminal e of the base chain and replace it with the suffix $-ol$ preceded by the number of the hydroxyl position[1]. For example:

Figure 40.2: Propan-1-ol ($CH_2CH_2CH_2OH$).

---

[1]Note: the interposition of the hydroxyl position number is not necessary for methanol and ethanol.

4. For organic molecules with more than one hydroxyl group, the prefixes "di-" or "tri-" are used:

Figure 40.3: Ethane-1,2-diol (ethylene glycol) CH_2OHCH_2OH.

What are the three types of alcohols?

1° (primary) alcohols; in which the carbon bonded to the hydroxyl group is either bonded to one (or less) other carbons.

2° (secondary) alcohols; in which the carbon bonded to the hydroxyl group is bonded to two other carbons.

3° (tertiary) alcohols; in which the carbon bonded to the hydroxyl group is bonded to three other carbons.

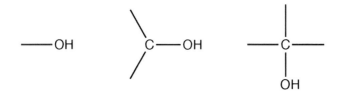

Figure 40.4: Methanol, a 1° alcohol (left), isopropanol, a 2° alcohol (center), and 2-methylpropan-2-ol, a 3° alcohol (right).

What would these three types of alcohols be oxidized to?

	Oxidized to...
1° alcohols	Aldehydes
2° alcohols	Ketones
3° alcohols	Resistent to oxidation because there are no attached hydrogens on the carbon attached to the hydroxyl group

Table 40.1: Oxidative products of 1°, 2° and 3° alcohols.

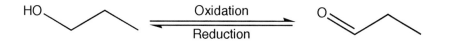

Figure 40.5: Oxidation of propanol to propanal (and the reduction of propanal to propanol).

40.2   Physical and Chemical Properties

What are three physical properties of alcohols?

1. Hydroxyl groups

   - Confer polarity

   - Can form hydrogen bonds

2. Solubility - A tug of war:

   - Polar hydroxyl group increases water solubility

     – The hydroxyl group of methanol, ethanol, and propanol dominates and these alcohols **are** miscible in water

   - Non-polar carbon chains decrease water solubility

     – Although the smallest alcohols are water soluble, the presence of hydrocarbon chains makes alcohols miscible in organic solvents, esp. pentanol and longer chains

3. Hydrogen bonding increases the boiling point when compared to ethers or other similar-sized hydrocarbons

What chemical properties does the hydroxyl group confer to alcohols?

1. Nucleophilicity

   - This allows alcohols to react with each other to form ethers and esters

2. Ability to undergo elimination

   - At high temperatures

What is the infrared absorption of the hydroxyl group $(C - OH)$?

Bond	Frequency (cm^{-1})
$C - OH$	~3300

40.3   Key Principles

What are two effects of hydrogen bonding among alcohols?

1. Increases boiling point

2. Increases miscibility in water

What contributes to the acidity of alcohols?

- The hydroxyl groups of alcohols makes them protic solvents, i.e. solvents capable of donating a proton (hydrogen).

- The presence of stabilizing resonance structures, e.g. an aromatic ring with one hydroxyl group (aka phenols) makes aromatic alcohols more acidic than straight-chained alcohols.

What is the acidity of simple alcohols (e.g. CH_3OH) compared to water?

Quite similar: the pK_a of H_2O is 15.74 while the pK_a of methanol is 15.5:

$$pK_a\ H_2O \sim pK_a\ CH_3OH$$

What is the effect of hydrocarbon branching on the physical properties of alcohols?

Increasing hydrocarbon branching negates the effects of the hydoxyl group(s). Therefore, properties ascribed to hydrocarbons (non-polarity, hydrophobicity, miscibility in organic solvents) prevail and hydroxyl properties (polarity, hydrophilicity, hydrogen bonding) are less dominant.

40.4   Reactions Involving Alcohols

What are seven important reactions involving alcohols?

1. Nucleophilic substitution to form alkyl halides

   - Via alteration of the hydroxyl group to make it a better leaving group
     - Protonating to form H_2O (a much better leaving group than a hydroxyl group)
     - Converting it to an ether (ROR')
   - S_N1 reactions in the formation in alkyl halides

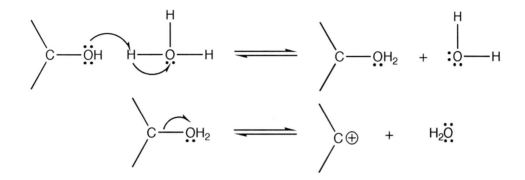

Figure 40.6: $2°/3°$ alcohols in S_N1 reactions.

- $2°/3°$ alcohols and benzylic alcohols can form carbocations resulting in S_N1 reactions with the carbocation serving as a substrate:

- S_N2 reactions in the formation of alkyl halides
  - $1°$ alcohols and methanol

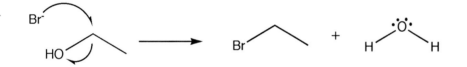

Figure 40.7: $1°$ alcohols and the formation in alkyl halides: an S_N2 reaction using
ethanol to create 1-bromo-ethane and water.

2. A lone pair of electrons from the hydroxyl's oxygen acts as a nucleophile

- Reactions with PBr_3 and $SOCl_2$
  - A $1°$ or $2°$ alcohol will react with PBr_3 to form an alkyl bromide

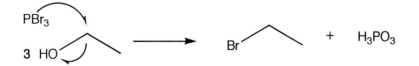

Figure 40.8: $1°$ or $2°$ alcohol reactions with PBr_3. Note, in this reaction, three alcohols
are needed for the reaction to proceed in the forward direction, which creates three
primary alkyl halides for every one phosphoric acid.

  - A $1°$ or $2°$ alcohol will react with $SOCl_2$ to form an alkyl chloride

- Mesylates and tosylates preparation

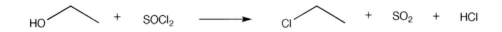

Figure 40.9: 1° or 2° alcohol reactions with SOCl$_2$. In this example, ethanol reacts with SOCl$_2$ to form 1-chloro-ethane.

      – Mesylates and tosyltates are very useful as substrates in S_N2 reactions because sulfonate ions are excellent leaving groups:

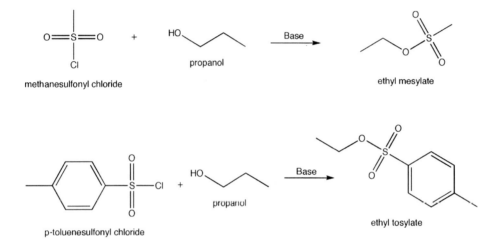

Figure 40.10: Alcohols and mesylate/tosylate preparation.

• Fischer Esterification, i.e. the synthesis of esters through the reaction of a carboxylic acid with an alcohol:

$$H_3C - COOH + HOCH_2CH_3 + H_2SO_4 \rightarrow$$
$$H_3C - COO - CH_2CH_3 + H_2SO_4 + H_2O$$

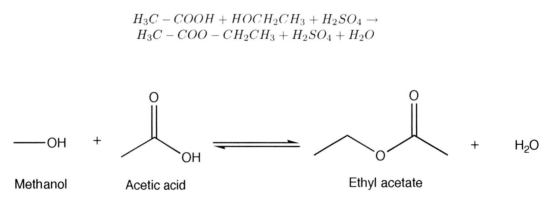

Figure 40.11: Fischer Esterification: synthesis of esters through the reaction of a carboxylic acid with an alcohol.

- Reaction with inorganic acids to form esters of inorganic acids, e.g. ATP

- Other S_N2 reactions that attack sp^3 carbons

3. Elimination reactions

- Alcohol dehydration to produce alkenes ($E1$ elimination):

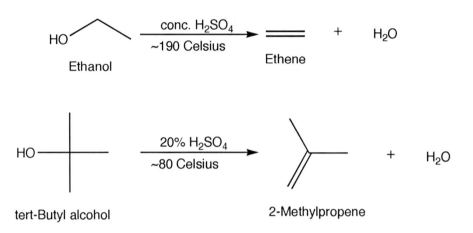

Figure 40.12: Alcohol dehydration. This process occurs most easily for tertiary alcohols, followed by secondary alcohols and then primary alcohols.

4. Oxidation reactions

- Oxidation occurs in the presence of a strong oxidation agent - usually a molecule with a oxidizing metal, e.g. $KMnO_4$, $Na_2Cr_2O_7$ or PCC ($C_5H_6NCrO_3Cl$)

- Alcohols oxidize to alkanes or aldehydes depending on the R group. If the R group is a hydrogen, oxidation will produce an aldehyde; if the R group is an alkyl, oxidation will produce a ketone:

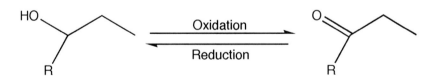

Figure 40.13: Oxidation of alcohols.

5. Reduction reactions

- Reduction occurs in the presence of a strong reducing agent, e.g. $LiAlH_4$ and $NaBH_4$

- In this example, a carboxylic acid is converted to an alcohol:

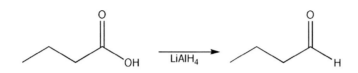

Figure 40.14: Reduction of alcohols.

- Generally speaking, the trend among organic molecules in regards to oxidation and reduction can be predicted as seen below:

Figure 40.15: Reduction of organic molecules.

6. The pinacol rearrangement[2]

- The hydroxyl group can also act as a weak acid
- The acid-catalyzed elimination of water from a 1,2-diol to yield a ketone:

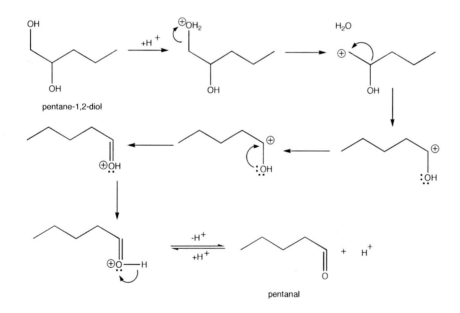

Figure 40.16: Pinacol rearrangement: acid-catalyzed elimination of water from a 1,2-diol to yield an aldehyde.

---

[2]Note: for the MCAT you do not need to know mechanisms. This is just FYI; knowing the reactant and the product is more than enough.

Chapter 41

Aromatic Compounds & Their Reactions

What are aromatic compounds?

Cyclic organic compounds which have delocalized π electrons and therefore increased stability.

What is Hückel's rule?

Hückel's rule determines the number of π electrons in aromatic, planar monocylic rings:

$$(4n + 2) \ \pi \text{ electrons, where n = is 0, 1, 2, 3, 4}$$

Therefore, planar monocyclic rings with 2, 6, 10, and 14 delocalized electrons will be aromatic. Further, carbons of aromatic rings are sp^2 hybridized carbons.

What aromatic ring has 6 π electrons?

Benzene.

Figure 41.1: Benzene.

What are some common benzene derivatives?

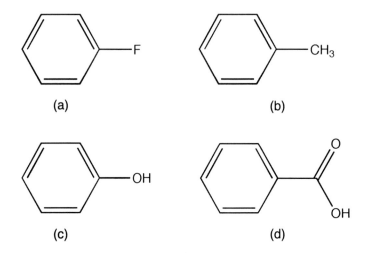

Figure 41.2: Common benzene derivatives: Fluorobenzene (a), toluene (b), phenol (c) and benzoic acid (d).

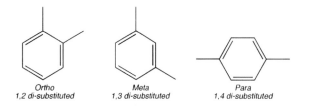

Figure 41.3: Methyl phenyl ketone (left) and benzyl bromide (right).

How are the relative positions of substituents on benzene rings identified?

Figure 41.4: Relative positions of substituents on benzene rings.

What are the effects of substituent positioning on the benzene ring?

Depending on the substituent, the effect can be either activating from an electron-donating groups or deactivating from an electron-withdrawing group:

Ortho-Para Directors	Meta Directors
Strongly activating (e^- donating)	Strongly activating (e^- donating)
$-NH_2$	
$-NR_2$	
$-OH$	
$NHCOR$	N/A
$-OCOR$	
$-OR$	
$-R$	

Table 41.1: Activating electron-donating groups for benzene substituent groups.

Ortho-Para Directors	Meta Directors
Deactivating (e^- withdrawing)	Deactivating (e^- withdrawing)
$-F,\ -Cl,\ -Br,\ -I$	$-NO_2$
	$-SO_3$H
	Carbonyls[1]

Table 41.2: Deactivating electron-withdrawing groups for benzene substituent groups.

41.1 Reactions Involving Benzene

What are four important reactions involving benzene?

1. Halogenation

   • In the presence of a Lewis acid catalyst:

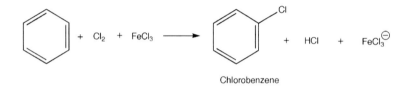

Figure 41.5: Benzene reactions: Halogenation.

2. Nitration

   • In the presence of nitric acid, sulfuric acid, and heat:

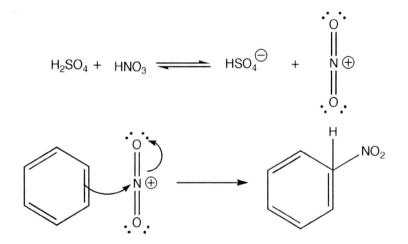

Figure 41.6: Benzene reactions: Nitration.

3. Sulfonation

   • In the presence of fuming sulfuric acid:

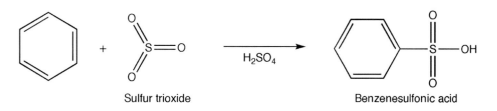

Figure 41.7: Benzene reactions: Sulfonation.

4. Friedel-Crafts acylation:

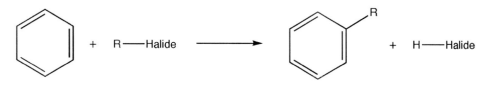

Figure 41.8: Friedel-Crafts acylation: Addition of the acyl group to benzene and the formation of a halide acid.

Chapter 42

Aldehydes & Ketones

What are aldehydes?

Aldehydes are organic functional groups that consist of a terminal carbonyl (C=O) bonded to a hydrogen. The general molecular formula of an aldehyde is $RCH = O$ and the carbon bonded to the carbonyl carbon is called the α carbon and the hydrogen bonded to the α carbon is called the α hydrogen.

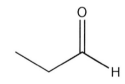

Figure 42.1: Aldehydes: propanal.

What are ketones?

Ketones are organic functional groups that consist of a carbonyl (C=O) that is bonded between two carbons. The general molecular formula for a ketone is R_1COR_2:

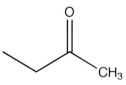

Figure 42.2: Ketone.

42.1   General

How are aldehydes named?

Count the number of carbons in the carbon chain and then change the alkane suffix from "-e" to "-al," see Figure 42.3 below.

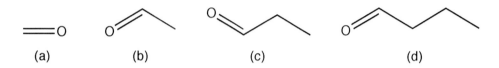

(a)   (b)   (c)   (d)

Figure 42.3: Aldehydes: (a) methanal (formaldehyde), H_2CO; (b) ethanal (acetaldehyde), CH_3CHO; (c) propanal, CH_3CH_2CHO; (d) butanal, $CH_3CH_2CH_2CHO$.

How are ketones named?

Change the alkane suffix from "-e" to "-one." If the ketone is within a chain, then the molecule can be named alkyl alkyl ketone; additionally, if there are two carbonyls within the chain, number them and add the suffix "-dione". See Figure 42.4 below.

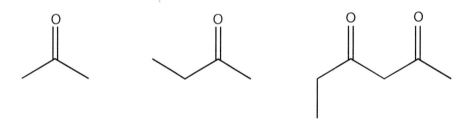

Figure 42.4: Ketones: 2-propanone (Acetone), CH_3COCH_3 (left); ethyl methyl ketone, $CH_3COCH_2CH_3$ (center); 2,4 hexadione, $CH_3COCH_2COCH_3CH_2$ (right).

42.2   Physical and Chemical Properties

What are two physical properties of aldehydes and ketones?

1. The carbonyl confers polarity and allows for hydrogen bonding with water.

   - Smaller aldehydes and ketones are very soluble in water, while larger aldehydes/ketones (including aromatic aldehydes/ketones) are insoluble in water
   - 1,3-dicarbonyls allow for internal hydrogen bonding

2. Boiling point:

 - Higher than similarly sized alkanes and alkenes

 - Lower than corresponding alcohols

What is the infrared absorption of the aldehyde C-H and the ketone carbonyl bonds?

Bond	Frequency (cm^{-1})
(O)C-H	~2800
C=O	~1700

Table 42.1: Infrared absorption of the aldehyde C-H and the ketone carbonyl bonds.

42.3 Key Principles

What demonstrates significant acidity in aldehydes and ketones?

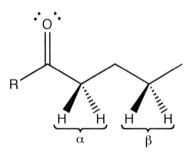

Figure 42.5: The acidity of hydrogens in aldehydes and ketones: The α-hydrogen has considerably more acidity than the β-hydrogen (α-hydrogen pK_a $\approx$ 20 vs. β-hydrogen pK_a $\approx$ 50).

Explain this acidity in terms of resonance.

The electron-withdrawing carbonyl group allows for the removal of the α-hydrogen. Subsequent electron delocalization results in a resonance-stabilized anion, see Figure 42.6 below:

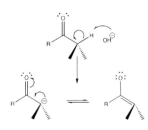

Figure 42.6: Role of electron-withdrawing carbonyl in α-hydrogen acidity.

Why are organometallics commonly used in aldehyde/ketone reactions?

Organometallics - aka Grignard reagents - are useful because they react well with the carbonyl carbons of aldehydes or ketones. Common organometallics include $R - Li$ or $R - MgBr$.

What are the products observed when organometallics (Grignard reagents) are reacted with methanal, and other aldehydes and ketones?

Methanal	1° alcohols
Longer chain aldehydes (i.e. longer than methanal)	2° alcohols
Other ketones	3° alcohols

Table 42.2: Products observed from specific organometallic reactions.

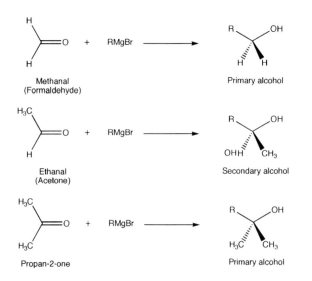

Figure 42.7: Role of electron-withdrawing carbonyl in α-hydrogen acidity.

How do carbonyl substituents affect reactivity?

Intuitively, larger substituents cause more steric hinderance and result in less-reactive reactants. Conversely, smaller substituents create less steric hinderance and result in more reactive reactants.

42.4 Reactions Involving Aldehydes and Ketones

42.4.1 Synthesis

- Aldehydes

    1. Oxidation of a 1° alcohol (the main technique for aldehyde synthesis):

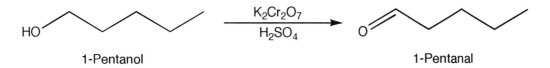

1-Pentanol   1-Pentanal

Figure 42.8: Aldehyde synthesis: oxidation of a 1° alcohol.

- Ketones

    1. Oxidation of a 2° alcohol:

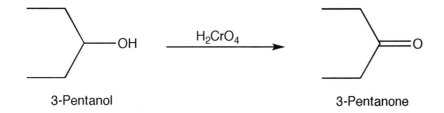

3-Pentanol   3-Pentanone

Figure 42.9: Ketone synthesis: oxidation of a 2° alcohol.

    2. Ozonolysis of alkenes:

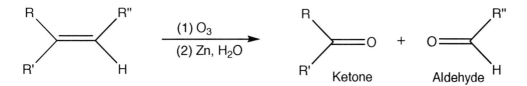

Figure 42.10: Ozonolysis of alkenes creates ketones and aldehydes depending on the R-group.

3. Friedel-Crafts acylation:

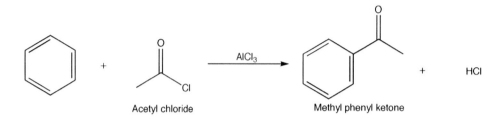

Figure 42.11: Friedel-Crafts acylation.

42.4.2   Nucleophilic Addition at the C=O Bond

- These reactions transform a trigonal planar carbonyl that is sp^2 hybridized to an sp^3 hybridized tetrahedral carbon.

- Hemiacetals and acetals

    - Hemiacetals are unstable molecules that are created when an aldehyde is dissolved in one equivalent of an alcohol (Note: acid- and base- catalyzed hemiacetal formation is also possible, but alcohol mediated hemiacetal formation is most common). Acetals are the products observed when a hemiacetal is combined with another molar equivalent of an alcohol.

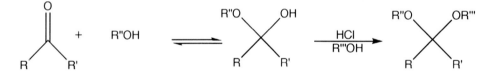

Figure 42.12: Hemiacetal and acetal formation. Depending on the R' of the initial reactant, an aldehyde (R' = H) or ketone (R' = alkyl) can be used in this reaction.

- Imines and enamines

    - Imines are produced by reacting an aldehyde or ketone with a 1° amine while enamines are produced by reacting an aldehyde or ketone with a 2° amine. See Figure 42.13 below.

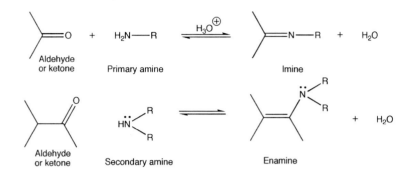

Figure 42.13: Imines and enamines.

42.4.3 Keto-enol Tautomerism

Keto-enol tautomerism is a process by which water added to an alkyne creates a very unstable vinylic alcohol which then rearranges (or tautomerizes) to a ketone:

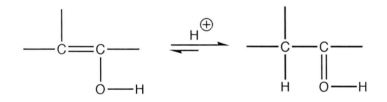

Figure 42.14: Keto-enol tautomerism.

42.4.4 Reactions at the α Carbon

- Aldol addition: The formation of β hydroxy aldehydes or ketones when an enolate reacts with an α-carbon of another carbonyl (*Note: this can occur in the presence of a base or an acid*). See Figure 42.15 below.

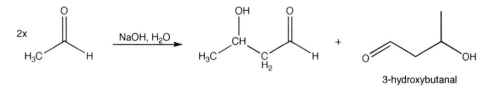

Figure 42.15: Aldol addition.

- Aldol condensation: The formation of a conjugated system in aldehydes or ketones (*Note: this can occur in the presence of a base or an acid*). See Figure 42.16 below.

- Haloform reactions: Reaction of a methyl ketone with halogens (in the presence of a base) which produces a methyl group with multiple halogens. See Figure 42.17 below.

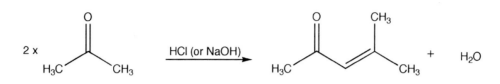

Figure 42.16: Aldol condensation.

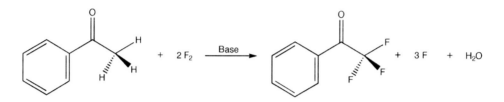

Figure 42.17: Haloform reactions.

- Oxidation

  - Aldehydes are easier to oxidize than ketones

  - Common, strong oxidizing agents include potassium permanganate ($KMnO_4$) or silver oxide (AgO):

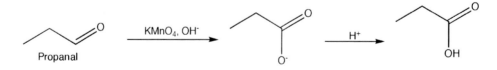

Figure 42.18: Aldehyde oxidation.

42.4.5   Wittig Reaction

- A mechanism to prepare alkenes by reacting an aldehyde or ketone with a phosphonium salt ylide[1].

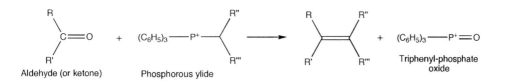

Figure 42.19: Wittig reaction.

42.4.6   Claisen Condensation

- First off, a condensation reaction is a reaction in which two molecules are joined with the elimination of alcohol or water. Secondly, the Claisen condensation is the synthesis of β-keto esters.

- For the synthesis of a β-keto ester, ethyl acetate and sodium ethoxide are "condensed" and then acidified. This produces ethyl acetoacetate (aka acetoacetic ester):

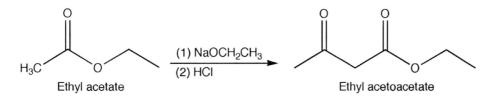

Figure 42.20: Claisen condensation.

---

[1] Ylides are molecules that have a positively-charged phosphorous and a negatively-charged carbon, which makes the net charge neutral.

42.4.7 Wolff-Kishner reduction

- By way of this reaction, the carbonyl of aldehydes or ketones can be reduced to a -CH_2- group:

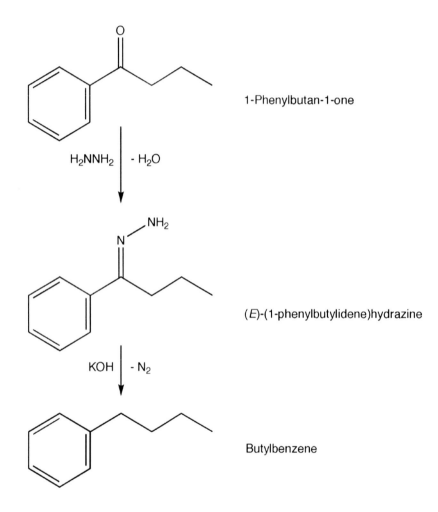

Figure 42.21: Wolff-Kishner reduction.

Chapter 43

Ethers, Epoxides & Esters

What are ethers (ROR)?

Ethers are organic molecules that have a $C - O - C$ bond:

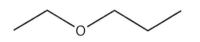

Figure 43.1: An ether: Ethyl propyl ether.

What are epoxides?

Epoxides are a sub-class of ethers in which the $C - O - C$ bond is contained in a heterocyclic system:

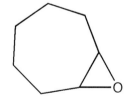

Figure 43.2: Epoxides: 1,2-epoxycycloheptane.

One of the oxygen's lone pair of electrons of an epoxide molecule can readily react in an S_N1 fashion.

What are esters (RCO_2R' aka $RCOOR'$)?

Esters are organic molecules in which a carbon atom is (a) double-bonded to an oxygen, and, (b) single bonded to an oxygen. Often, esters are sweet-smelling substances.

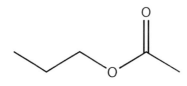

Figure 43.3: An ester: Propyl acetate.

43.1   General

What is the IUPAC alkoxyalkane convention for naming ethers?

1. Find and name the R and R' chains.

2. Identify the number at which the R and R' chains bond to the oxygen.

    • If the oxygen is bonded at the 1 position, disregard the numbering.

3. Name the ether by choosing the shorter chain as the prefix, interposing "oxy" and using the longer chain as the suffix:

Figure 43.4: (left) Methoxyethane, CH_3CH_2-O-CH_3; (right) 2-methoxybutane.

43.2   Physical and Chemical Properties

What is a notable physical property of ethers?

Ethers can not form hydrogen bonds and so they have lower boiling points - remember how quickly ether evaporated from your orgo lab bench top?

What is a notable chemical property of ethers?

Relative lack of chemical reactivity which makes them particularly good solvents.

What is the infrared absorption of $C - O - C$?

Bond Frequency	(cm^{-1})
$C - O - C$	~ 1100

Table 43.1: Infrared absorption of $C - O - C$ bond.

43.3 Key Principles

How are ethers used to "protect" alcohols?

Because ethers lack significant reactivity, conversion to ethers can be used as an intermediary step in an experiment. This is commonly done with alcohols to "protect" the hydroxyl.

43.4 Reactions Involving Ethers

What is an important reaction involving ethers?

1. Williamson ether synthesis

    - The first step of the Williamson Ether Synthesis is the reaction of a metal with an alcohol to form an alkoxide ion plus hydrogen gas
    - The alkoxide ion in turn is a powerful nucleophile which reacts in an S_N2 fashion

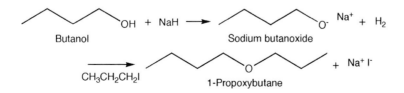

Figure 43.5: Williamson ether synthesis.

43.5   General

What is the IUPAC alkoxyalkane convention for naming esters?

1. To name the alkyl alkanoate (i.e. ester), identify the carbon chains that are separated by an "ether" oxygen, i.e. $C - O - C$.

2. Naming the two halves:

   - Name the chain without the carbonyl group: this is the "alkyl" chain; with the suffix of "-yl"

   - Name the chain with the carbonyl group: this is the "alkanoate" chain; with the suffix of "-oate"

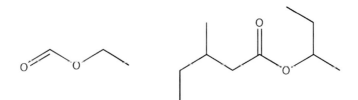

Figure 43.6: Esters: (left) Ethyl methanoate and (right) but-2-yl 3-methylpentanoate. *Note: the location of the carbonyl group determines which is the alkanoate chain.*

What is a notable physical and chemical property of esters?

Esters can participate in hydrogen bonds as hydrogen bond accepters, e.g. an ester and a water molecule, but *cannot* act as hydrogen bond donors and therefore cannot hydrogen bond to each other. Esters also have higher boiling points and smell sweet. Different esters smell like various fruits, including raspberries, apples, bananas, pears and oranges.

43.6   Reactions Involving Esters

What is an important reaction involving esters?

1. Esters are synthesized through esterification through the reaction of carboxylic acids with an alcohol:

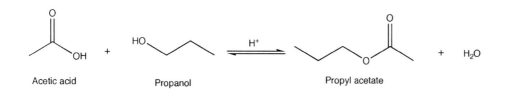

Figure 43.7: Ester synthesis through esterification.

2. Esters readily undergo hydrolysis

   • Acid-catalyzed hydrolysis

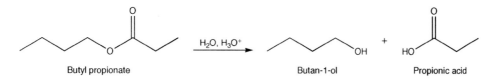

Figure 43.8: Acid-catalyzed hydrolysis of esters.

   • Base-catalyzed hydrolysis, aka saponification

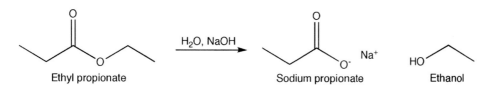

Figure 43.9: Base-catalyzed hydrolysis of esters: Saponification.

Chapter 44

Keto Acids & Keto Esters

What are keto acids and keto esters?

Keto acids are exactly what the name states: organic molecules with a carbonyl ("keto") and a carboxylic acid group:

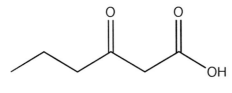

β keto acid

Figure 44.1: Keto acids: 3-oxohexanoic acid.

Keto esters are exactly what the name states: organic molecules with a carbonyl ("keto") and an ester:

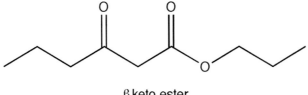

β keto ester

Figure 44.2: Keto esters: propyl 3-oxohexanoate.

Note: in both keto acids and keto esters, the "β" designation is made to identify the location of the carbonyl.

44.1 Reactions Involving Keto Acids and Keto Esters

What key reaction is associated with β-keto acids?

Decarboxylation, a reaction whereby a carboxylic acid loses a carbon dioxide. β-keto acids can decarboxylate easily when heated above $100^{o}C$:

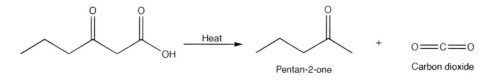

Figure 44.3: Decarboxylation of keto acids.

What key reaction is associated with β-keto esters?

1. Claisen condensation: synthesis of β-keto esters

   - First off, a condensation reaction is a reaction in which two molecules are joined with the elimination of an alcohol or water.
   - For the synthesis of a β-keto ester, ethyl acetate and sodium ethoxide are "condensed" and then acidified. This produces ethyl acetoacetate aka acetoacetic ester:

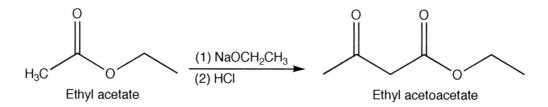

Figure 44.4: Claisen condensation.

44.2 Key Principles

In β-keto esters, what is associated with considerable acidity - why?

The α-hydrogen between both carbonyl groups. Because there is considerable "pull" from the electronegative carbonyl oxygens, the α-hydrogen "comes" off easily:

What type of rearrangement leads to the keto form?

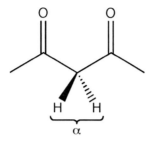

Figure 44.5: Acidity of α-hydrogen in keto esters: The α-hydrogen has a p$K_a \approx 10$.

Keto-enol tautomerism.

This process adds water to an alkyne creating a very unstable vinylic alcohol which then rearranges (or tautomerizes) to a ketone:

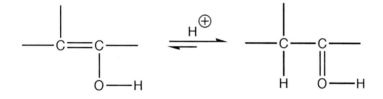

Figure 44.6: Keto-enol tautomerism.

Chapter 45

Carboxylic Acids

What are carboxylic acids?

Carboxylic acids are organic functional groups that consist of a terminal carbonyl ($C = O$) bonded to a hydroxyl group. The general molecular formula for carboxylic acids is $R - COOH$. When the hydrogen dissociates from the carboxylic acid it turns into its anionic (salt) form called a carboxylate.

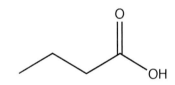

Figure 45.1: Carboxylic acids: Butanoic acid.

45.1 General

How are carboxylic acids named?

Carboxylic acids are in the alkanoic acid family, and the identifying suffix - "-oic acid" is derived from this family designation.

1. The carbonyl group in the alkanoic acid family will always be positioned at the end of a carbon chain, i.e. at the "1" position. For this reason, the "1" is omitted from naming.

2. The suffix "-oic acid" replaces the terminal "-e" of the alkane name.

3. The dissociated form of carboxylic acids, $R - COO$, has a suffix which changes from "-oic acid" to "-ate," e.g. ethanoic acid (acetic acid) becomes an acetate ion.

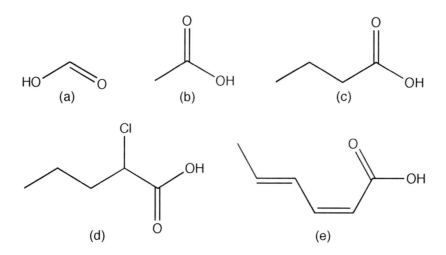

Figure 45.2: Examples of carboxylic acids: (a) Methanoic acid (formic acid), (b) ethanoic acid (acetic acid), (c) butanoic acid, (d) 2-chloropentanoic acid, and (e) hexadionic acid.

45.2   Physical and Chemical Properties

What are three physical properties of carboxylic acids?

1. Acidity

   - Typically weak acids.
   - The ability to release hydrogen is increased by the existence of the two electronegative oxygen atoms attached to the carbonyl/hydroxyl carbon. Moreover, the addition of other electronegative groups near the carboxylic group, e.g. chloride, will increase the acidity of the carboxylic acid and is an example of an inductive effect:

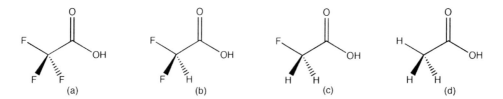

Figure 45.3: Inductive effects in carboxylic acids: (a) has the highest acidity ($pK_a \approx$ 0.7), followed by (b) ($pK_a \approx$ 1.5), (c) ($pK_a \approx$ 3.0), and (d) ($pK_a \approx$ 5.0).

2. Boiling point

   - Exceptionally high because of hydrogen bonding. The unique positioning of two oxygens allows for dimeric hydrogen-oxygen associations:

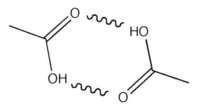

Figure 45.4: Hydrogen bonding in carboxylic acids.

3. Solubility

- Solubility is directly related to polarity and the ability to undergo hydrogen bonding.

- Lower than corresponding alcohols but the first four carboxylic acids (i.e. methanoic acid to butanoic acid) are soluble in water. As expected, as the carbon chain grows, water solubility decreases.

What role does resonance play in carboxylic acids?

Stabilizing the anionic form:

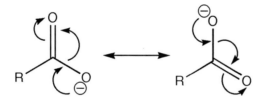

Figure 45.5: Resonance in carboxylic acids.

What is the infrared absorption of carboxylic acids?

Bond Frequency	(cm^{-1})
$RCOOH$	~1700

Table 45.1: Infrared absorption of carboxylic acids.

How do carbonyl substituents affect reactivity?

Intiuitively, larger substituents cause more steric hindrance and decrease reactivity.

45.3   Reactions Involving Carboxylic Acids

45.3.1   Synthesis

- Oxidation

  - Oxidation of many organic molecules can be used in the synthesis of carboxylic acids, including alkenes, aldehydes, $1°$ alcohols, alkyl-benzenes and methyl ketones. Again, a strong oxidant is used to complete this reaction, e.g. $KMnO_4$:

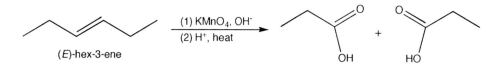

Figure 45.6: Oxidation to synthesize carboxylic acids.

- Hydrolysis of nitriles

  - Hydrolysis of the $-CN$ group to a $-COOH$ group:

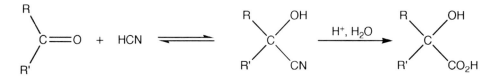

Figure 45.7: Hyrdolysis of nitriles to synthesize carboxylic acids.

- Carbonation of Grignard reagents

  - This reaction takes tertiary alkyl halides and turns them into carboxylic acids:

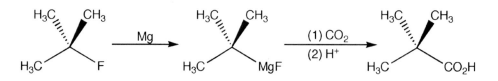

Figure 45.8: Carbonation of Grignard reagents to synthesize carboxylic acids.

45.3.2   Reactions at the Carbonyl Group

- Nucleophilic attack

  - Nucleophilic attack leading to nucleophilic substitution is a two part process whereby (1) nucleophilic addition and (2) elimination occurs. This latter step causes the $C = O$ to re-form:

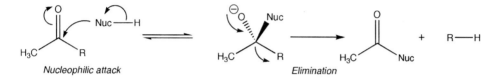

Figure 45.9: Nucleophilic attack and elimination at the carboxylic acid carbonyl.

- Reduction

  - Reduction of carboxylic acids by a reducing agent, e.g. LAH, produces an aldehyde. Further reduction produces an alcohol:

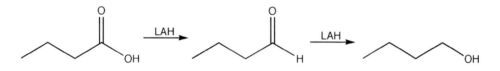

Figure 45.10: Reduction of carboxylic acids with LAH.

- Decarboxylation

  - Reaction in which a carboxylic acid loses CO_2. This is a slow reaction that requires a significant amount of heat.

- Fischer esterification

  - The synthesis of esters by the reaction of a carboxylic acid with an alcohol:

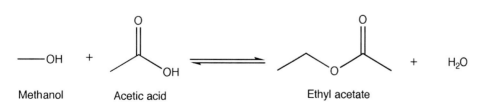

Figure 45.11: Fischer esterification.

45.3.3   Reactions at the α position

- Halogenation (Hell-Volhard-Zelinski reaction - aka HVZ)

    - Bromine and phosphorus can react to form an α-halide carboxylic acid (aka α-halo acid):

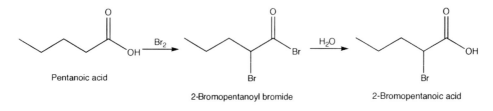

Figure 45.12: Carboxylic acid halogenation: The Hell-Volhard-Zelinski (HVZ) reaction. Halogenation occurs at the α-carbon of a carboxylic acid.

Chapter 46

Carboxylic Acid Derivatives: Acid Chlorides, Anhydrides, Amides & Amines

What are four derivatives of carboxylic acids, i.e. acyl compounds?

The four acyl compounds (acid derivatives):

1. Acyl chlorides (aka acid chlorides)

2. Anhydrides

3. Esters

4. Amides

What are acyl chlorides?

Acyl chlorides are the most reactive derivatives of carboxylic acids, and they have a general molecular formula of $R - COCl$:

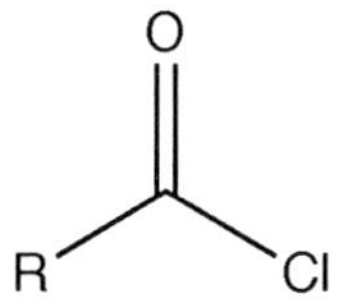

Figure 46.1: Acyl chloride.

What are acid anhydrides?

The 2nd most reactive derivative of carboxylic acids which has a general molecular formula of $(RCO)_2O$:

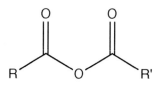

Figure 46.2: Acyl anhydrides.

What are esters?

The 3rd most reactive derivative of carboxylic acids which has a general molecular formula of RCO_2R' aka $RCOOR'$:

Figure 46.3: Esters.

What are amides?

The 4th most reactive derivative of carboxylic acids which has a general molecular formula of $R - CONH_2$:

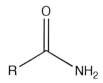

Figure 46.4: Amides

46.1   General

What are the relative reactivities of acyl compounds?

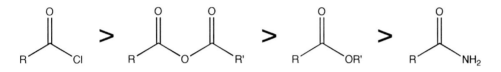

Figure 46.5: Relative reactivities of acyl compounds.

How are acyl chlorides named?

Acyl chlorides have the suffix "-oyl" plus the name of the halide.

1. The carbon of the acyl halide will always be positioned at the end of a carbon chain, i.e. at the "1" position. For this reason, the "1" is omitted from naming.

2. The suffix "-oyl" replaces the terminal "-e" of the alkane name. After this, the name of the halide is added.

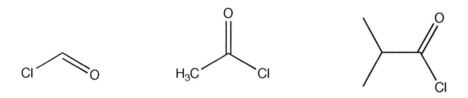

Figure 46.6: Examples of acyl chlorides: (left) methanoyl chloride, (center) ethanoyl chloride, (right) 2-methylpropanoyl chloride.

How are anhydrides named?

Anhydrides have the suffix "-oic anhydride", which denotes a $-OCOR$ group that replaces the $-OH$ of a carboxylic acid.

1. The $-OCOR$ will always be positioned at the end of a carbon chain, making a number designation unnecessary.

2. Most anhydrides are named by dropping the word "acid" from the carboxylic acid and replacing it with "anhydride."

3. If two alkane moieties (halves) exist, name both and arrange the shorter chain first

4. Cyclic anhydrides are named as alkanedioic anhydrides

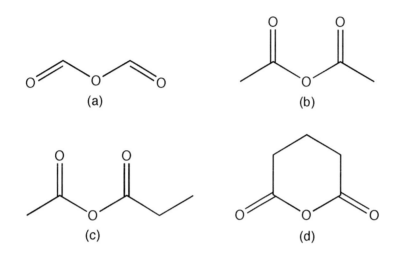

Figure 46.7: Examples of anhydrides: (a) methanoic anhydride (formic anhydride), (b) ethanoic anhydride (acetic anhydride), (c) ethanoic propanoic anhydride, (d) pentanedioic anhydride.

How are esters named?

1. To name the alkyl alkanoate (i.e. ester), identify the carbon chains that are separated by an "ether" oxygen

2. Naming the two halves:

    - Name the chain without the carbonyl group - this is the "alkyl" chain - with the suffix of "-yl"

    - Name the chain with the carbonyl group - this is the "alkanoate" chain - with the suffix of "-oate"

Note: the location of the carbonyl group determines which is the alkanoate chain.

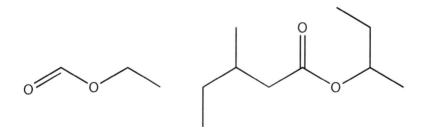

Figure 46.8: Examples of esters: (left) ethyl methanoate and (right) but-2-yl 3-methylpentanoate.

How are amides named?

1. The "amide" suffix is added to the end of an alkane chain

2. When two amides exist at each end of an alkane, the "diamide" suffix is used. Because a consonant is used ("d"), the vowel is preserved in the alkane chain (see Figure 46.9(c) below for an example)

3. Cyclic amides are called lactams designated β-lactam (2 non-carbonyl carbons), γ-lactam (3 non-carbonyl carbons), and δ-lactam (4 non-carbonyl carbons)

Note: Amines will be reviewed in another chapter.

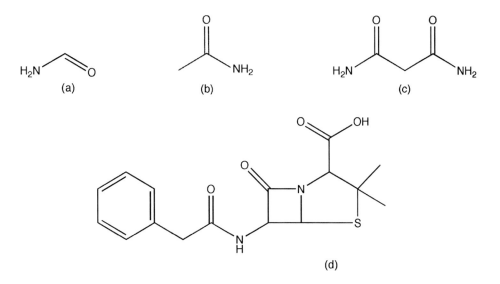

Figure 46.9: Examples of amides: (a) methanamide, (b) ethanamide, (c) propanediamide, (d) β-lactam (penicillin G).

46.2   Physical and Chemical Properties

What are some notable properties of the four derivatives of acyl compounds?

1. Acyl chlorides

   - They are very reactive and have practical synthetic purposes.
   - Chlorine makes the carbonyl carbon a very good electrophile that even weak nucleophiles can attack.
   - Chlorine is a good leaving group.

2. Anhydrides

   - They are usually not water soluble (anhydrides commonly react with water).

3. Esters

   - Esters can form hydrogen bonds with water but not with themselves.

4. Amides

   - Amides can form hydrogen bonds and therefore have higher boiling points.

− β-lactams have significantly more strain since they have only two non-carbonyl carbons.

What are the relative reactivities of acyl compounds?

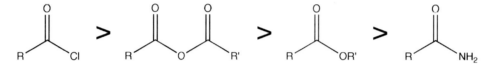

Figure 46.10: Relative reactivities of acyl compounds.

How can the carbonyl carbon of acyl carbons be modified?

Electron withdrawing groups make the carbonyl carbon more electrophilic, and therefore more susceptible to nucleophilic attack. This phenomenon explains a lot about the relative reactivities of the acyl compounds illustrated above.

What are two differences between amides and amines?

	Amides	Amines
pH	Less basic	More basic
e⁻ withdrawing effects	Greater (from carbonyl oxygen)	Less

Table 46.1: Two key differences between amides and amines.

Note: the decreased pH of amides is a result of the greater withdrawing effects from the amide's carbonyl oxygen.

What is the infrared absorptions of carboxylic acids and their derivatives?

	Bond	Frequency	(cm^{-1})
Carboxylic acids		RCOOH	~1700
Acyl chlorides		RCOCl	~1800
Acid anhydrides		$(RCO)_2O$	~1800
Esters		RCOOR	~1700
Amides		$RCONH_2$	~1600

Table 46.2: Infrared absorption of carboxylic acids and derivatives.

46.3 Reactions Involving Carboxylic Acids

46.3.1 Synthesis

- Acyl chlorides

    - Reacting carboxylic acids with acid chlorides ($SOCl_2$ or PCl_3) produces acyl chlorides:

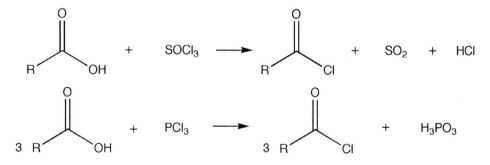

Figure 46.11: Acyl chloride synthesis.

- Acid anhydrides

  - Reacting carboxylic acids with acyl chlorides:

Figure 46.12: Acyl anhydride synthesis.

- Esters

  - Esters are synthesized through esterification through the reaction of carboxylic acid with an alcohol:

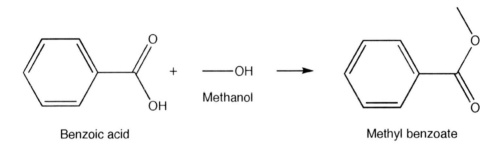

Figure 46.13: Ester synthesis

- Amides

  - Amides can be synthesized in multiple ways using acyl chlorides, anhydrides, and esters. All involve nucleophilic attack:

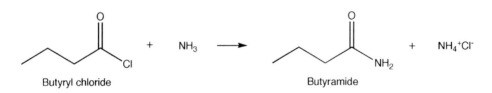

Figure 46.14: Amide synthesis from the nucleophilic attack of a primary amine to the carbonyl carbon of an acyl chloride.

46.3.2 Nucleophilic substitution

- The most reactive carboxylic acid derivative (acyl chloride) can be used to create progressively less-reactive derivatives: anhydrides, esters and amides. But the reverse cannot happen.

- Table 46.3 below shows how one can use an acyl chloride to produce a specific product, i.e. anhydrides, esters and amides using the nucleophiles (RCO_2, $R'OH$ and R_2NH).

Acyl chlorides reacts with...	... to yield:
RCO_2	Anhydrides
$R'OH$	Esters
R_2NH	Amides

Table 46.3: What to react with an acyl chloride to yield a specific product.

46.3.3 Transesterification

- The process of exchanging an ester's alkoxy group using another alcohol.

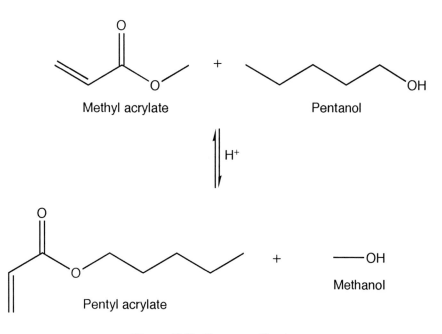

Figure 46.15: Transesterification.

Note: Transesterification can occur in the presence of a base or an acid.

46.3.4 Saponification

- Saponification is the base-catalyzed hydrolysis of esters (aka the hydrolysis of fats and glycerides).

- This is in contrast to acid-catalyzed hydrolysis of esters (See Ethers, Epoxides and Esters). Base-catalyzed hydrolysis of esters is irreversible:

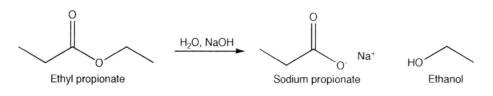

Figure 46.16: Saponification.

46.3.5 Reactions specific to amides

- Hydrolysis

    - Hydrolysis of amides can occur when amides are heated either with an acid or a base:

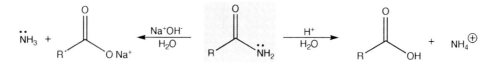

Figure 46.17: Hydrolysis of amides.

- Hofmann degradation of amides (aka Hofmann rearrangement)

    - Amides with an unsubstituted nitrogen can react with chlorine or bromine in a base to produce an amine:

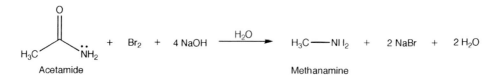

Figure 46.18: Hofmann degradation of amides.

Chapter 47

Amines

What are amines?

Organic molecules that are derivatives of ammonia and are classified as primary (N is attached to 1 carbon), secondary (N is attached to 2 carbons) or tertiary (N is attached to 3 carbons):

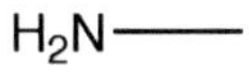

$$H_2N\text{——}$$

Figure 47.1: Amines: methanamine.

47.1   General

What is the IUPAC convention for naming amines?

1. For terminal amines (1° amines), identify the alkane and add the suffix $-amine$.

2. For 2° and 3° amines, identify the alkane chains and arrange with the shorter alkane first followed by the longer alkane and amine.

   - If the alkane chains are the same, use di- or tri-.

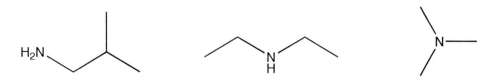

Figure 47.2: Amine nomenclature and the number of alkane chains: (left) 2-methyl-1-propanamine, (center) diethylamine, (right) trimethylamine.

3. If the amine group is an $-NH_2$ group, use the prefix "amino".

Figure 47.3: Amine nomenclature and using the amino prefix: aminomethanol (left) and 2-aminoethanol (right).

- "Amino" prefixes are often used when a molecule has an $-OH$ or $-CO_2H$ group:

What is the stereochemistry and hybridization of amines and the nitrogen atom?

The amine geometry is trigonal pyramidal, the bond angles are tetrahedral, and the nitrogen is sp^3 hybridized:

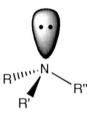

Figure 47.4: Amine stereochemistry and hybridization: trigonal pyramidal stereochemistry with tetrahedral bond angles and an sp^3 hybridized nitrogen.

What can occur to amines because they are sp^3 hybridized?

They can "flip", i.e. undergo an interconversion between amine enantiomers:

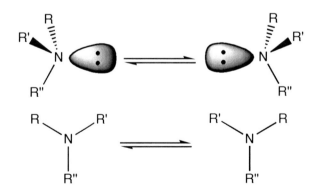

Figure 47.5: Amine enantiomers.

47.2 Physical and Chemical Properties

What are three physical properties of amides?

1. Basicity

    - Amines are weak bases

    - Electron withdrawing groups decrease basicity (aromatic rings, NO_2), electron donating groups increase basicity (e.g. OH, $-CH_3$)

2. Lone pair of electrons

    - Hydrogen bonding

	Can form hydrogen bonds with each other	Can form hydrogen bonds with H_2O
1° amines	⋆	⋆
2° amines	⋆	⋆
3° amines		⋆

Table 47.1: Hydrogen bonding by 1°, 2° and 3° amines.

What is the infrared absorption of the amine group $(-NH)$?

Bond Frequency	(cm^{-1})
N-H	~ 3300

Table 47.2: Infrared absorption of the amine group $(N-H)$.

47.3 Key Principles

How are carbocations in amines stabilized?

Electron delocalization.

What are two differences between amides and amines?

	Amides	Amines
pH	Less basic	More basic
e⁻ withdrawing effects	Greater (from carbonyl oxygen)	Less

Table 47.3: Two key differences between amides and amines.

Note: the decreased pH of amides is a result of the greater withdrawing effects from the amides carbonyl oxygen.

What are five biologically active amines?

Acetylcholine, dopamine, serotonin, amphetamine and morphine.

47.4   Reactions Involving Amines

47.4.1   Synthesis

- Hofmann degradation (aka Hofmann rearrangement) of amides to amines

    - Amides with an unsubstituted nitrogen can react with chlorine or bromine in a base to produce an amine:

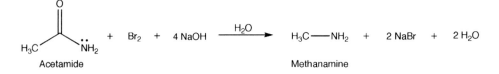

Figure 47.6: Hofmann degradation.

- Hofmann elimination

    - *E*2 elimination when a quaternary ammonium hydroxide is heated to produce an alkene, water and a tertiary amine:

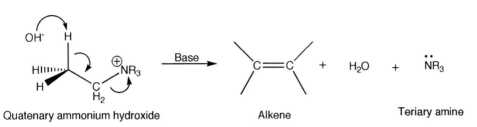

Figure 47.7: Hofmann elimination.

- Primary amine synthesis from reacting ammonia with alkyl halides (aka Gabriel synthesis)

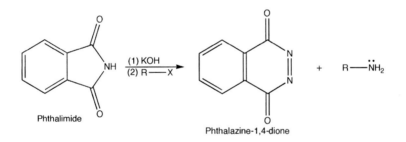

Figure 47.8: Primary amine synthesis: Gabriel synthesis.

- Reduction of nitro compounds

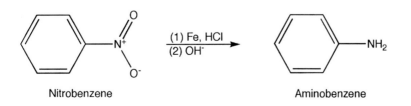

Figure 47.9: Reduction of nitro compounds.

- Reductive animation of aldehydes or ketones.

  - Formation of 1°, 2° and 3° amines

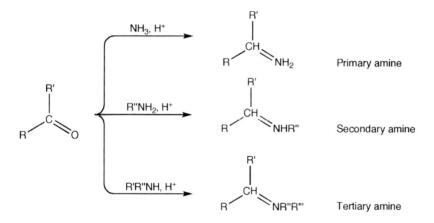

Figure 47.10: Amine synthesis: Reductive animation of aldehydes or ketones to create primary, secondary or tertiary amines. For secondary and tertiary amines, a ketone needs to be used as the substrate reactant.

- Reduction of nitriles, oximes and amides

  - Formation of 1° and 3° amines

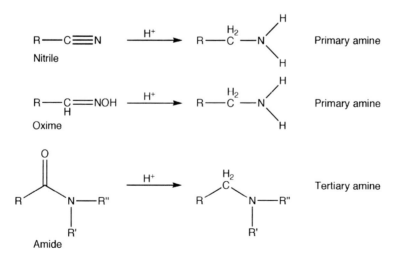

Figure 47.11: Formation of 1° amines from the reduction of nitriles or oximes and the formation of 3° amines from the reduction of amides.

47.4.2 Amine Reactions with Nitrous Acid

- Primary amines
  - Primary aliphatic amines reacted with nitrous acid

R—NH2
Nitrous acid, H2O
NaNO2, HX
R—N≡N: X-
Unstable diazonium salt
:N≡N: + R+ + X-
Alkenes
Alcohols
Alkyl halides

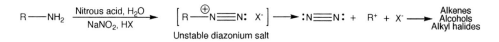

Figure 47.12: Primary amine reaction with nitrous acid.

  - Primary arylamines with nitrous acid

Ar—NH2
Nitrous acid, H2O
NaNO2, HX
Ar—N≡N: X-
Stable diazonium salt
+ NaX + 2 H2O + X-

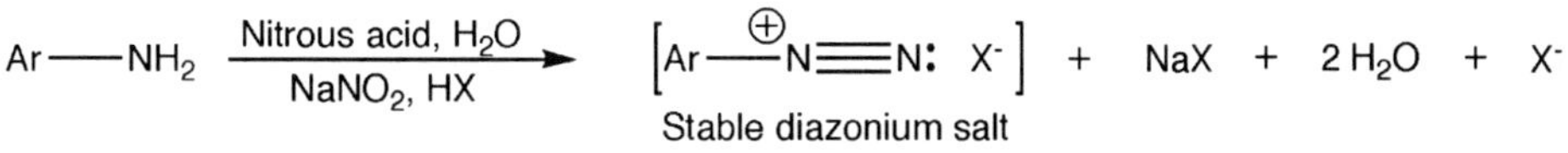

Figure 47.13: Primary arylamine reaction with nitrous acid.

- Secondary amines with nitrous acid

N
H
Diethylamine
Nitrous acid, NaNO2
HCl, H2O
O
N
N
N-Nitrosodiethylamine

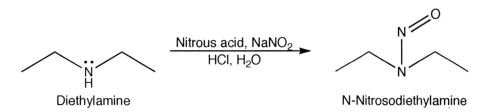

Figure 47.14: Secondary amine reaction with nitrous acid.

47.4.3   Alkylation of amines

- Nucleophilic substitution

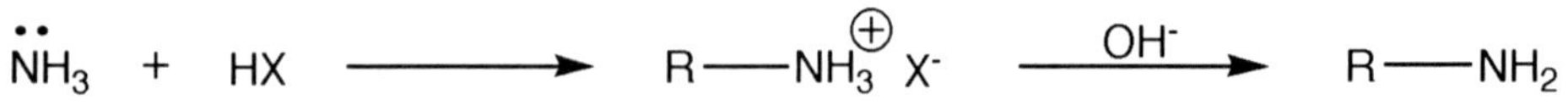

$$\overset{\cdot\cdot}{\text{NH}}_3 \;+\; \text{HX} \;\longrightarrow\; \text{R}\!-\!\!\overset{\oplus}{\text{NH}}_3 \; \text{X}^- \;\xrightarrow{\text{OH}^-}\; \text{R}\!-\!\text{NH}_2$$

Figure 47.15: Alkylation of amines: nucleophilic aubstitution.

Chapter 48

Amino Acids & Proteins

What are amino acids?

Amino acids are the building blocks of proteins which contain an amino group, a carboxylic group and a unique "-R" group. This specific arrangement about a carbon creates an α-amino acid:

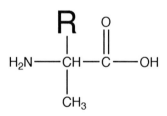

Figure 48.1: An amino acid.

Which amino acid has the simplest $R-$ group?

Glycine, whose $R-$ group is an $H-$. This makes glycine achiral and not optically active, while the 20 other amino acid $R-$ groups get increasingly more complex and chiral.

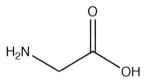

Figure 48.2: Glycine.

What is the absolute stereo configuration of most amino acids?

L configuration:

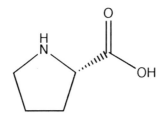

Figure 48.3: *L*-configuration of amino acids: *L*-proline.

Note: There are some D-configured amino acids that are found in bacteria, but the **overwhelming majority** *of amino acids are L-configured.*

What are two ways in which amino acids can be drawn?

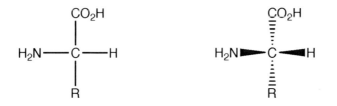

Figure 48.4: Amino acid projections: The Fischer projections have the amino group on the left, and the equivalent wedge-dashed-wedge line projection is depicted on the right.

What makes amino acids bipolar ions?

The basic amino group and the acidic carboxyl acid group. Based on the *pH* of the solution, the degree of protonation can vary:

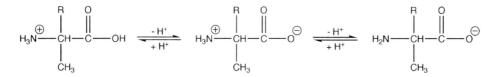

Figure 48.5: Amino acids have a basic amino group and an acidic carboxylic acid group. Additionally, the $-R$ group can also have acidic or basic properties.

What links two amino acids and what is released when two amino acids polymerize?

A peptide linkage attaches two amino acids. When polymerization occurs between two amino acids to form a dipeptide, H_2O is released:

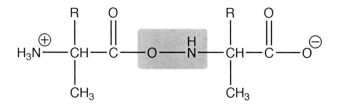

Figure 48.6: Peptide linkage (within the shaded region).

Note: Therefore, hydrolysis of a peptide linkage results in the addition of H_2O and cleavage of the bond.

48.1 Protein structure

What is the primary structure ($1°$) of a protein?

The amino acid sequence of a polypeptide chain

- For example, Leucine-Valine-Glutamic acid

What is the secondary structure ($2°$) of a protein?

The folding pattern of a polypeptide chain

- Two main types:

    1. α-helix
    2. β-pleated sheet

- Mediated by hydrogen bonds

48.2 Amino Acids: Classification

Try not to get too bogged down with the amino acid classifications. In general, this may be beyond the scope of the MCAT. If you take anything away from this chapter, focus on amino acid structure and reactions (above) with less emphasis on classification (below).

In fact, this section might help you out more for a biochem exam or in medical school.

Amino acid characteristics are numerous, so if you want to be super hard core, you can memorize this jingle that is sung to the tune of the Beverly Hillbillies theme[1]:

Come an' listen to my story about the a-mi-nos
Five Al-i-phats kick off our show
Glycine, Alanine, Valine and then
Leucine and Iso make up half of ten

Well the next thing you know are three aromats
phenylalanine (F) is right off the bat
tYrosine has alcohol next to its ring
And tryptophan (W) has indole double ring thing.

Sulfur in Cysteine; it loves to bond
Sulfur Methionine is much more a snob
Alcoholic Serine, well wouldn't you know,
And Threonine's OH gives a warm glow.

Acid-aspartic (D) and glutamic (E) are ionized
With pK of 4, their protons are lysed,
asparagine (N) and glutamine (Q) play a different role
With amides they're neutral but they both have poles

lysine(K) and aRginine are the basic kind,
But Histidine's imidazole can't make up its mind,
Proline, the last one, coming at the end
It's imine, an oddball, proteins use to bend.

Classification by pH: basic and acidic amino acids:

HAL. is G.As.sy spoken *"Hal is gassy!"*

Histidine	**G**lutamic acid
Arginine	**A**spartic acids
Lysine	

---

[1]From http://www.medicalmnemonics.com/

Classification by essential amino acids for humans:

PVT TIM HALL spoken *"PriVaTe TIM HALL"*

Phenylalanine	**T**hronine	**H**istidine
Valine	**I**soleucine	**A**rginine
Tryptophan	**M**ethionine	**L**eucine
		Lysine

Chapter 49

Carbohydrates

What are carbohydrates?

Organic molecules that have a general formula of $C_x(H_2O)_y$.

What are the general categories of carbohydrates?

Monosaccharides	single saccharide
Disaccharides	2 monosaccharides
Oligosaccharides	2 to 10 monosaccharides
Polysaccharides	>10 monosaccharides

Table 49.1: Categories of monosaccharides.

How are monosaccharides classified?

1. Based on the number of carbons they have:

Triose	3 carbons
Tetrose	4 carbons
Pentose	5 carbons
Hexose*	6 carbons

Table 49.2: Carbon number of common monosaccharides.

Hexoses can form five-membered rings

2. Based on their functional groups:

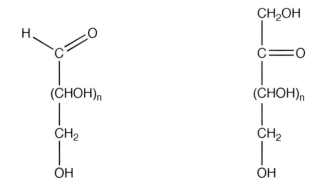

Figure 49.1: **Al**doses and **keto**ses: **al**doses contain an **al**dehyde (left) and **keto**se contains a **keto**ne (right).

What are some common monosaccharides?

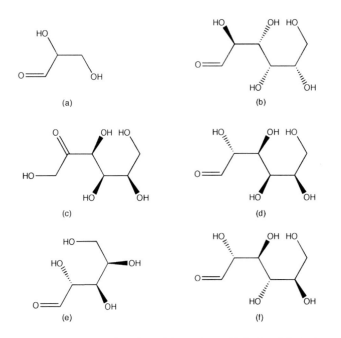

Figure 49.2: Common monosaccharides: (a) L-glyceraldehyde, (b) L-glucose, (c) D-fructose, (d) D-glucose, (e) D-ribose, (f) D-galactose.

What are the D and L designations for monosaccharides?

A system of distinguishing the enantiomers of a carbohydrate with a stereocenter. This system was created before the R and S classification in the early 1900s using glyceraldehyde.

Figure 49.3: D (left) and L (right) designations for glyceraldehyde.

How are the D and L designations made?

1. Remember how glyceraldehyde looks:

   - Note that the the *dextro* classification puts the $-OH$ on the right and the *levatory* classification puts the $-OH$ on the left.

2. Draw your monosaccharide with the same orientation as the glyceraldehydes, i.e. with the highest stereocenter at the bottom such that the aldehyde (CHO) is at the top:

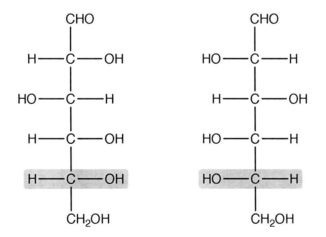

Figure 49.4: Stereocenter orientation. The highest stereocenter is highlighted.

What are epimers and anomers?

Epimers are diastereomers (stereoisomers that are not mirror images of each other) that differ in the configuration of one stereoisomer:

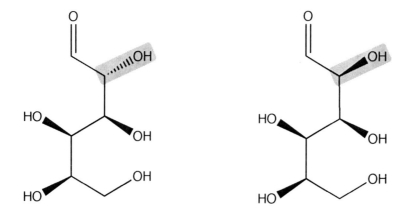

Figure 49.5: Epimers: *D*-glucose (left) and *D*-mannose (right).

Anomers are special types of epimers that occur *after cyclization* and reflect a change in configuration at the hemiacetal or hemiketal carbon. This carbon is also called the anomeric carbon, and the two variants are identified with an α or β:

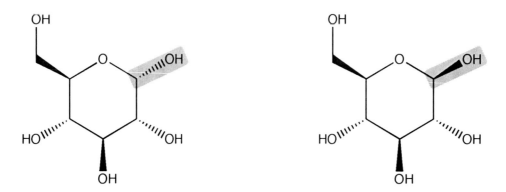

Figure 49.6: Anomers: α-D-(+)-glucopyranose (left) and α-D-(+)-glucopyranose (right).

What is meant by the absolute versus relative configurationof a molecule?

Absolute configurations: When the arrangement around a stereocenter is precisely determined by experiment, e.g. X-ray crystallography, to be R or S.

Relative configurations: When the arrangement in an optically active molecule is determined (by experiment) to be "+" (*D*) or "-" (*L*) but it is unknown to what R or S configuration they are matched to.

How do straight-chain monosaccharides create rings?

1. The aldehyde or ketone group reacts with the hydroxyl group on the carbon chain

2. This creates a hemiacetal (from aldehydes) or a hemiketal (from ketones), resulting in an oxygen bridge between the two carbon atoms

3. A heterocyclic ring is formed

   - Five-membered rings are called furanose rings
   - Six-membered rings are called pyranose rings

What are acetals?

The product of reacting glucose with a small amount of methanol. Acetals are also called glycosides.

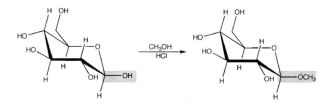

Figure 49.7: Acetals (glycosides).

What are glycosidic linkages?

Connections between glycosides, i.e. carbohydrate acetals or ketals.

What is the product of glycoside hydrolysis?

A sugar and an alcohol:

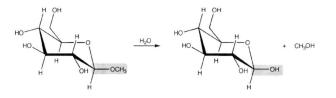

Figure 49.8: The product of glycoside hydrolysis: a sugar and an alochol.

Chapter 50

Lipids

What are lipids?

Non-polar compounds of biologic origin that are insoluble in water.

What are four lipids that you should be familiar with for the MCAT?

1. Steroids

2. Terpenes

3. Triacyl glycerols

4. Free fatty acids

What are steroids?

Very important lipids involved in regulating biological functions, which have a characteristic four-carbon ring system - memorize the shape of steroids and be able to recognize it!

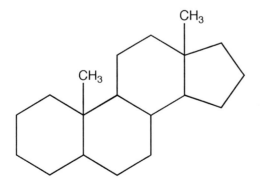

Figure 50.1: The general structure of a steroid.

What steroid is found in cell membranes and contributes to membrane fluidity?

Cholesterol.

What are three other important steroids?

Sex hormones, vitamin D and cortisol.

What are terpenes and terpenoids?

Also collectively called "essential oils," terpenes are hydrocarbons that include carotenes (precursors for vitamin A). Terpenoids are similar to terpenes but are derived from isoprene units and have odoriferous characteristics (e.g. cinnamon):

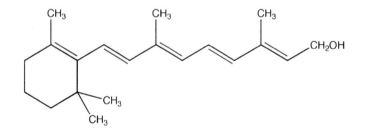

Figure 50.2: Retinol (vitamin A).

What are triacylglycerols?

Esters of glycerols:

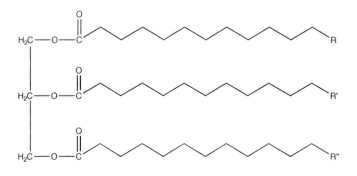

Figure 50.3: Triacylglycerols.

What unique physical properties do triacylglycerols have?

Hydrophilic and hydrophobic moieties which can be used to create a barrier between polar and non-polar regions, e.g. cell membranes and micelles in the gut:

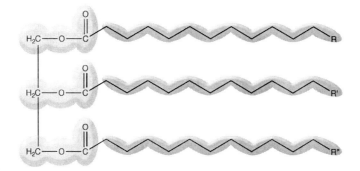

Figure 50.4: Triacylglycerols: Hydrophilic heads (left) and hydrophobic tails (right).

What is created when triacylglycerols undergo hydrolysis?

Free fatty acids and glycerol:

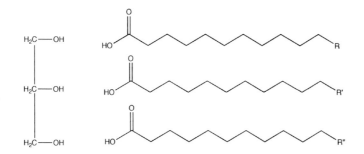

Figure 50.5: Products of triacylglycerols hydrolysis in the presence of a base and water followed by an acid: one glycerol molecule and three free fatty acids.

What are three properties of fatty acids?

1. Unbranched

2. An even number of carbons

3. Unsaturated vs. saturated fats

   - Unsaturated fats have not met their saturation point of hydrogens and always have *cis*-double bonds

– *Cis*-double bonds result in lower boiling points because they pack less efficiently

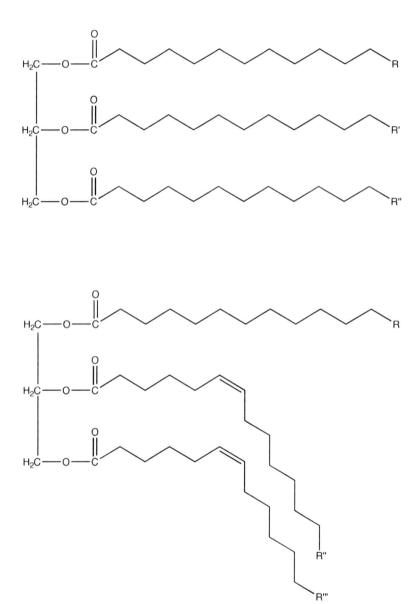

Figure 50.6: Saturated (top) vs. unsaturated fats (bottom).

Chapter 51

Phosphorous Compounds

51.1 General

What are alkyl phosphates?

The products of reacting an alcohol with phosphoric acid to yield an alkyl phosphate:

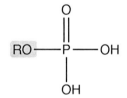

Figure 51.1: An alkyl phosphate.

This reaction can be repeated to form a dialkyl hydrogen phosphate and ultimately a trialkyl phosphate.

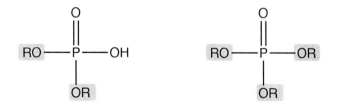

Figure 51.2: Addition to alkyl phosphates to make di- and trialkyl phosphates.

What are two types of linkages found in a trialkyl phosphate?

Ester and anhydride linkages. Hydrolysis of these linkages is an exothermic process and is a key reason why adenosine triphosphate is the predominant energy currency of most living cells.

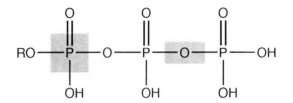

Figure 51.3: Ester linkages (square) and anhydride linkages (rectangle).

51.2   Reactions Involving Phosphorous Compounds

What is the Wittig reaction?

A mechanism to prepare alkenes by reacting an aldehyde or ketone with a phosphonium salt ylide.

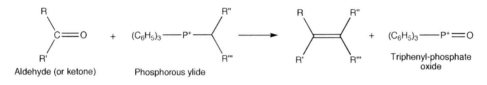

Figure 51.4: Wittig reaction.

Note: ylides are molecules that have a positively-charged phosphorous and a negatively-charged carbon, making the net charge neutral.

Chapter 52

Separation Techniques

What are four techniques used to separate organic molecules?

1. Extraction

2. Distillation

3. Chromatography

4. Recrystallization

What property is used to separate substances with extraction?

Solubility.

The goal in separating a solution of two substances is to identify a solvent in which each solute is miscible in, e.g. one substance can dissolve in an aqueous solution and the other can dissolve in an organic solvent.

The success of extraction is dependent on the difference in solubilities of the substances in solution.

What property is used to separate substances with distillation?

Boiling points.

Going back to orgo lab, the key is to heat solutions slowly so that you don't overshoot the boiling point of one of the substances. Slow and steady warming of the distilling flask will ensure that as the temperature increases, only one substance at a time will boil/vaporize and get collected through the condenser.

What are three ways in which distillation can be performed?

1. Simple distillation

   - This is the typical distillation that we did in orgo lab with a distillation flask, distilling column/thermometer, condenser and collecting flask.

   - Boiling temperatures of the substances differ by a significant amount, e.g. 40°.

2. Fractional distillation

   - The key for this is providing a large surface area for condensation to form on. As the substance evaporates and condenses as it goes through the column, it becomes more and more concentrated until it reaches the top of the column and "spills" over into the condenser.

   - This technique is useful when differences in boiling temperatures between the two substances are smaller, e.g. $< 40^o$.

3. Vacuum distillation

   - By applying a vacuum to the system, the boiling points are decreased. This can protect sensitive substances from decomposing under the duress of high boiling temperatures.

What is chromatography?

The process of separating compounds by passing the mobile phase, i.e. the analyte or sample, through a stationary phase, i.e. a substance that provides some resistance to "filter" the mobile phase.

A compound can be identified by:

- The rate at which it travels

- The distance it travels through the assay

What are three types of chromatography?

1. Column chromatography

   - Mobile phase: analyte which is vaporized and transported in an inert gas, e.g. He_2 or N_2

   - Stationary phase: a layer of liquid that lines a column or capillary tube

   - The vaporized analyte is carried through the columns or capillary tubes and, at the other end, is recorded by a device

2. Paper chromatography

   - Mobile phase: a solvent, e.g. ethanol or water

   - Stationary phase: analyte applied above the level of the solvent

- Over time, the solvent rises through the vertically positioned paper and pulls apart the analyte

3. Thin-layer chromatography

    - Similar to paper chromatography, but the stationary phase is an adsorbent substance (e.g. silica gell or cellulose) which is fixed onto a hard, flat, thin surface

    - Sometimes UV light is used to help reveal spots that are not apparent to the naked eye

How is recrysallization used to purify organic solvents?

An impure crystal is dissolved in a hot solvent to create a saturated solution. As the solvent cools, the solubility of the dissolved crystal decreases; it precipitates out of solution as a crystal, leaving the impurities behind in solution.

What are factors that should be considered when choosing a solvent?

- The compound should be soluble in the solvent at high temperatures and insoluble at low temperatures

- The solvent should dissolve the impurities (if they are known) equally well at high or low temperatures to ensure that they stay in solution and do not re-crystallize with the compound of interest

Chapter 53

Spectroscopy: Infra red, Mass & NMR

What is spectroscopy?

Generally speaking, spectroscopy is the study of frequency distributions (spectra).

Specifically, the type of spectroscopy depends on the form of frequency being measured, e.g. absorption spectroscopy (infrared, visible or UV regions of the electromagnetic radiation), mass spectroscopy (mass-to-charge ratio of ions), and nuclear magnetic resonance (analysis of hydrogen and carbon nuclei).

53.1   Infrared Spectroscopy (Absorption Spectroscopy)

How does infrared (IR) spectroscopy identify organic molecules?

An organic molecule is exposed to infrared radiation and absorbed. In turn, this "sun burn" of sorts causes the molecule to vibrate. This intramolecular vibration, specifically bond rotation, bending and stretching, is unique for each type of bond.

In IR spectroscopy what must change for vibration to occur?

The dipole moment of the molecule.

What does infrared spectroscopy measure?

Intramolecular vibrations that are quantified in wavenumbers (cm^1).

How does the polarity of a bond relate to its vibration frequency?

More polar bonds will vibrate "faster," i.e. more polar bonds will have larger IR vibrations.

		Bond Frequency (cm^1)
Alkanes	$C - H$	~ 1200
	$C - C$	~ 2900
Alkenes	$C = C$	~ 1600
Alkynes	$C \equiv C$	~ 2200
Ethers	$C - O - C$	~ 1100
Alcohols	$C - OH$	~ 3300
Ketones	$C = O$	~ 1700
Aldehydes	$(O)C - H$	~ 2800
Carboxylic Acids	$RCOOH$	~ 1700
Acyl chlorides	$RCOCl$	~ 1800
Acid anhydrides	$(RCO)_2O$	~ 1800
Esters	$RCOOR'$	~ 1700
Amides	$RCONH_2$	~ 1600
Amines	$N - H$	~ 3300
Aromatics	$C - H$	~ 3000
	$C - C$	~ 1500

Table 53.1: Infrared absorption for organic bonds.

53.2   Visible Region Spectroscopy (Absorption Spectroscopy)

What is visible region spectroscopy?

Another method used to identify organic molecules which uses the visible region of the electromagnetic spectrum to characterize molecules.

One commonly found compound in nature appears in the visible region - β-carotene from carrots.

What bond properties significantly affect visible spectroscopy readings?

Conjugated bonds.

The presence of conjugated bonds shifts the maximum absorption to an increasing wavelength. Moreover, extensively conjugated electron pairs are commonly visualized with visible region spectroscopy.

53.3 Ultraviolet Region Spectroscopy (Absorption Spectroscopy)

How does ultraviolet (UV) spectroscopy identify organic molecules?

An organic molecule is exposed to UV radiation and this energy is absorbed. UV light has enough energy to excite electrons in conjugated bonds. When a molecule absorbs UV light of sufficient energy (remember, the shorter the wavelength, the more energy is contained in the wave), the electrons jump from their higher occupied molecular orbitals (HOMO) to their lower occupied molecular orbitals (LOMO).

How does HOMO and LOMO relate to orbitals?

In most alkenes, HOMO is a bonding (π) orbital and LOMO is an antibonding (π^*) orbital.

How does the amount of conjugated bonds in a compound relate to the wavelength at which it absorbs light?

The greater the number of conjugated multiple bonds, the longer the absorbed wavelength of light.

53.4   Mass Spectroscopy

How does mass spectroscopy identify organic molecules?

Mass spec, as it's commonly called, can be used to identify molecules in two ways:

1. Identifying compounds by the mass of one or more elements within the compound

2. Identifying the isotopic composition of one or more elements in a compound

There are many types of mass specs, but gas chromatography (mass spectrometers) is common. Remember, once a sample is put in a mass spec, you can not get it back.

How do mass specs sort molecules?

By their mass/charge (m/z) ratios.

What is the name of the highest peak on a mass spec and what can be calculated from it?

The parent peak.

The molecular weight can be calculated from the parent peak. Because the parent peak has an intensity (y-axis) close to 100%, the molecular weight can be extrapolated from the m/z.

53.5   Nuclear Magnetic Resonance (NMR) Spectroscopy

NMR is pretty complex and not a high-yield topic for the MCAT. We will talk briefly about it, but refer to a prof, a text or your class notes for a more in-depth discussion of NMR.

How does NMR identify organic molecules?

NMR recognizes the spin of protons (^{1}H or ^{13}C) in their normal states (a lower "α" energy state) and in a state excited by a magnetic field (a higher "β" state).

Applying a magnetic field results in resonance of ^{1}H or ^{13}C nuclei, and each give a distinct pattern, depending on their locations in a molecule and in relation to other atoms.

This pattern has been analyzed and allows us to identify molecules.

How do NMR spikes relate to each other?

The area under a curve is directly related to the number of nuclei which it represents.

Therefore, for a given plot, one can compare one spike to another. If one has an area of, let's say X, and another has an area three times X, then the latter exists three-fold more than the former (see Figure 53.1 below).

Can two nuclei interact with each other?

Yes, nuclei within three bonds of each other can influence each other.

When nearby nuclei are in different energy states they can "shift" each other's resonance, causing a normal spike to split; this is also called spin-spin splitting.

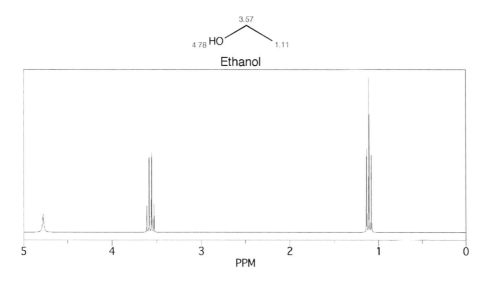

Figure 53.1: NMR ^{1}H of ethanol.

Part IV

Physics

Chapter 54

Translational Motion

Translational motion is the movement of an object through space *without* rotation. One dimensional motion is completely specified by its magnitude and has no direction, i.e. scalars, while two-dimensional motion is completely specified by a magnitude and a direction, i.e. vectors. An object moving along a straight line moves along one dimension of length. So, the position of the object can be described by providing its distance from a reference point on the line, the origin. Distance has the dimensions of length and its SI unit is the meter (m).

What is the difference between distance and displacement?

Displacement is a vector relationship which describes the net change of an objects position and *depends only on the initial and final positions of the object*, not on the path taken between them - i.e. the space between P and Q in Figure 54.1 below.

On the other hand, distance is a scalar relationship that takes into account the sum of position changes. In Figure 54.1 below, the distance travelled is equal to the sum of the length of the individual segments PA, AB, BC, CD, and DQ.

Suppose the object went around in a circle and returned to its initial position. In this case, the *net displacement* is zero, whereas the total distance travelled is not.

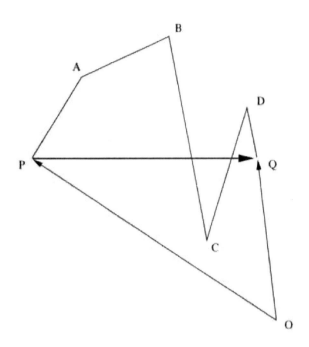

Figure 54.1: Distance and displacement: an object initially at point P moves along the path ABCD to O. The position vectors of points P and Q are shown with respect to the origin O, as is the displacement vector $\vec{PQ}$.

What is speed?

Speed is the *rate at which the distance is changing*, and has the SI unit of meter/second (m/s). In other words, "speed" allows us to describe how rapidly or slowly distance is changing.

What are the first two derivatives of distance and time?

Velocity and acceleration are in fact the first and second derivatives of distance with respect to time. Therefore, the rate of change of distance is speed (m/s) and the rate of change of speed is acceleration (m/s^2).

$$\frac{\Delta \, Distance}{\Delta \, Time} = Speed = \frac{m}{s} \tag{54.1}$$

$$\frac{\Delta \, Velocity}{\Delta \, Time} = Acceleration = \frac{m/s}{s} = \frac{m}{s^2} \tag{54.2}$$

How do you calculate average velocity?

Average velocity $(\bar{v})$is defined as the total distance travelled by total time taken:

$$\bar{v} = \frac{x_2 - x_1}{t_2 - t_1} = \frac{\Delta x}{\Delta t} \qquad (54.3)$$

When average acceleration is **constant**, the average velocity is also given by:

$$\bar{v} = \frac{v_o + v}{2} = \frac{v_i + v_f}{2} \qquad (54.4)$$

Average velocity ($\bar{v}$) is the total displacement over the total time, e.g. the average speed for an entire road trip (Equation 54.3). Equation 54.4 is another approach to calculating average velocity provided that acceleration is held constant (v_o is the velocity at the beginning and v is the velocity at the end).

How do you calculate instantaneous velocity?

$$v = \lim_{\Delta t \to \infty} \frac{\Delta x}{\Delta t} \qquad (54.5)$$

Instantaneous velocity (v) is average velocity over an infinitesimally small time interval, e.g. the actual speed you see on your speedometer when you are on the highway (*Note the difference in notation between average velocity ($\bar{v}$) and instantaneous velocity (v)*).

What is the difference between instantaneous and average speed?

Instantaneous speed is the rate of change of distance with time and is equivalent to the first derivative of distance with respect to time:

$$v = \frac{dx}{dt} \qquad (54.6)$$

The average speed is defined as the total distance traveled divided by the total time taken to travel the distance:

$$v_{avg} = \frac{v_{final} + v_{initial}}{2} = \frac{x_{final} - x_{initial}}{t_{final} - t_{initial}} = \frac{\Delta x}{\Delta t} \qquad (54.7)$$

When does the instantaneous speed equal average speed?

Only when speed does not change with time.

At constant acceleration, what three equations describe how velocity is related to acceleration and time?

$$v = v_o + at \tag{54.8}$$

$$x = x_0 + v_o t + \frac{1}{2}at^2 \tag{54.9}$$

$$v^2 - v_o^2 = 2a(x - x_o) \tag{54.10}$$

Where v_o is the velocity at the beginning and v is the velocity at the end.

What is the difference between speed and velocity?

Speed is the rate of change of distance and velocity is the rate of change of displacement. Both these quantities have the same SI unit (meter/second), but the latter is a vector quantity, because it is the time derivative of a vector quantity (displacement).

54.1   Projectile motion

The motion of a projectile through the air under the influence of gravity is an example of motion in two dimensions with constant acceleration.

The fundamental concept to understand is that the x-component of projectile motion remains unaffected[1], while the y-component changes linearly with time due to gravity. Therefore gravity acts **only** on the y-component of the velocity. We can therefore treat the x- and y-components of the velocity separately.

Suppose a projectile is released into the air at an angle θ with the horizontal, and an initial velocity of zero ($\vec{v}(0) = (v_x(0), v_y(0))$). If the y-axis is taken to be pointing upward, then the acceleration vector ($\vec{g}$) points towards the Earth and is equal to $-g$. Using equation 54.8 for $v_x(t)$ and $v_y(t)$, the components of the velocity at time t,

$$v_x(t) = v_x(0) \quad \text{(because } a_x = 0) \tag{54.11}$$

$$v_y(t) = v_y(0) - gt \quad \text{(because } a_y = -g) \tag{54.12}$$

Similarly, we can use equation 54.9 to get the components of the displacement at time t:

---

[1]Assuming the absence of air resistance.

$$x(t) = x(0) + v_x(0)t \qquad (54.13)$$

$$y(t) = y(0) + v_y(0)t - \frac{1}{2}gt^2 \qquad (54.14)$$

What is Galileo's hypothesis regarding free-falling objects?

Law 4 *At a given location on Earth, and in the absence of air resistance, all objects fall with the same constant acceleration provided the height it falls through is very small compared to the size/radius of the Earth.*

Clearly, the "constant acceleration" that Galileo referred to is the acceleration due to gravity, g, which equals $10 \ m/s^2$ *(Note: for MCAT purposes, make your life easier by rounding 9.80 m/s^2 to 10 m/s^2).*

How can distance, time and acceleration be related in regards to free fall calculations?

$$y = \frac{1}{2}at^2 \qquad (54.15)$$

54.2 Questions

1. A projectile is released from the ground with an initial speed 5 m/s at an angle 30° to the horizontal. How long does it take to hit the ground again?

   Answer: The projectile's initial and final y-positions are the same. Let us choose our coordinates such that the origin is at the initial point, so that $x(0) = y(0) = 0$. If the initial speed is 5 m/s and the angle is 30°, we have:

   $$v_y(0) = v_0 \sin\theta = 5\sin(30°) = 5/\sqrt{3} \ \text{m/s} \qquad (54.16)$$

   Also, since it hits the ground again, $y(t) = 0$. From the information given, it is clear that we have to use equation 54.14:

   $$0 = 0 + \frac{5}{\sqrt{3}}t - \frac{1}{2} \times 10 \times t^2 \qquad (54.17)$$

   Solving this for t gives $t = \frac{1}{\sqrt{3}}$ s.

Chapter 55

Force & Motion

55.1 Newton's Laws of Motion

What is Newton's first law of motion?

Law 5 *If no net force acts on an object, it does not accelerate.*

This profound law has its roots in Aristotelian and Galilean work and explains why objects begin to move, stay in motion or remain at rest.

How does Newton's first law of motion relate to inertia?

Intimately: Inertia is the tendency for a body to maintain its current state of motion (or lack thereof) and Newton's first law is also referred to as the *Law of inertia.*

What is Newton's second law of motion?

Law 6 *If a known net force is applied on an object, the acceleration is known.*

In Newton's second law of motion, F is the force in Newtons (N), m is the mass in kilograms (kg) and a is the acceleration in m/s^2:

$$\Sigma F = ma \tag{55.1}$$

Assuming the force applied and the mass of the object is constant, then the acceleration of the object is directly proportional to the force applied (e.g. twice the force results in twice the acceleration) and inversely proportional to the mass of the object (e.g. twice the mass results in half the acceleration).

Based on Newton's second law of motion what is a *force*?

An action capable of accelerating an object. This can take the form of changing or direction of an objects velocity.

What is Newton's third law of motion?

Law 7 *If, in spite of the application of a known force, a body does not accelerate, there must be an equal and opposite second force that balances the forces to result in a net force equal to zero.*

$$F_{A \to B} = -F_{B \to A} \qquad (55.2)$$

Or, for every action, there is an equal and opposite reaction as seen in Equation 55.2 above.

What is the day-to-day application of Newton's third law of motion?

Newton's third laws explains why motion occurs. For example, if you are in a dingy next to a dock; when you push against the dock with a certain force, the dock exerts an equal force on to you and the dingy. Because the force you applied is on to a massive dock that has been secured with many pilings, its movement is imperceivable (albeit still occurs). You, on the other hand, are in a dingy floating on a relatively frictionless surface and your movement will be pretty apparent.

55.2   Weight

What is weight?

The special name given to the gravitational force exerted (by the earth, for example) on an object of mass m acted on by the acceleration of gravity, g:

$$F_{gravity} = mg \qquad (55.3)$$

What is F_N?

The force that opposes the downward force of an object. In other words, if an object exerts a force on a second object, but produces zero acceleration, it means the second object is exerting an equal and opposite force on the first object. This equal and opposite reaction force is called the *normal reaction* and is usually represented by F_N, $\vec{N}$ or simply N.

What is the relationship between F_N and F_G?

Equal in magnitude, opposite in direction and acting on the same object, e.g. a piece of chalk placed on a table.

55.3   Friction: Kinetic and Static

What is kinetic and static friction?

Kinetic friction is the force that a surface applies to an overlying, *moving* object in a direction to the applied force/motion.

Static friction is the force that a surface applies to an overlying, *non-moving* object and must be overcome to move the object.

The magnitude of kinetic friction is relatively constant and the magnitude of static friction is variable. For example, if you want to pull an airplane with a rope, before you pull, the static force is zero. As you increase the applied force, the force of static friction increases, keeping the net force zero and the plane immobile. It can not, however, match the applied force beyond a critical (maximum) value. Once the applied force exceeds this value, the airplane starts to feel a non-zero force and moves. Once the plane begins to move, kinetic friction takes over. Commonly, the force to keep an object moving - especially a heavy one - is less than the force to move it in the first place.

How are kinetic and static friction calculated?

First off, the relationship between the force of friction (F_{fr}) is based on the characteristics of the two objects that are in contact with each other. Further, the F_{fr} is perpendicular to the F_N and can be calculated using a predetermined coefficient (μ) which is always less than 1:

$$\text{Kinetic friction} \qquad F_{fr} = (\mu_{kinetic})\,(F_N)$$
$$\text{Static friction (max. value)} \quad F_{fr} = (\mu_{static})\,(F_N)$$

Table 55.1: Kinetic and Static Friction.

Note: $F_{Kinetic\ fr.}$ is usually less than $F_{Static\ fr.}$ (i.e. $\mu_{kinetic} < \mu_{static}$)and μ is directly related to the amount of friction between the two objects, i.e. the more friction, the higher the μ, the higher the F_{fr} and the more closely it resembles F_N.

55.4   Motion on an inclined plane.

Label the forces involved in an inclined plane:

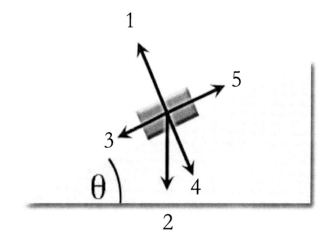

Figure 55.1: The Inclined Plane: (1) F_N, (2) F_G, i.e. weight, (3) F_{G_X}, i.e. $W_\parallel$ - the component parallel to the surface of the inclined plane of the weight, (4) F_{G_Y}, i.e. $W_\perp$ - the component perpendicular to the surface of the inclined plane of the weight (5) F_{fr}, (θ) The critical angle of the incline which may also be represented as θ_c.

There are three forces or vectors acting on a block on an inclined plane:

Weight (W or $\vec{W}$)	The weight of the block always acts in the vertical direction and points towards the Earth ("down") depicted as 2 above with its individual components 3 and 4.
Friction (F_{fr} or $\vec{F}_{fr}$)	The contact betwen the inclined plane and the block results in a force which opposes relative motion. That is, points in a direction opposite to the direction of motion of the block.
Normal reaction (F_N or $\vec{N}$)	If the block's weight were the only force (at rest), then the block would "fall through" the inclined plane. The force that prevents this is the normal reaction, so called because it always acts perpendicular to the surface.

Table 55.2: Three key forces or vectors of the inclined plane.

What is the relationship between the angle of inclination of the inclined plane and force calculations?

$$F_N = mg \cos \theta$$

$$F_{Gx} = mg \sin \theta$$
$$F_{Gy} = -mg \cos \theta$$

$$F_{fr} = (\mu_{kinetic})(F_N)$$

$$\mu_{kinetic} = \frac{mg \sin \theta_c}{mg \cos \theta_c} = \tan \theta_c$$

Table 55.3: Inclined Plane: Relationship between angle of inclination and force calculations.

55.5   Solving an incline plane problem

Solving an incline plane problem involves separating the three forces - $\vec{W}$, $\vec{F_{fr}}$ and $\vec{N}$ - into components $\parallel$ and $\perp$ to the surface of the plane *instead* of $\parallel$ and $\perp$ to the ground:

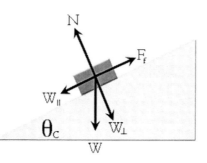

Figure 55.2: The inclined plane: components of the forces.

We immediately see that:

- The normal reaction, N, is balanced by the $\perp$ component of the weight:

$$N = W_\perp \tag{55.4}$$

- Any motion $\parallel$ to the plane is due to the imbalance between $W_\parallel$ and F_f. Once again, we usually expect a block to slide down a plane. This will occur if gravity is the only force other than N and F_f such that the acceleration, a, (and net force) along the plane is given from Newton's second law:

$$ma = W_\parallel - F_f \tag{55.5}$$

We can also see that:

$$F_f = \mu N = \mu W_\perp \tag{55.6}$$

Therefore, we can put equations 55.5 and 55.6 together to get:

$$ma = W_\parallel - \mu W_\perp \tag{55.7}$$

- Another important aspect of inclined planes is using the correct angle because this affects the calculation of the components of W:

  Finally for completion sake, if we use the standard convention for θ to determine the individual components of W, i.e. left half of Figure 55.3 where $W_\perp = W\cos\theta$ and $W_\parallel = W\sin\theta$. and replace appropriate variables in Equation 55.7, we get:

$$W_\perp = W\cos\theta \qquad W_\| = W\sin\theta \qquad\qquad W_\perp = W\sin\theta \qquad W_\| = W\cos\theta \quad (55.8)$$

Figure 55.3: Using the correct angle is of paramount importance. The inclined plane to the left reflects $W_\perp = W\cos\theta$ and $W_\| = W\sin\theta$ and is the most common depiction seen in probelms. The inclined plane to the right may be used to trick you during exams and the actual angle of the inclined plane is actually $90° - \theta$. Therefore, $W_\perp = W\sin\theta$ and $W_\| = W\cos\theta$ (right).

$$ma = W(\sin\theta - \mu\cos\theta) \qquad\qquad (55.9)$$

In the end though, it is better to remember the more general form seen in Equation 55.7 where by the following conclusion can be made:

Principle 2 *If gravity is the only external force on the system, the acceleration down an inclined plane is proportional to the parallel component of the weight minus μ times the perpendicular component.*

Chapter 56

Gravitation

56.1   Uniform Circular Motion

What is uniform circular motion?

When an object moves in a circular pattern with a constant speed (v). Additionally, although v is constant, its direction changes continuously.

Does acceleration change in uniform circular motion?

Yes. Because acceleration, a, is defined as the rate of change of the velocity vector, a changes constantly in uniform circular motion. In fact, a uniformly circularly moving object is accelerating constantly towards the center, i.e. *centripetal acceleration* or *radial acceleration*.

How can centripetal acceleration (a_C) be calculated?

$$a_C = \frac{v^2}{r} \tag{56.1}$$

Again, the vector of acceleration is towards the center of the orbit. If you had a bird's eye vantage point of an orbiting object, this would make sense: The spinning object is always coming around 'back' towards its axis of rotation.

What force keeps a rotating object moving about a fixed axis?

Centripetal force, an application of Newton's second law of motion (see page 385 for a review of Newton's second law):

$$\Sigma F_R = ma_R = m\frac{v^2}{r} \qquad (56.2)$$

What counters centripetal force?

For an object tied to a string spinning around a center point, the tension in the string provides the centripetal force.

What trajectory does a spinning object follow if released?

The velocity vector, i.e. a direction tangential to the orbit: Think of a softball pitcher and the direction the softball travels once the ball is released. In other words, in circular motion, the velocity vector, $\vec{v}$, is always $\perp$ to the acceleration vector, $\vec{a}$.

56.2   Newton's Law of Gravitation

What is a Newton's law of universal gravitation?

Law 8 *Every particle in the universe attracts every other particle with a force that is proportional to the product of their masses and inversely proportional to the square of the distances between them. This force acts along a straight line joining the two particles.*

In Newton's law of universal gravitation, F is the force in Newtons (N), G is the universal gravitation constant $(N \cdot m^2/kg^2)$, m_1 and m_2 are the masses of the two objects in kilograms (kg), and r^2 is the distance between the two objects in meters (m):

$$F = G\frac{m_1 m_2}{r^2} \qquad (56.3)$$

Chapter 57

Equilibrium of Forces

57.1   Translational Equilibrium

What is the center of mass (CM)?

Because it is difficult to follow the motion of a system of particles, it is convenient to replace these many particles with a single "equivalent" point mass that is subjected to the same motion, forces, etc. This unique point, (CM, on an object will move along a certain path whether simply moving in a fixed orientation (translational motion) or also rotating (translation plus rotational motion).

What is the center of gravity (CG)?

Very similar to CM, CG is the unique point on an object that gravity is considered to act upon.

What is translational motion equilibrium?

Translational motion in which the vector sum of the forces acting on an object equals zero ($\Sigma \vec{F} = 0$) and therefore the object is not accelerating.

57.2   Rotational Equilibrium

What is rotational motion equilibrium?

Rotational motion in which the vector sum of the torques acting on an object equals zero ($\Sigma \vec{\tau_{net}} = 0$) and therefore the object is not rotating, or, at least rotating at a constant speed.

57.2.1   Torque

What is torque (τ)?

Anything that causes rotational acceleration around a pivot point is a torque. For example, the torque you apply on a crowbar to loosen a lug nut when changing a tire. As opposed to force which causes translational acceleration, e.g. a cart rolling down an inclined plane.

How do you calculate the magnitude of torque?

$$\vec{\tau} = \vec{r} \times \vec{F} \tag{57.1}$$

Where τ is the torque in Newton-meters (N·m), r is the length of the lever in meters (m), and F is the force applied to the lever in Newtons (N).

Based on this, one can appreciate that torque is directly proportional to the perpendicular distance from the axis of rotation, i.e. it is easier to close a door by pushing on the door knob instead of one inch away from the hinge.

57.3   Weightlessness

What is weightlessness?

Whenever gravity is the *only* force acting on a body. Usually, the ground opposes our free fall and "pushes" us upward, i.e. normal force, F_N. But in a satellite in a geosynchronous orbit, the satellite is continually falling towards earth but 'just missing it' or Michael Jordan's famous 1988 Slam Dunk title where he lifts off from the free-throw line and experiences a split second of weightlessness.

Chapter 58

Linear Momentum

58.1 General

What is linear momentum?

Momentum (p) is the product of an object's mass and velocity:

$$\vec{p} = m\vec{v} \tag{58.1}$$

Where p is momentum in kilogram-meters per second (kg· m/s), m is the mass of the object in kilograms (kg), and v is the velocity in meters per second (m/s).

What is Newton's second law in terms of momentum?

$$\Sigma F = ma = m\,\frac{\Delta v}{\Delta t} = \frac{m\,(v - v_o)}{\Delta t} = \frac{mv - mv_o}{\Delta t} = \frac{\Delta p}{\Delta t} \tag{58.2}$$

$$\vec{F} = \frac{\vec{p}}{t} \tag{58.3}$$

Therefore, an applied force is equal in magnitude and direction to the rate of change of momentum it causes.

What is the law of conservation of momentum?

Law 9 *In the absence of external forces, the total momentum*

This is an application of the conservation of energy and explains why the momenta before and after a collision are equal. That is not to say that the momentum for each object can not change, but the overall total momentum will be conserved before and after the collision.

58.2   Impulse

What is impulse?

Impulse (Δp) is the total change in momentum due to an external force acting over a certain time duration:

$$Impulse \ = F\Delta t = \Delta p \tag{58.4}$$

Where F is the force in Newtons (N), Δt is the duration of time during which the force acts in seconds (s) and Δp is the change in momentum which occurs in newton-seconds. *Note: F and Δt are inversely related for a given impulse. Also, a no-brainer, but don't forget that $F = ma$ where m is the mass in kilograms (kg) and a is the acceleration in m/s^2.)*

A real-world example is car airbags: Airbags increase the Δt of the impact and thereby decrease the magnitude of the force transmitted to the vehicle occupant.

58.3   Elastic and Inelastic Collisions

What elastic and inelastic collisions?

An **elastic collision** is one in which *kinetic energy is conserved* and is usually seen on a *microscopic, sub-atomic scale*. For example, if two objects A and B collide then the kinetic energy will be conserved (Equation 58.5) as well as the momentum [1] (Equation 58.6):

$$\underbrace{\frac{1}{2}m_A v_A^2 \ + \ \frac{1}{2}m_B v_B^2}_{Before\ collision} = \underbrace{\frac{1}{2}m_A v_A^2 \ + \ \frac{1}{2}m_B v_B^2}_{After\ collision} \tag{58.5}$$

$$\underbrace{m_A v_A \ + \ m_B v_B}_{Before\ collision} = \underbrace{m_A v_A \ + \ m_B v_B}_{After\ collision} \tag{58.6}$$

An **inelastic collision** is one in which *kinetic energy is **not** conserved* and is more often seen on a *macroscopic scale*, e.g. a ballistic test in which a bullet is fired into a tank of water. Energy can be released or added in inelastic collisions and can take a variety of forms, e.g. chemical, thermal, etc.

---

[1] This is assuming that there are no external forces acting on the system and the mutual forces acting during the collisions last for a very short duration so that impulse ≈ 0.

*Note: Although kinetic energy is not conserved, total energy **is** conserved.*

When presented with a problem that deals with an inelastic collision, a common objective will be to calculate the amount of energy that was "lost." To do this, calculate the total kinetic energy before the collision and subtract it from the total kinetic energy after the collision - the difference is the energy that was "lost" inelastically:

$$\underbrace{(\frac{1}{2}m_A v_A^2 \; + \; \frac{1}{2}m_B v_B^2)}_{Total \; KE \; Before} - \underbrace{(\frac{1}{2}m_A v_A^2 \; + \; \frac{1}{2}m_B v_B^2)}_{Total \; KE \; After} = Energy \; lost \; inelastically$$

$$(58.7)$$

.

Chapter 59

Work

59.1 Work

What is work?

Definition 1 *Work, W, is said to be done **by** a force **on** an object if the force displaces the object. The magnitude of the work done W is given by:*

$$W = \vec{F} \cdot \vec{d} = F d_{\parallel} \tag{59.1}$$

Where $d_{\parallel}$ is the component of the displacement vector parallel to $\vec{F}$. When $\vec{F}$ is not parallel to the displcement and seen in Figure 59.1, then Equation 59.2 seen below is used:

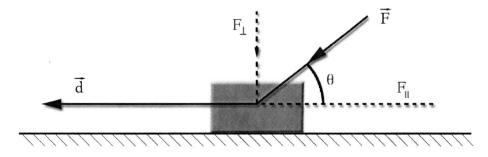

Figure 59.1: Work and its component vectors.

$$W = \vec{F} \cdot \vec{d} = F d_{\parallel} = F d \cos\theta \tag{59.2}$$

What are the units of work?

Joules (J), which are Newton-meters (N·m). Therefore in Equations 59.4 and 59.2 above, W is the work in Newton-meters (N·m), F is the force applied to the object in Newtons (N), d is the displacement of the object in meters (m), and θ is the angle between the applied force and the displacement in degrees (^{o}).

What are the sign conventions for work?

If A does work W on B, then $-W$ is the work done by B in A. Or, another way of seeing this is relationship:

$$Work\ done\ by\ system = -\ Work\ done\ on\ system \qquad (59.3)$$

59.2   Gravity & Work

What determines the work done by gravity?

The vertical height of the incline. *Note: The path up the incline is of little consequence; only the vertical height is important:*

Figure 59.2: Work done by gravity: In the above illustration, all variables are constant except for height - the determinant of work done by gravity as explained by equation 59.4 below.

How is work done by gravity calculated?

$$W = -\vec{F} \cdot \vec{d} = Fd_{\parallel}$$
$$\Downarrow$$
$$W_{Gravity} = -mgh \qquad (59.4)$$

Where W is the work in Newton-meters (N·m), "$-$" is the sign convention, mg is the conversion of F according to Newton's second law with g corresponding to the acceleration due to gravity, and h is the substitution of d (see Figure 59.2).

What is the work done by the earth on the orbiting moon?

Zero. If you draw out the vectors, the force of gravity is perpendicular to the direction of travel (i.e. tangential to the orbit) and no work is done because, by definition, for work to occur, force and displacement must be parallel to each other. See Figure 59.3 below.

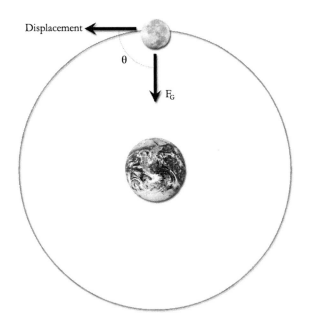

Figure 59.3: Absence of work done by gravity on the orbiting moon because the angle of displacement and the force of gravity (F_G) is equal to zero ($\cos 90° = 0$).

59.3   Kinetic Energy & Work

What is the Work-Energy principle?

Principle 3 *The net work done on an object is equal to the change in its kinetic energy.*

$$W_{Net} = \underbrace{\frac{1}{2}mv^2}_{After} - \underbrace{\frac{1}{2}mv^2}_{Before} = \Delta KE \qquad (59.5)$$

Therefore, if the kinetic energy of an object is greater after than before, then
W was added to the system. Conversely, if the kinetic energy of an object is
less after than before, then W was removed from the system.

59.4   Mechanical Advantage

What is mechanical advantage?

Definition 2 *The factor by which a machine multiplies the force put into it.*

In Figure 59.4 below, you can see a beam in equilibrium on a fulcrum:

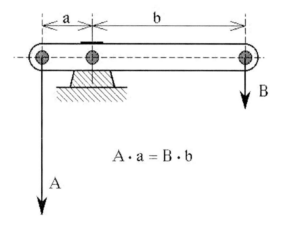

Figure 59.4: Mechanical advantage seen in a beam in equilibrium. This is due to the
momentum $A \cdot a$ created by $\vec{A}$ being in equilibrium with momentum $B \cdot b$ created by
$\vec{B}$. The ratio of the forces $A : B$ is equal to the ratio of the distances to the fulcrum
$b : a$. This ratio is called the mechanical advantage.

What are pulleys?

A pulley is a wheel with a groove along its edge capable of holding a rope or
cable with certain similar features:

- Pulleys are to reduce the amount of force needed to lift a load.

- With or without a pulley, the same amount of work is still necessary to
  move the load

- Pulleys reduce the magnitude of the force needed but in return it must
  act through a longer distance.

- The effort needed to pull a load up is roughly the weight of the load divided by the number of wheels.

- The more wheels there are, the less efficient a system is, because of increased mechanical friction

What are three common types of pulleys?

1. A fixed pulley has and axle which is fixed or anchored in place. A fixed pulley is used to redirect the force in a rope and has a mechanical advantage of 1.

2. A movable pulley has an axle which is free to move in space. A movable pulley is used to transform forces and has a mechanical advantage of 2. For example, if one end of the rope is anchored, pulling on the other end of the rope will apply a doubled force to the object attached to the pulley.

3. A compound pulley is a combination fixed and movable pulley system.

See Figure 59.6 on page 406 for illustrations of various pulleys.

How is mechanical advantage calculated for an inclined plane?

By dividing the length of a slope by the height of slope.

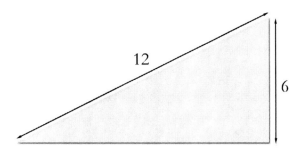

Figure 59.5: In this inclined plane, the mechanical advantage corresponds to 2 (length of slope, 12, divided by height, 6). Invariably, the higher the height for a given slope, the less the mechanical advantage.

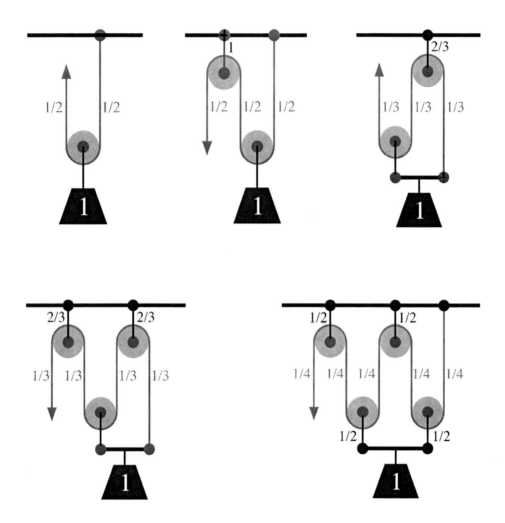

Figure 59.6: Pulleys: *Top, left:* Single movable pulley lifting a unit weight with the tension in each line half the unit weight (advantage = 2). *Top, middle:* A simple pulley system similar to the one on the left in which the lifting force is redirected downward (advantage = 2). *Top, right:* A simple compound pulley system in which the tension in each line is one third the unit weight (advantage = 3). *Bottom, left:* A simple compound pulley system with an additional pulley redirecting the lifting force downward yielding tension in each line one third the unit weight (advantage = 3). *Bottom, right:* A compound pulley system with an additional pulley redirecting the lifting force. Here the tension in each line is one quarter of the unit weight (advantage = 4). *Public domain image obtained from www.wikipedia.org .*

Chapter 60

Energy

What is energy?

Although not easily definable, energy will be regarded as the ability to do work: mechanical energy has two forms: (1) kinetic energy, and (2) potential energy.

60.1 Kinetic Energy

What are the units of kinetic energy?

Joules (J), which are Newton-meters (N·m) or, in the case of the kinetic energy formula below, Joules are also equivalent to kg·m^2/s^2.

How is kinetic energy calculated?

A no-brainer at this point:

$$KE = \frac{1}{2}mv^2 \qquad (60.1)$$

60.2 Potential Energy

What is potential energy?

Depending on the mechanism of energy involved, potential energy is energy stored in a system that can be used to do work.

How are gravitational and spring potential energies calculated?

- Gravity

$$PE_{Gravity} = mgh \tag{60.2}$$

- Spring

$$PE_{Spring} = \frac{1}{2}kx^2 \tag{60.3}$$

Where k is a proportionality constant which appears from Hooke's law (see page 438), and x is the displacement from equilibrium in meters.

60.3   Conservation of Mechanical Energy

What is the principle of the conservation of mechanical energy?

Principle 4 *The total mechanical energy of a system is conserved if :*

$$\underbrace{KE + PE}_{Before} = \underbrace{KE + PE}_{After} \tag{60.4}$$

If this is violated, than a non-conservative force is present, e.g. friction.

Chapter 61

Fluids & Solids

61.1   Fluids

What is the difference between density and specific gravity?

Density (ρ) is the mass per unit volume of a given substance:

$$\rho = \frac{m}{V} \tag{61.1}$$

Specific gravity (SG) is the density of substance with respect to the density of water at the *same* temperature and pressure:

$$SG = \frac{\rho_{Substance}}{\rho_{Water}} \tag{61.2}$$

At standard temperature and pressure, $\rho_{Water} \approx 1.0 \ g/cm^3$ or $1000 \ kg/m^3$. Because SG is a ratio, it is dimensionless and has no units. For example, the density of blood is $\approx 1.035 \ g/cm^3$, therefore:

$$SG_{Blood} = \frac{1.035 \ g/cm^3}{1.0 \ g/cm^3} = 1.035$$

Thus, making blood thicker than water.

What is pressure?

A force. F, exerted perpendicularly on a surface of area A. In water, the *Pascal (Pa)* is commonly used:

$$P = \frac{F}{A} \tag{61.3}$$

Where P is the pressure in Pascals (1 Pa = 1 N/m^2), F is the force applied to the object in Newtons (N) and A is the object's surface area in meters squared (m^2).

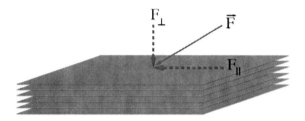

Figure 61.1: Force vector on water: Each component of this force vector will result in pressure ($F_\perp$) and a shear effect ($F_\parallel$).

In the context of fluids, imagine a "layered" fluid as illustrated above in Figure 61.1. If a force $\vec{F}$ is exerted on a layer at an angle to it, two immediate observations can be made:

1. The perpendicular component of this force, $F_\perp$, causes the layers to be "squashed" together. $F_\perp$ divided by the area A of the layer over which the force is distributed is called pressure.

2. The parallel component of this force, $F_\parallel$, causes the layers to move *horizontally* with respect to each other. This type of force is called shear force and causes the fluid to flow. Ideal fluids offer no resistance to a shear force and flow freely. Real fluids do resist flow by exerting an opposing force similar to friction called viscosity. See below for a more depth discussion on flow.

61.1.1   Hydrostatics

What is hydrostatics?

The study of fluids at rest.

What is Pascal's Principle?

Principle 5 *Pressure applied to small region in a confined fluid increases the pressure throughout the fluid by the same amount.*

Pascal's Principle helps us understand that fluids exert pressure in all directions - when an imbalance in this occurs, movement in the fluid occurs.

How do you calculate the pressure of a liquid with density ρ at varying depths?

$$P = \rho g h \tag{61.4}$$

The excess pressure observed at increasing depths due to the fact that for a given depth within a column of fluid, the overlying fluid contributes to the pressure exerted at the surface.

61.1.2   Buoyancy & Archimedes' Principle

What is buoyancy?

The upward force generated by a fluid to counter the downward force (weight) of a body immersed in it. The magnitude of this force is given by Archimedes' principle:

Principle 6 *A body immersed in a fluid is buoyed up by a force equal to the weight of the displaced fluid.*

Therefore, if V is the volume of the submerged body, then V is also the volume of the displaced fluid. The mass of this amount of fluid is its density ρ_f times V. In sum the bouyant force, F_B, is equal to:

$$F_B = \rho_f g V \qquad (61.5)$$

61.1.3   Viscosity & Poiseuille Flow.

What are the general types of flow?

Laminar, i.e. Poiseuille flow, and turbulent flow. Velocity, radius of the vessel, presence of obstructions, and viscosity all contribute to how a fluid flows.

What is viscosity?

A frictional force that exists between "layers" of a fluid. The viscous force is directly related to a quantity called the *coefficient of viscosity* denoted by η. η has units Pascal - second ($Pa \cdot s$). For example at room temperature, the viscosity of water is $1.0 \ x \ 10^{-3}\eta$ while the viscosity of glycerine is $1500 \ x \ 10^{-3}\eta$ - 1500 more dense than water.

What are four characteristics of laminar flow (Poiseuille Flow)?

1. Flow is directly proportional to the fourth power of the radius of the tube, e.g. if the radius increases by a factor of two, the flow increases by a factor of 2^4 or 16-fold.

2. Flow is directly proportional to the pressure difference existing between the beginning and end of a tube.

3. Flow is inversely proportional to the viscosity of the fluid.

4. Flow is inversely proportional to the length of the tube.

Where in a vessel is flow the fastest and the slowest?

Flow is fastest in the center of a vessel and slowest at the sides. Kind of like a stream or river, the water flows by much slower at the banks than in the middle.

What is the equation of continuity?

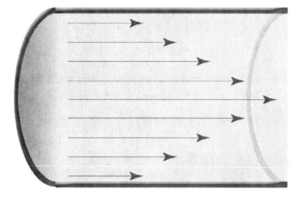

Figure 61.2: Flow in a vessel: Longer vectors (arrows) represent faster flow/velocity vectors, while shorter arrows represent slower flow/velocity vectors.

$$A_1 v_1 = A_2 v_2 \qquad\qquad (61.6)$$

Where A is the area of the vessel and v is the velocity of flow; provided that ρ is held constant. The equation of continuity arises from conservation of mass in any flow. Simply stated, what goes in one end, must all come out the other end provided there are no sources (or sinks) within the tube as can be seen in Figure 61.3 below:

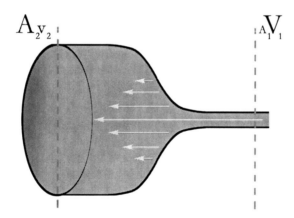

Figure 61.3: Conservation of mass during flow: Flow enters the system at a high velocity and through a small surface area (right) and leaves at a low velocity through a larger surface area (left). Note that longer vectors (arrows) represent faster flow/velocity vectors, while shorter vectors represent slower flow/velocity vectors.

61.1.4   Bernoulli's Principle.

What is Bernoulli's Principle?

This principle arises from the equation of continuity:

Principle 7 *In fluid flow, an increase in velocity occurs simultaneously with a decrease in pressure.*

The utility of Bernoulli's Principle is seen in many real-world examples, including the generation of lift by a wing and the ability of a sailboat to move forward against the wind (see Figure 61.4 on page 415).

61.1.5   Surface Tension & Capillary Action.

What is surface tension?

Surface tension results from the attractive forces of a fluid and is the interesting ability of a fluid at rest to have a "membrane" that can support weight.

What is capillary action?

The phenomenon by which fluid rises in a small-diameter tube, and which results from the adhesive/cohesive forces between the liquid/capillary tube.

61.2   Solids

61.2.1   Elasticity

What is elasticity?

Elasticity is the property of a material to preserve its original configuration after a configuration-altering external force has been removed. For small forces less than the elastic limit, the material regains its original shape. Beyond the limit, the material becomes "plastic" and is unable to return to the initial state. If the external force is increased further, a breaking point is eventually met.

Elasticity is the elongation of an object by a given force. Until the elongation reaches a particular point (*the elastic limit*), the object will reach a certain point. After which, *plasticity* is seen whereby the object does not return to its original form. Eventually, if elongation continues, a *breaking point* is met.

What law predicts the length changes seen in the elastic region?

Hooke's Law[1]:

$$F = -kx \tag{61.7}$$

Where F is the force applied to the object, the "$-$" sign convention indicates that the force is opposite to the direction of travel, k is the propotionality constant (unique to each object), and x is the displacement of the object in meters (m).

61.2.2   Shear, Compression & Thermal Expansion

What is shear, compression and thermal expansion?

Shear is a form of stress that an object may be exposed to that causes it to be spread *like butta on toast*. Placing a telephone book on a table and pushing along the binding and deforming the profile of the book into a parallelogram is an example of shear stress.

Compression is a form of stress that is pretty self-explanatory but occurs in objects that support weight such as columns or vertical beams.

Thermal expansion is the elongation of an object when subjected to heat. For a given object, the change in size is correlated to an expansion coefficient specific to a given material. Of note, although the expansion coefficient stays constant, the change in size is more noticeable for a larger object than a smaller object of similar composition.

---

[1]Although the "law" designation is used, it is not entirely appropriate because this is in actuality a *relation*. See page 438 in the Periodic Motion chapter for a review of simple harmonic motion and Hooke's Law).

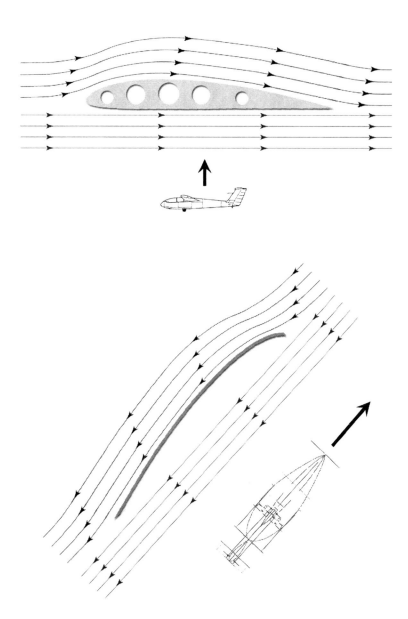

Figure 61.4: Applications of Bernoulli's Principle: Generation of lift by a wing (top) and a sailboat moving forward against the wing (bottom). Air flow over a wing (curved, black arrows) is faster and creates a negative pressure *above* the wing; making the force of lift (F_{Lift}) greater than the force of gravity (F_G) and a resultant upward motion. For the sailboat, wind traveling behind the sail (straight, blue arrows) is slower and creates positive pressure while the wind traveling over the sail (curved, black arrows) is faster and creates a negative pressure. Similar to a wing, this creates the force vector in a forward direction (F_{Wind}). Underneath the sailboat there is vertical extension called a keel which naturally resists the opposing F_{Wind}. Combining the vectors will make the boat move in the forward, diagonal direction (F_{Fwd}).

Chapter 62

Electrostatics

62.1   Electrostatics

What is electrostatics?

The study of forces exerted by unchanging (i.e. static) electric fields upon a charged object.

What is electrostatic induction?

Electrostatic induction occurs when there is a separation of charges in an object with the total charge remaining *zero*, e.g. this is what happens to you with static cling.

What is the charge of an electron?

The electron has a *negative* charge of 1.6×10^{-19} Coulomb. Charge has the SI unit of the Coulomb (C); 1 Coulomb is a very large amount of charge and corresponds to the charge on 6.25×10^{18} electrons.

What is an electrical charge?

An electrical charge, Q, is actually a quantum flavor[1]. Electrical charge obtains its properties from two main charged subatomic particles: electrons and protons which possess negative (-) and positive (+) charges, respectively. Neutrons are neutral subatomic particles which have a Q equal to zero. When an object has a balance of electrons and protons the object is neutrally charged ($Q = 0$), when there are more protons than electrons, the object has a positive Q, when there are more electrons than protons, the object has a negative Q. Moreover, free charges are transmitted by conductors (e.g. copper) and prevented from transmission by insulators (e.g. rubber).

---

[1]There are several quantum flavors including *electric charge (Q)*, *Charm*, *Strangeness*, *Topness*, and *Bottomness* to name a few.

What is the law of conservation of electrical charge?

Law 10 *The net amount of electrical charge produced in any process is zero.*

Like the other laws of conservation we have seen, the same theme persists: electrical charge can neither be created nor destroyed. Instead, electrical charge transfers from one object to another.

What is an electric current?

A flow of charges from one point to another. Moreover, any moving charge can constitute a current.

Since protons, atoms and ions are at least about two thousand times heavier than electrons, electric currents inside most bulk matter consist of flowing electrons (i.e. it is a lot easier to move lighter objects than heavier ones). Atoms that have lost a single electron and protons have the same *magnitude* of charge as an electron. Therefore, we can think of a flow of electrons in a certain direction as a flow of protons (or positively charged ions) in the opposite direction. Just remember that this is just a way to simplify things, and this may not represent the actual physical situation inside macroscopic objects carrying current.

62.2   Coulomb's Law

What is Coulomb's Law?

An expression that quantifies the electrostatic force of attraction (or repulsion) between two *point* charges:

Law 11 *The magnitude of the electrostatic force between two charges Q_1 and Q_2 is directly proportional to the product of the charges and inversely proportional to the square of the distance r between them.*

This force is a vector and its direction is always along the line joining the two charges. $F < 0$ is an attractive force and $F > 0$ is a repulsive force:

$$F = k\frac{Q_1 Q_2}{r^2} \tag{62.1}$$

Where F is the force exerted between the two objects in Newtons (N), k is the electrostatic constant ($k \approx 9.0 \; x \; 10^9 \, N \cdot m^2/C^2$), Q_1 and Q_2 are the charges of each object in Coulombs (C), and r^2 is the square of the distance between the two objects in meters (m).

Since the force F depends on the inverse square of the distance between the charges, Coulomb's Law is an inverse square law, just like Newton's Law of Gravitation (see page 394).

What are point, source and test charges?

A *point charge* is exactly that, it possesses a charge, but no dimensions (it has zero size). A *source charge* is a charge (or set of charges) that influences everything around it through its electrostatic force. A *test charge* is usually a unit positive charge (+1 C) that "feels" the force exerted by the source charge, and it is used to determine the quantitative effect of the source charge.

62.3   Electric Field

What is an electric field?

An electric field, E, is the extension of an object's charge into its surrounding space and is defined as the electric force given by Coulomb's Law per unit charge.

$$E = \frac{k \frac{Q_1 Q_2}{r^2}}{q} = \frac{F}{q} \tag{62.2}$$

Where E is the electric field in Newtons/Coulombs (N/C), F is the force exerted on a test charge in Newtons (N), and q is the magnitude of a test charge in Coulombs (C). This equation allows us to appreciate that the electric field E at a distance r from a source charge Q is equal to the electrostatic force experienced by a unit charge placed a distance r away from Q.

Just like the electrostatic force, the electric field is also a vector and the magnitude has the same direction as that of the electrostatic force between the source and test charge. Another way of understanding this is by the following analogy: electric field is to charge as acceleration is to mass.

What are electric field lines?

At any point in space, the effect of a source charge Q is described by the electric field vector. In order to represent the electric field in a region of space, we draw what are called electric field lines as depicted in Figure 62.1 below. These represent curves along which a positive test charge will move if placed in that region such that:

1. The direction of the electric field at any point on a field line can be found by drawing a tangent at that point.

2. The magnitude of the electric field at any point is directly proportional to the number of field lines per unit area.

3. Since electric fields represent forces on unit positive charges, field lines always start on (and point away from) positive source charges and end on (and point towards) negative source charges.

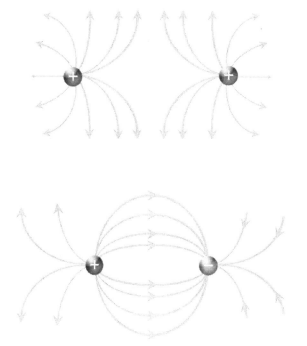

Figure 62.1: Electric field lines in various settings: two positive charges (top) and one positive and one negative charge (bottom).

How is the electric field due to a point charge calculated?

$$E = k\frac{Q}{r^2} \tag{62.3}$$

Where E is the electric field in Newtons/Coulombs (N/C), k is the electrostatic constant ($k \approx 9.0 \ x \ 10^9 N \cdot m^2/C^2$), Q is the charge in Coulombs (C) and r^2 is the square of the distance between the two objects in meters (m).

Note: Equation 62.2 allows you to define an electric field needed for a given process; whereas Equation 62.3 allows you to calculate the magnitude and direction of an electric field at a certain distance from a particular point.

62.4   Electric Potentials

What is an electric potential?

An electric potential is the potential energy that exists across a space that can be measured, and, theoretically, be harnessed to do work. Mathematically, this can be calculated with Equation 62.4 below:

$$V_A = \frac{PE_A}{q} \tag{62.4}$$

Where V is the electric potential in Volts (J/C), PE is the potential energy in Joules (J) and q is the magnitude of the charge in Coulombs (C).

How do you calculate a change in voltage, i.e. work?

$$\underbrace{\frac{PE_B}{q}}_{V_B} - \underbrace{\frac{PE_A}{q}}_{V_A} = \Delta V = Work \tag{62.5}$$

How is the electric potential of a point charge calculated?

$$V = k\frac{Q}{r} \tag{62.6}$$

Where V is the electric potential in Volts (J/C), k is the electrostatic constant ($k \approx 9.0~x~10^9 N \cdot m^2/C^2$), Q is the charge of point charge in Coulombs (C) and r is the square of the distance between the two objects in meters (m).

Because of the inverse relationship of potential with respect to r, the closer the distance, the higher the potential. This is graphically depicted in Figure 62.2 below:

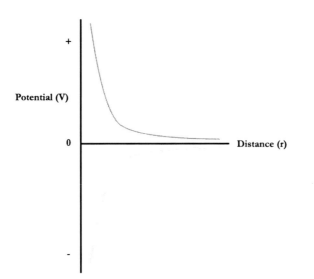

Figure 62.2: The graphical relationship between voltage (V, *y-axis*) and the distance between the potential (r, *x-axis*) for a given charge Q that is positive (top, blue line) or negative (bottom, yellow).

How can the presence of an electric potential be depicted?

Through the use of equipotential lines which are perpendicular to an electric field (see Figure 62.3 below).

62.5   Electric Fields vs. Electric Potentials

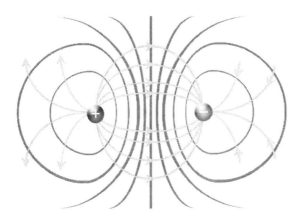

Figure 62.3: Equipotential lines (lines with arrowheads) represent the electrical potential created by an electrical field (lines without arrowheads). *Note: equipotential line are always perpendicular to the electrical field.*

	Electric fields	Electric potentials
Definition	An electric field is the extension of an object's charge into its surrounding space.	An electric potential is the potential energy that exists across a space that can be measured, and, theoretically, be harnessed to do work.
Unit	Coulombs (C)	Volts (V)
General Calculation	$E = \frac{k\frac{Q_1 Q_2}{r^2}}{q} = \frac{F}{q}$	$\frac{PE_B}{q} - \frac{PE_A}{q} = W$
Point charge calculation	$E = k\frac{Q}{r^2}$	$V = k\frac{Q}{r}$

Table 62.1: Electric fields vs. electric potentials.

62.6 Electric Dipole

What is an electric dipole?

An electric dipole occurs when two equal point charges Q are of opposite signs and are separated by a specified distance.

What occurs when an electric dipole encounters an electric field?

A dipole moment is created in which there a separation of charge; creating a polar molecule as seen in hydrogen fluoride in Figure 62.4 below:

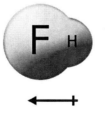

Figure 62.4: Dipole moment and e^- charge distribution in HF.

Chapter 63

Magnetism

Generally speaking, what is a magnetic field?

A magnetic field is the extension of an object's ability to attract iron into its surrounding space and is measured in Tesla (T) or Gauss units $(1G = 10^{-4})$. Much like electric fields, magnetic fields can be depicted using magnetic field lines as seen below in Figure 63.1. As with electric fields, conventions exist for illustrating magnetic field lines: (1) the direction of the magnetic field is tangent to any point on the magnetic field line, (2) the magnitude of the magnetic field is directly related to the number of depicted lines, and (3) lines begin at the north pole and terminate on the south pole of the magnet:

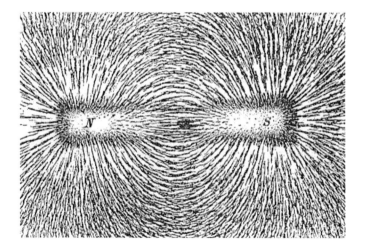

Figure 63.1: Magnet with magnetic field lines. *Public domain image obtained from www.wikipedia.org .*

What is a "B magnetic field"?

A B magnetic field is the formal designation of a magnetic field. Magnetic fields are *vectors* that exhibit a magnitude and direction. Magnetic are the consequence of a source charge moving over a given time frame, e.g. current moving through a copper wire. The relationship between current is intimate: current creates a magentic field but, in turn, a nearby magnetic field can affect a current.

What creates magnetic fields?

Many naturally-occurring substances can but, given the name of this chapter, so can an electric current traveling in a wire. The **right-hand rule** in Figure 63.2 below illustrates how the magnetic field lines travel in relation to the electric current.

What is the direction of the force created by the magnetic field from an electric current?

Principle 8 *The direction of the force is always perpendicular to the direction of the current and also perpendicular to the direction of the magnetic field.*

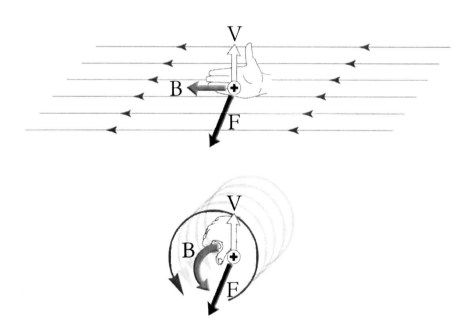

Figure 63.2: Right-hand rule: Top: The thumb points in the direction of the velocity (V), which is often current (*I*); the fingers will point in the direction of the magnetic vector (B) which flows in the *N-S* direction; the outward vector from the palm is the direction of force on a charge (F). Bottom: The modified right hand rule is useful to understand rotating vectors. For this, the thumb points in the direction of the force (F); the fingers will point in the direction of rotating vector and will "curl" into the magnetic vector (B), and the outward vector will come from the dorsum of the hand (V).

What is the force exerted on an electric charge moving in a magnetic field?

$$F = qvB \sin \theta \qquad (63.1)$$

Where F is the force exerted on the electric charge in Newtons (N), q is the charge of the particle in Coulombs (C), v is the velocity of the particle in meters per second (m/s), B is the magnetic field in Tesla (T), and θ is the angle between v and B in degrees (^{o}).

What is Ampère's Law?

The law which allows us to determine the magnetic field around a current-containing wire:

$$\Sigma B_{\parallel} \Delta l = \mu_0 I \qquad (63.2)$$

Where $\Sigma B_{\parallel} \Delta l$ is the total of each magnetic field parallel to the length of the wire, μ_0 is a constant ($\approx 13 \ x \ 10^{-7} T \cdot m/A$) and I is the current in the wire in amperes (A).

Therefore, if the wire is a circle, the sum total of the lengths would be $2\pi r$ and Ampère's law would be:

$$\Sigma B_{\parallel} 2\pi r = \mu_0 I \qquad (63.3)$$

What is a solenoid and how would you apply Ampère's law to derive its magnetic field?

A solenoid is simply a coil of wire. Equation 63.4 below would allow you to calculate the magnetic field:

$$B = \mu_0 n I \qquad (63.4)$$

Where the new term "n" is equal to the number of loops per unit length ($n = N/l$).

Chapter 64

Electric Circuits

64.1 Electric Circuits

What is an electric circuit?

A continuous conducting path between the terminals of a battery to allow the flow of current.

What is the difference between electron flow and conventional current flow?

Electric currents are produced by a flow of electrons, not positive charges - given that electrons have more freedom to move being that they are about two thousand times lighter than protons, atoms and ions. With that said, a flow of electrons in one direction can also be thought of as flow of positive charges in the opposite direction. This current of positive charges is called conventional current.

64.2 Batteries

What is a battery?

A device that stores energy that can be used in an electrical form. Batteries can take many forms, e.g. the common electrochemical battery that runs a radio or a battery which stores energy in an electrostatic form (see capacitors on page 434). The schematic symbol for a battery is seen in Figure 64.1 below:

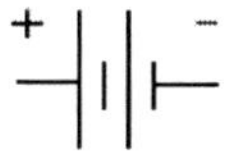

Figure 64.1: Schematic symbol for a battery.

What is electromotive force (*emf*)?

emf is the work done by the battery in bringing a unit positive charge from the negative terminal of the battery to the positive terminal within the battery (as opposed to through the external circuit). You may recall this is the same definition as potential difference (see page 421). As such, we can say that *emf* is the potential difference between the terminals of a battery not connected to an external circuit and has the same units as the potential difference, i.e. Volts. The *emf* of a battery is usually provided by the manufacturer, e.g. a 9V battery.

Note: The term "electromotive force" is misleading because emf is a not a force, it is a potential difference.

64.3   Current (I)

What is an electric current (I)?

The amount of charge that passes though a wire, motor, etc. per unit time. That is, current is the time-derivative of charge similar to the relation between velocity and displacement:

$$I = \frac{\Delta Q}{\Delta t} \qquad\qquad 1\ A = \frac{C}{s} \qquad\qquad (64.1)$$

Where I is the current in amperes (A), and ΔQ is the amount of charge that passes through the conductor in Coulombs (C) for a given time interval Δt in seconds (s).

64.3.1   Direct vs. Alternating Current

What is a direct current (DC)?

A current, I, or voltage, V, which is constant with time (as shown in Figure 431 below).

What is an alternating current (AC)?

A periodically varying current, usually with a known function of time such as a sine, triangle, sawtooth or square wave with an average value over a whole period equal to zero. Therefore, it spends equal amounts of time being positive and negative.

In daily usage, AC refers specifically to sinusoidally alternating current as shown in Figure 64.2 below. The AC current/voltage obtained from power outlets in our homes alternates 50 times per second, i.e. 50 Hertz (Hz).

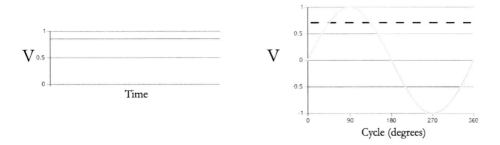

Figure 64.2: Direct current is a continuous current per unit time (left) and alternating current is current that reverses multiple times per second (right).

What is the utility of the root mean square for alternating current and voltage and how is it calculated?

AC voltage as shown above has a mean value of zero. To measure the current or voltage, an alternate way was developed. Because the square of V will always be positive, the issue regarding the mean value of zero is addressed, albeit a V^2 answer. Now, taking the square root of the mean of the square of the voltage will return the value in Volts. This can also be applied for currents as well:

$$V_{rms} = \sqrt{\overline{V^2}} \tag{64.2}$$

$$I_{rms} = \sqrt{\overline{I^2}} \tag{64.3}$$

64.4   Power

What is power?

Power is defined as the rate at which work is done. In other words, it is energy per unit time, and has the units Joule/second. This unit is also called a Watt, W.

A kiloWatt-hour, or kWh, is a unit of energy and not power. KiloWatt-hours are calculated by multiplying 1000 W by an hour (3600 seconds). Converting kWh into Joules:

$$1 \ kWh = (1000 \ J/s)(3600 \ s) = 3.6 \ \times \ 10^6 \ J = 3.6 \ MegaJoules \tag{64.4}$$

How do you calculate the power in a circuit?

$$\bar{P} = I_{rms}^2 R \tag{64.5}$$

$$\bar{P} = \frac{V_{rms}^2}{R} \tag{64.6}$$

64.5 Resistance

What is electrical resistance?

Any material that, while a current flows through it, allows a potential difference to develop across its ends. The physical quantity, resistance, is denoted by the symbol R or r and has the SI unit, Ohm (Ω). Schematically, resistors are represented with the symbol is seen in Figure 64.1 below:

Figure 64.3: Schematic symbol for a resistor.

What is resistivity?

Resistivity (ρ) is a constant which reflects the resistance to electrical conduction by a particular substance. Copper has a very low resistivity (1.59×10^{-8}) and rubber has a very high resistivity ($\sim 10^{14}$). Resitivity (ρ) has units $\Omega \cdot m$ and its relationship to resistance, R, surface are, A, and length, L,is appreciated:

$$\rho = R\frac{A}{L} \tag{64.7}$$

What is Ohm's law?

Law 12 *The potential drop, V, across a resistor is directly proportional to the current, I, through it, and the proportionality constant relating them is the resistance, R.*

$$V = IR \tag{64.8}$$

Where V is the voltage in volts (V), I is the current flowing in the circuit in amperes (A), and R is the resistance in ohms (Ω).

What is the expression for power dissipated across resistors?

$$P = IV \qquad\qquad P = I^2R \qquad\qquad P = \frac{V^2}{R} \tag{64.9}$$

Depending on which of the three quantities (V, I, or R) are known, we can use the corresponding equation for power.

Illustrate resistors in series and in parallel.

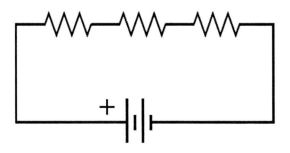

Figure 64.4: Resistors in series.

$$R_{Total} = R_1 + R_3 + R_3 \qquad (64.10)$$

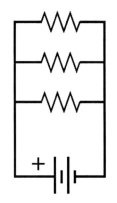

Figure 64.5: Resistors in parallel.

$$\frac{1}{R_{Total}} = \frac{1}{R_1} + \frac{1}{R_3} + \frac{1}{R_3} \qquad (64.11)$$

Note: Remember to invert the answer to get R_{Total}

64.6   Capacitance

What is capacitor?

A capacitor is an electrical device that stores charge Q while developing a potential difference V across parallel plates or terminals, e.g. a camera flash. In comparison, a resistor which allows a current I through it while developing a voltage V across itself. The amount of charge stored is directly proportional to the voltage V, and the constant of proportionality, C, is called the capacitance of the capacitor:

$$Q = VC \quad \Rightarrow \quad C = \frac{Q}{V} \tag{64.12}$$

Where Q is the amount of charge in Coulombs (C), V is the voltage of the circuit, C is the capacitance in Farads (F). The schematic symbol is seen below:

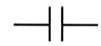

Figure 64.6: Schematic symbol for a capacitor.

What is a dielectric?

A dielectric is an insulating substance that can be put in-between the plates of a capacitor to (1) allow for higher voltages to be applied without allowing a discharge between the plates of a capacitor, (2) allow for "space-savings" and to bring the plates of the capacitor closer together while still preserving the same desired capacitance, and (3) increase the capacitance of the capacitors.

How much energy can a capacitor store?

$$Energy = U = \frac{1}{2}QV = \frac{1}{2}\left(\frac{Q^2}{C}\right) \tag{64.13}$$

Illustrate capacitors in series and in parallel.

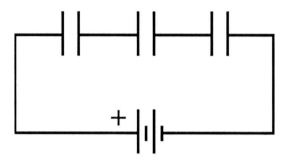

Figure 64.7: Capacitors in series.

$$\frac{1}{C_{Total}} = \frac{1}{C_1} + \frac{1}{C_3} + \frac{1}{C_3} \qquad (64.14)$$

Note: Remember to invert the answer to get C_{Total}

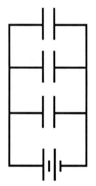

Figure 64.8: Capacitors in parallel.

$$C_{Total} = C_1 + C_3 + C_3 \qquad (64.15)$$

Chapter 65

Periodic Motion & Waves

65.1 Periodic Motion

What is periodic motion?

Motion which repeats itself over a certain fixed interval of time, i. e. the period T. Examples of periodic motion: a regular heartbeat, a swinging pendulum, revolution of the earth around the sun, etc.

What is amplitude, period, frequency and phase?

- **Amplitude** (A): The maximum value achieved during periodic motion. On a graph, the amplitude is the vertical distance between the peak of a wave and its mean position.
- **Period** (T): The time required to complete one wave or cycle.
- **Frequency** (f): The number of complete cycles in one second where 1 cycle per second (s^{-1}) equals 1 Hz:

$$f = \frac{1}{T} \tag{65.1}$$

- **Phase**: The actual position of a body undergoing periodic motion, with respect to a reference position - usually the equilibrium or mean position. If, for example, at time $t = 0$ the object is not at the mean position,it is said to be "out of phase". Phase can be quoted in terms of the time after or before $t = 0$ at which the object returns to (or was at) the reference position, but it is usually written in terms of angles (dimensionless quantities).

Figure 65.1: Comparison of phase among waves: waves are in-phase (left) and waves are out-of-phase (right).

65.2   Elasticity & Hooke's Law

What is elasticity?

The property of materials to oppose external forces that cause change in configuration or shape. Elasticity can also be defined as the property of materials to revert to their original configuration once the external deforming force has been removed. For example, a spring resists changes in length because the elastic force (or restoring force) counteracts the external force. Depending on the magnitude of the external force three situations are generally seen:

1. Elastic region: For very small forces, the object is able to regain its original configuration once the force is removed. This region is therefore called the elastic region. The relationship between the extension and the applied force in this region is given by Hooke's Law (discussed below).

2. Plastic region: Beyond a certain value of the applied force, the object is unable to regain its original shape once the force is removed.

3. Breaking point: As the applied force keeps increasing, the object ultimately reaches a breaking point.

What is Hooke's Law[1]?

Hooke's Law relates the restoring force to the change in length, i.e. extension, caused by an external force. Equivalently, since the restoring force is equal in magnitude to the external force, this law also relates the extension to the amount of force applied:

Law 13 *For small extensions produced in a material is directly proportional to the external force applied to it.*

In other words, the restoring force is directly proportional to the extension:

$$F_{Restoring} = F_{Extension} = \quad kx \tag{65.2}$$

Where F is the force applied to the object, the "−" sign convention indicates that the force is opposite to the direction of travel, k is the propotionality constant (unique to each object), and x is the displacement of the object in meters (m).

What type of motion is seen in an object following Hooke's Law?

Simple harmonic motion (SHM). *Simple harmonic displacement has a sinusoidal function over time* as seen below in Figure 65.2. Objects that exhibit SHM are called simple harmonic oscillators.

---

[1]Although the "law" designation is used, it is not entirely appropriate because this is in actuality a *relation*.

Figure 65.2: Sinusoidal characteristic of simple harmonic motion.

What is the total energy of a simple harmonic oscillator?

$$E = \underbrace{\frac{1}{2}mv^2}_{KE} + \underbrace{\frac{1}{2}kA^2}_{PE} \qquad (65.3)$$

Most of the variables are straightforward except A which is the amplitude and corresponds to the displacement (x) of the spring that was seen in Hooke's Law (Equation 65.2) . Because this equation combines the KE and PE, there will be a point at which each will equal zero and you can calculate the maximum amplitude (when $KE = 0$) or maximum velocity (when $PE = 0$). See Figure 65.3 below:

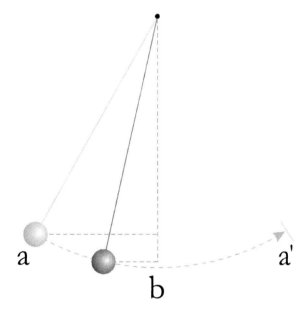

Figure 65.3: Total energy in simple harmonic oscillators: maximum amplitude and potential energy where KE = 0 (a and a') and maximum velocity and kinetic energy where PE = 0 (b).

Random question - what determines the frequency of a pendulum?

The length of the cord attached to the pendulum bob, *not the mass of the bob.*

65.3   Wave motion

What is a wave?

A disturbance that propagates through space, often transferring energy to particles in the region.

What are two types of waves?

1. Transverse waves - a wave that oscillates perpendicular to the direction it advances, e.g. electromagnetic radiation.

2. Longitudinal waves - are waves that oscillate along or parallel to their direction of travel, e.g. sound waves and earthquakes.

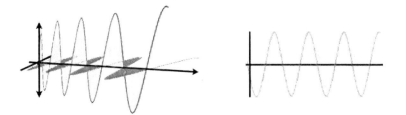

Figure 65.4: Transverse electromagnetic waves (left) with magnetic (yellow), electromagnetic waves (blue) and direction of radiation (arrow head); see Figure 63.2 on page 426 for a review of the right-hand rule. Longitudinal simple harmonic motion waves (right).

Define wavelength, amplitude, period, node, antinode, frequency, velocity and intensity?

- **Wavelength (λ):** The distance between two wave crests (or troughs).

- **Amplitude (A):** The maximum displacement of a particle from its mean position when disturbed by a wave.

- **Node:** A point along the wave that has zero displacement from the mean position.

- **Antinode:** A point along the wave that suffers maximum displacement from the mean position - i.e. its displacement is equal to the amplitude.

- **Period (T):** The time required to complete one wave or cycle.

- **Frequency (f):** The number of complete cycles in one second where 1 cycle per second (s^{-1}) equals 1 Hz:

$$f = \frac{1}{T} \tag{65.4}$$

- **Velocity (v):** The distance travelled by the wavefront per unit time, i.e. umber of waves per period:

$$v = \frac{\lambda}{T} = \lambda f \tag{65.5}$$

- **Intensity** (I): The power transmitted per unit area perpendicular to the direction of wave propagation. The intensity depends on the energy and the wave velocity, and, therefore, also proportional to the square of the amplitude[2]:

$$I = \frac{Power}{Area} \qquad (65.6)$$

Intensity has the SI unit Watt per square meter ($\mathrm{W/m^2}$). Sound intensity is measured on a logarithmic scale. An intensity I in $\mathrm{W/m^2}$ corresponds to a value:

$$I = \log_{10}\left(\frac{I}{I_0}\right) \qquad (65.7)$$

Where I is in Bels, B, units. I_0 here is the threshold of human hearing ($\tilde{1}0^{-12}$ $\mathrm{W/m^2}$). The better-known deciBel (dB) is one-tenth of a Bel. Normal conversation, for example, happens at about 60 dB ($\mathrm{I}{=}10^6 I_0 = 10^{-6}$ $\mathrm{W/m^2}$).

What is the superposition principle?

Principle 9 *If a point undergoes displacements due to more than one wave, the resultant displacement as a function of time is equal to the vector sum of the displacements produced by each wave.*

So, for example, at a time t, if one wave is causing a displacement of $\vec{y_1} = 5\hat{j}$ cm, and another wave is causing a displacement of $\vec{y_2} = -2\hat{j}$ cm, the net displacement at that point is $\vec{y} = \vec{y_1} + \vec{y_2} = (5-2)\hat{j} = 3\hat{j}$ cm.

What is interference?

Interference is a phenomenon that results when two waves that differ in phase cause different displacements at the same point.

Constructive interference is said to occur when the two waves are in phase at a point in space, they reinforce each other at that point and the resultant amplitude is greater than the amplitudes of the individual waves.

Destructive interference is said to occur when the two waves are out of phase and the resultant amplitude is reduced.

With regards to interference, what are nodes and antinodes?

For a given frequency, *nodes* are points of destructive interference where no movement occurs, while *antinodes* are points where constructive interference occurs and maximum wave movement occurs.

If you oscillate a rope between you and a fixed point and at a fixed frequency, a *standing wave* will be formed. Nodes will appear where there is no movement in the

---

[2]The relevance of this is that to calculate the intensity at a point, we must first calculate the amplitude at that point and then square it.

rope, and antinodes will appear at the crests and troughs of the oscillating rope.

What is another name for frequencies that produce standing waves?

Resonant or natural frequencies.

What are fundamental frequencies?

A wave with only one antinode:

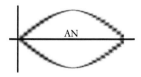

Figure 65.5: The fundamental frequency has one antinode (AN) and no nodes. Therefore the wavelength is equal to $1/2\lambda$.

How are integral multiples of fundamental frequencies calculated?

The fundamental mode is the 1st harmonic, the 2nd harmonic is the first overtone, the nth harmonic is the $(n-1)^{th}$ overtone, and so on. The fundamental frequencies can be calculated with Equation 66.2 below:

$$L = n\left(\frac{\lambda}{2}\right) \tag{65.8}$$

Where L is the length of the string in meters (m), n is any integral number, and λ is the wavelength of the wave in meters (m). Note that each half-wavelength extra is an extra harmonic. Examples of the second and third harmonics can also be seen below in Figure 65.6.

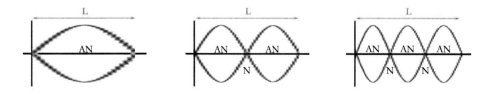

Figure 65.6: The first harmonic with a wavelength of $2L$ (left), second harmonic with a wavelength of L (center), and third harmonic with a wavelength of $\frac{2}{3}L$ (right) where AN means antinode and N means node.

What is refraction?

The change in direction of propagation (and velocity) of a wave at an interface separating two different media. Snell's Law of refraction, as discussed on page 451 and illustrated with Figure 67.4 on page 451, gives the relation between the incident and refracted angles and wave velocities.

What is diffraction?

When a huge obstacle is placed in front of a wave, the wave is unable to reach points behind the obstacle. This region is now part of the "shadow" of the obstacle. However, diffraction is observed when the size of the obstacle is comparable to the wavelength of the wave, the wave bends around the obstacle. This phenomenon is called diffraction. Visible light has very small wavelengths (about 400 - 700nm) and requires very small obstacles for diffraction to be observed (see Figure 68.4 on page 459), but diffraction can be observed daily with sound, e.g. an ambulance's siren can sometimes be observed around the corner of buildings.

Chapter 66

Sound

66.1 Characteristics of Sound

What is sound?

Energy in the form of longitudinal pressure waves transmitted through a medium from a vibrating object. For example, a clap changes air pressure around it. This disturbance propagates through the air and reaches your ear.

What affects the transmission of sound?

1. *Density (ρ)*: The denser the object the faster the transmission of sound. Therefore, sound transmission is greatest for solids and liquids and less so for gases.

2. *Temperature*[1]: The warmer a gas, the faster the sound transmission.

3. *Elastic modulus (B)*: The relative stiffness of a material, B is also directly related with the rate of sound transmission.

What is sound attenuation?

The decrease in sound intensity resulting from sound wave scattering and absorption by the transmitting medium.

66.2 Quantifying Sound

What is the difference between pitch and frequency?

Pitch is the qualitative nature of sound, i.e. high pitch like a flute or low pitch like a bass guitar. Frequency is the quantitative nature of pitch and assigns a number in Hz to the pitch. For example, the pitch of a "C" note is equivalent to a frequency of

---

[1]Temperature affects sound transmission particularly in gases; less so for solids and liquids.

262 Hz.

How is sound intensity measured?

In decibels (dB) that can be calculated with Equation 66.1 below:

$$\beta = 10 \log \frac{I}{I_o} \qquad (66.1)$$

Where β is the sound intensity measured in dB[2]. I is the sound intensity measured in W/m^2 and I_o is the sound intensity of a reference value and is also measured in W/m^2. I_o is the threshold of human hearing is 10^{-12} (corresponding to $\approx 2.5 \ x \ 10^{-5}$!).

Because dB's represent a log relationship, a 10-fold increase in dB's results in a 10-fold (10^1) increase in intensity, a 20-fold increase in dB's will result in a 100-fold (10^2) increase in intensity, a 30-fold increase in dB's will result in a 1000-fold (10^3) increase in intensity, etc.

66.3   Doppler Effect

What is the Doppler effect?

Principle 10 *When there is a relative motion between a source of sound and an observer, the observed frequency is different from the frequency emitted by the source.*

In other words, when a sound source is moving towards an object, the frequency of the sound will increase. When a sound source is moving away from an object, the frequency of the sound will decrease. For light, when light moves towards an observer, the frequency will increase (also known as a blue shift). When the observer moves away from the source, the frequency will decrease (also known as a red shift).

66.4   Sound in Pipes and Strings

What differences in sound transmission exist between a tube open at one end and a tube open at both ends?

Sound transmission can be viewed in two ways: (1) displacement, the flow of air, or (2) pressure, the compression or expansion of air. Table 66.1 and figure 66.1 below outlines the salient differences of each. HIgh pressure results in a *node* making the air contract and restricting its movement. Conversely, an *antinode* is an area of low pressure and high displacement.

---

[2]1 B = 10dB; this is taken into account by the "10" on the right side of Equation 66.1

	Open at one end (e.g. a flute)	Open at **both** ends (e.g. a saxophone)
Fundamental frequency (First harmonic)	$\lambda_1 = 4L$	$\lambda_1 = 2L$
Air displacement **antinode** of fundamental	Antinodes at open end	Antinodes at both ends
Air displacement **node** of fundamental	Node at closed end	Nodes at the middle
Air pressure **antinode** of fundamental	One antinode at closed end	One antinode in the middle
Air pressure **node** of fundamental	One node at open end	Nodes at both ends
Harmonics produced	Odd harmonics	All harmonics

Table 66.1: Sound transmission in a tube open at one end vs. a tube open at both ends. In both examples, L is held constant and λ_n changes with n.

Sound is depicted below as a transverse wave for ease of visualization (although normally it is a longitudinal wave and should strictly be represented by enhanced and rarified region of density of air):

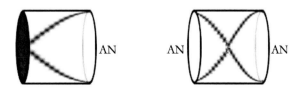

Figure 66.1: Sound transmission in a tube open at one end (left) and a tube open at both ends (right). Think of the antinode (AN) as a point with the maximal air movement (low pressure) which invariably has to occur at the open end (this would correspond to position "b" of the pendulum in figure 65.3 on page 439).

How are harmonic frequencies calculated?

Harmonics (all λ) or overtones (any λ_n where $n > 1$) are fundamental frequencies with decreased wavelengths that can be calculated with Equation 66.2 below:

$$L = \frac{n}{2}\lambda_n \qquad\qquad (66.2)$$

Where L is the length of the string in meters (m), n is any integral number, and λ_n is the wavelength of the wave in meters (m). Diagrams of harmonics can be seen in Figure 65.6 on 442. In this situation, L is being held fixed and different waves of different λ_n values (depending on n) can "fit" into this L. The longest λ_n has $n = 1$, corresponding to one AN.

66.5   Ultrasound

How does ultrasound work?

A pulse of sound is emitted by a transmitter. The sound waves enter the body and reflect off of internal organs. The transmitter records the echoes (sound reflections) and converts this information into an image. The Doppler effect can also be used to convey information on the direction of blood flow (see *Doppler shifts* on page 446 of this chapter).

Chapter 67

Geometrical Optics

What is geometrical optics?

The branch of physics that assumes that light travels in straight lines, i.e. rays.

67.1 Reflection

What is the law of reflection?

Law 14 *Given a plane, the angle of light incidence equals the angle of reflection.*

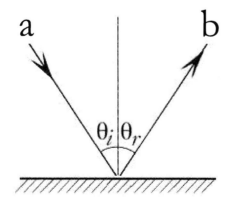

Figure 67.1: The law of reflection: Incident light ray (a) and reflected light ray (b).

What is the difference between a virtual image and a real image?

Light *does not travel through a virtual image* while light travels *through a real image.* Moreover, virtual images cannot be photographed and maintain the same orientation as the object. On the contrary, real images can be photographed and are usually inverted.

In finding the position of a virtual image, the rays of light reaching your eyes are said to "originate" from this virtual image, by tracing the path of this light backward. For example an apple in front of a mirror:

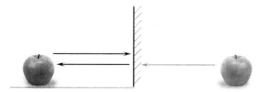

Figure 67.2: The virual image of the apple seems to be at a distance D behind the mirror, but if you placed a camera behind the mirror, it will not detect an image.

Real and virtual images are also created when light travels through lens and mirrors:

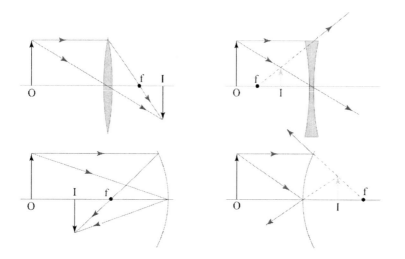

Figure 67.3: Real vs. virtual images: Real images (left): Formation of a real image using a convex lens (top) and a concave mirror (bottom). The image is formed by actual light rays and thus can form a visible image on a screen placed at the position of the image. Virtual images (right): Formation of a virtual image using a concave lens (top) and a convex mirror (bottom). Light rays appear to emanate from the virtual image but do not actually exist at the position of the virtual image. Therefore, an image cannot be formed by placing a screen at the position of the virtual image. In both diagrams, f is the focal point, O is the object, I is the image and *solid blue lines* indicate light rays [6].

67.2   Refraction

What is refraction?

Refraction is the bending of light as it passes from one medium to another provided that the angle of incidence is not perpendicular to the plane between the two mediums:

Figure 67.4: Refraction: Light (arrow) traveling from one medium to another. The perpendicular is the "normal".

What is Snell's law?

Also referred to as the basic law of refraction, Snell's Law provides a relation between the incident and refracted angles and the refractive indices of the two media, where θ_1 is the angle of incidence and θ_2 is the angle of refraction:

Law 15
$$n_1 \sin \theta_1 = n_2 \sin \theta_2 \tag{67.1}$$

What is the index of refraction and what is its effect on the direction of light travel during refraction?

The refractive index of an interface between light traveling from media 1 to 2 is equal to the ratio of the velocities of light in these media:

$$n_{1 \to 2} = \frac{v_1}{v_2} \tag{67.2}$$

Usually the first medium is chosen to be a vacuum so that v_1 equals c:

$$n_{1 \to 2} = n_2 = \frac{2}{v_2} \tag{67.3}$$

Note, the index of refraction changes for different wavelengths. Light will bend toward the normal if its speed is decreased, indicating that the medium has a higher index of refraction. Conversely, light will bend away from the normal if its speed is increased, indicating that the medium has a lower index of refraction.

67.3   Internal Reflection

What is total internal reflection?

In refraction, for very large incident angles, the light ray bends so much that it "bends back" into the original medium as seen below in Figure 67.6.

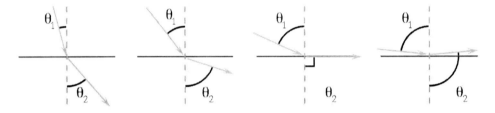

Figure 67.5: Total internal reflection: total internal reflection occurs when $\theta_1 < \theta_C$ (far left and left middle), reflection perpendicular to the normal occurs when $\theta_1 = \theta_C$ (right middle) and reflection off of the medium occurs when $\theta_1 > \theta_C$ (far right).

θ_C is the critical angle above which the light rays is effectively "reflected" into the original medium - a phenomenon called total internal reflection. Using Snell's law $\theta_1 = \theta_2$ and $\theta = 90^o$ gives:

$$\frac{n_2}{n_1} = \sin \theta_C \qquad (67.4)$$

As $\sin \theta_C \lesssim 1$ always, $n_2 \lesssim n_1$. Therefore, total internal reflection can only happen for light rays going from a denser to a rarer medium.

This concept has a real life application: optical fibers. Optical fibers consist of a dense core of refractive index n_1 surrounded by a rarer cladding of index n_2, so that total internal reflection can occur. Any light ray entering the core undergoes successive reflections to get to the other end:

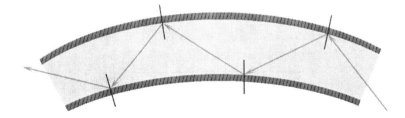

Figure 67.6: Optical fibers: A light ray entering the core will undergo successive reflections to get to the other end (blue lines reflect normals).

67.4 Spherical Mirrors

What are the key components of spherical mirrors?

- The **center of curvature (C)** is the center of a sphere in which the mirror makes a small part its circumference. The distance from C to any point on the mirror is the radius of curvature (r).

- The **focal length** is the distance between the spherical mirror and the points of all light ray intersections. The focal length can be calculated with Equation 67.5 below where r is the radius of curvature:

$$f = \frac{r}{2} \qquad (67.5)$$

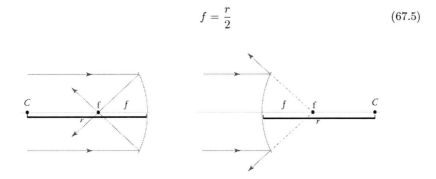

Figure 67.7: Key components of concave (left) and convex (right) mirrors: center (C) and radius (r) of curvature, focal point (f) and the focal length (f).

67.5 Thin Lenses

What are two types of thin lenses?

- **Converging lenses** are *thicker* in the middle of the lens and make parallel rays of light converge to a point called its focus.

- **Diverging lenses** are *thinner* in the middle of the lens and make parallel rays of light seem to diverge from an imaginary point called its focus.

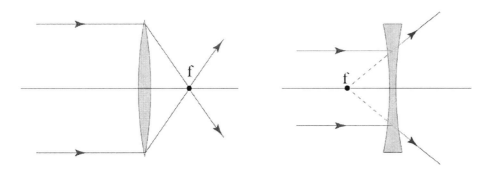

Figure 67.8: Converging (left) and diverging (right) lenses.

- **Magnification** (m): $m > 0$ for an erect, upright virtual image; $m < 0$ for an inverted real image:

$$m = \frac{h_o}{h_i} = -\frac{d_i}{d_o} \tag{67.6}$$

What is the lens equation?

$$\frac{1}{f} = \frac{1}{d_o} + \frac{1}{d_i} \tag{67.7}$$

Where f is the focal length, d_o is the distance of the object and d_i is the distance of the image.

What are the sign conventions for lenses?

- f is positive for converging lenses
- f is negative for diverging lenses
- d_o is positive if the object is on the same side of the lens as the light source
- d_i is positive if the object is on the *opposite* side of the lens as the light source
- d_i is positive for real images with the image on the other side of the lens
- d_i is negative for virtual images with the image on the same side of the lens
- Heights measured "upward" are positive and vice versa

How is lens strength calculated?

$$P = \frac{1}{f} \tag{67.8}$$

Where P is the lens power in diopters (D) and f is the focal length of the lens.

Chapter 68

Light

What is light?

The term "light" refers to electromagnetic (EM) waves (or EM radiation). Three main properties of EM waves are:

1. **E and B**: EM waves consist of E and B fields with simple harmonic oscillating in two mutually perpendicular planes. The "path" of propagation of the EM wave is the intersection of these two planes. At any point on this path, the $\vec{E}$ and $\vec{B}$ vectors are perpendicular to each other, and the direction of propagation of the EM wave is found using the right hand rule[1].

2. **Speed of light**: The speed of propagation of the wave depends on the amplitudes (maximum values) of the E and B - In a vacuum, it is approximately 3×10^8 m/s.

3. **No medium required**: EM waves do not need a medium for propagating through space. This is why they can travel through vacuum, unlike sound.

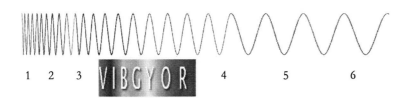

Figure 68.1: The electromagnetic spectrum: gamma rays (1), X-rays (2), gamma rays (3), the visible portion of the EM spectrum (ROY G BIV), infrared (4), microwaves (5) and radiowaves (6). As one moves from left to right, the wavelength increases and the energy decreases.

What is the relationship between wavelength, λ, and frequency, f?

$$f = \frac{c}{\lambda} \tag{68.1}$$

---

[1]Borrowing from the right hand rule, raise your right-hand as if you were giving a high five: your thumb pointing to the left would represent the pathway of the light, your fingers pointing towards the sky would represent the electric field (E) and a vector leaving the palm of your hand outward in front of you would represent the magnetic field (B).

68.1   Interference, Diffraction, Refraction & Young's Experiment

What is diffraction?

The apparent bending or spreading of light when it encounters an object.

What is diffraction grating?

Diffraction grating is a device with parallel, equally spaced grooves that allow for multiple diffractions and separate the incident light beam into its wavelength components to produce a spectrum of colors. This is visually similar to the spectrum produced by a prism, though the mechanism is very different. The mechanism behind prisms is the *slowing of light* by passing it from one medium to another, e.g. air to glass. In diffraction grating, the principle of wave-interference allows for the separation of light into its spectrum of colors.

What is refraction?

Discussed in the above answer, refraction is the change in direction of a wave due to a change in its velocity. This occurs when light passes from a medium with a different refractive incidence to another and explains the mechanisms behind prisms, the twinkle-twinkle of diamonds, etc. For for more information (including a review of Snell's Law), refer to page 451 in the *Geometrical Optics* chapter.

When do thin films refract light?

When a beam of light is reflected by a substance whose index of refraction is greater than that of the material in which it is traveling. This causes a change in phase by 1/2 a cycle. Such effects - i.e. thin-film refraction - can be seen when a puddle forms on freshly paved asphalt: the petroleum residue coats a thin film over puddles and one can see a spectrum of colors.

What is Young's double-slit experiment?

The landmark experiment which introduced the concept of *wave-interference* using visible light. Similar to wave interference covered on page 441 in the *Periodic Motion & Wave* chapter, Young's experiment revealed alternating lines of light and absence of light. The absence of light is the result of destructive interference while the presence of light indicates constructive interference. To achieve this, Young used two *closely-spaced* slits, as can be seen in Figure 68.3 on page 458.

How can the minima (i.e. points of zero light intensity) be determined in single-slit diffraction?

$$D \sin \theta = m\lambda \qquad (68.2)$$

Where D is the width of the single slit in meters (m), θ is the angle of the light compared to the perpendicular, m is the integer value and represents the *minima* (i.e. points of destructive interference and an absence of light), and λ corresponds to the wavelength of the light in meters (m). See Figure 68.2 below and 68.4 on page 459 for an illustration of this concept.

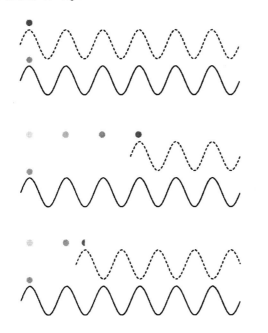

Figure 68.2: Path & phase differences between waves: Waves in phase (top), wave in phase with one moved to the right by three wavelengths, i.e. $6 \times \frac{\lambda}{2}$ (middle), wave out of phase with one moved to the right by one and a half wavelengths, i.e. $3 \times \frac{\lambda}{2}$ (bottom).

68.2   X-ray Diffraction

What is X-ray diffraction?

X-ray crystallography is a technique which takes advantage of the organized atomic lattice structure of crystals and uses x-ray beams to examine their structures. The physics behind x-ray crystallography is definitely beyond the scope of the MCAT but appreciate that it is a powerful technique that has allowed scientists to better understand the microscopic world. One amazing application of x-ray crystallography was by a woman scientist by the name of Dr. Rosalind Franklin who suggested that DNA is a helix before Watson and Crick's formal discovery.

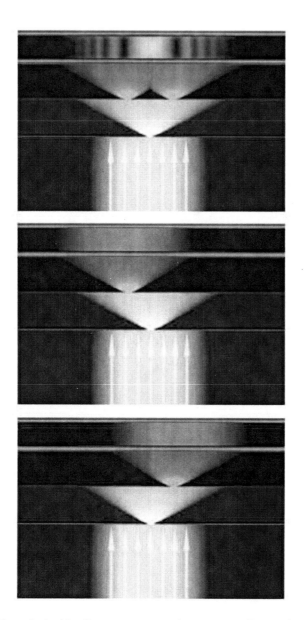

Figure 68.3: Young's double-slit experiment: right gate open (bottom), left gate open (middle) and both gates open (top). The absence of light is the result of destructive interference, while the presence of light indicates constructive interference.

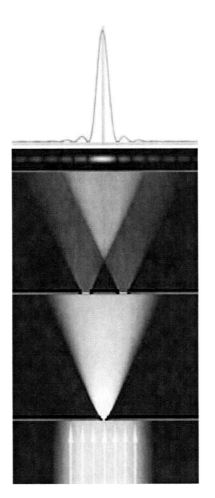

Figure 68.4: Single slit diffraction model with a plot of light intensity (y-axis) and θ (x-axis) above diffraction model.

Chapter 69

Radioactivity

69.1   Radioactive decay: α, β & γ Decay

What is radioactive decay?

The decay or disintegration of unstable atomic nuclei via three main mechanisms (alpha, α, beta, β, and gamma, γ, decay) outlined below:

- α decay occurs when a nucleus emits an α particle: $^{4}_{2}\text{He}$. Losing a $^{4}_{2}\text{He}$ results in an atom that has lost two protons and two neutrons[1].

- β decay occurs when a nucleus emits a β particle, i.e. an electron (e^{-}), $^{0}_{-1}e$, or a positron (e^{+}), $^{0}_{+1}e$. Unlike the formation of an ion where a valence shell electron is lost or gained, in β decay, the emitted particle **comes from the nucleus proper**.

- γ decay occurs when a nucleus falls to a lower state of excitation and emits high energy photons in the form of γ rays. Comparatively, when an electron falls to a lower excitation state X-rays are produced which are 1/1000 the strength of γ rays.

Type of decay	Particle released
α decay	$^{4}_{2}\text{He}$
β decay	$^{0}_{+1}e$ and $^{0}_{-1}e$
γ decay	γ rays

Table 69.1: Particles released during radioactive decay.

---

[1]See the inorganic chemistry chapter *Electronic Structure* for a review of conventional notation for electronic structure.

69.2   Half-life: $T_{1/2}$ & Exponential Decay

What is $T_{1/2}$?

A very important concept: $T_{1/2}$ is the time it takes for a substance to reduce in quantity by **half**.

Law 16

$$T_{1/2} = \frac{0.693}{\lambda} \qquad (69.1)$$

Where $T_{1/2}$ is the half-life of a given substance, 0.693 is derived number[2], and λ is the decay constant for a given substance. Using this equation, you can calculate the λ for a substance if given the $T_{1/2}$ or vice versa.

# of $T_{1/2}$	Percent of original remaining (%)	Fraction Left
0	100	1
1	50	1/2
2	25	1/4
3	12.5	1/8
4	6.25	1/16
5	~3.0	1/32
6	~1.5	1/64
7	~1.0	1/128
⋮	⋮	⋮
n	$\frac{1}{2^n}$ x 100%	$1/2^n$

Table 69.2: Percent of original substance remaining based on the numbers of $T_{1/2}$ that have transpired.

What is exponential decay?

Radioactive decay is an example of *exponential decay*. If we started with N_0 nuclei at time $t = 0$, the number of nuclei at time $t = t$ that have *not* undergone radioactive decay, $N(t)$ (usually abbreviated as N) is given by the exponential law:

$$N(t) = N_0 e^{-\lambda t} \qquad (69.2)$$

Abive, λ is the decay constant, and depends on the type of nucleus under consideration. The inverse of the decay constant, $\tau \equiv 1/\lambda$, is called the mean lifetime of the sample. With some manipulation of equation 69.3[3] you see that the mean lifetime is the time taken for about 100-37=63% of the nuclei in the original sample to have decayed. See Figure 69.1 below on page 463.

---

[2] $e^{-\lambda T_{1/2}} = \frac{1}{2} \Rightarrow T_{1/2} = \frac{\ln 2}{\lambda} \approx \frac{0.693}{\lambda}$
[3] $N(t = \tau) = N_0 e^{-\lambda/\lambda} = N_0/e \approx 37\%$ of N_0

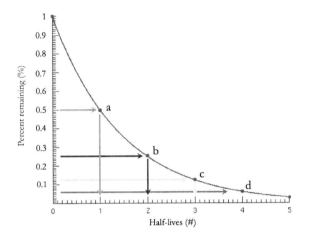

Figure 69.1: Exponential decay: Plot of decay over time where, after one half-life 50% remains (a), two half-lives 25% remains (b), three half-lives 12.5% remains (c), four half-lives 6.25% remains (d).

What is activity?

The number of disintegrations (i.e. number of nuclei decaying) per unit time. The activity A of a sample also decays according to the exponential law:

$$A(t) = A_0 e^{\lambda t} \qquad\qquad (69.3)$$

Where A_0 is the activity at time $t = 0$. Activity has the unit of Becquerel (Bq), which equals 1 disintegration per second $(1\ \mathrm{Bq} = 1\ \mathrm{s}^{-1})$.[4].

69.3   Fission & Fusion

What is nuclear fission and fusion?

Nuclear fission occurs when a nucleus splits into two or more smaller nuclei, releasing substantial amounts of energy and photons in the form of γ rays. Fission is the process used by nuclear reactors to make energy to heat water and produce steam.

Nuclear fusion occurs when two nuclei join, forming a larger nucleus. This process is believed to fuel the sun and depending on the size of the nuclei, energy can be released or absorbed.

The ^{56}Fe isotope of iron is the most stable nucleus and elements below iron undergo fusion preferentially to reach iron, while elements above iron undergo fission preferentially. Opposing this trend usually requires energy while following the trend releases

---

[4]Although not something you need to memorize, a more commonly used unit is the Curie (Ci) where $1\ Ci = 3.7 \times 10^{10}$ Bq.

energy.

What is mass deficit?

Mass deficit is seen in fusion and fission in which the products have less mass than the sum of the parts (i.e. the "parent" atoms): The "lost" mass is converted into energy. This relationship was made famous by a publication from Albert Einstein[5] in which he stated the equation $E = mc^2$.

69.4   Questions

What is mass deficit?

Mass deficit is seen in fusion and fission in which the products have less mass than the sum of the parts (i.e. the "parent" atoms): The "lost" mass is converted into energy. This relationship was made famous by a publication from Albert Einstein[6] in which he stated the equation $E = mc^2$.

Often times, it is not always necessary to invoke the exponential decay equation for every problem involving. The knowledge of the powers of two can be a very powerful problem solving tool:

1. ^{14}C has a half-life of about 5700 years. How long does it take for a sample to display only 25% of its original activity?

   Answer: 25% means only one fourth of the sample remains. $2^2 = 4$, so two half-lifes have passed. Each half-life is 5700 years, so the total time taken is 5700×2=11400 years.

2. In 1954, Kaufmann and Libby[7] used tritium[8] dating to date several French and Italian wines. The activities of a recently bottled wine and a 49.2 year-old bottle are respectively 1200 and 75 Bq. Find the half-life of tritium.

   Answer: The ratio of activities is 1200/75=16=2^4, so four half-lifes equals 49.2 years. Therefore, the half-life of tritium is about 12.3 years.

---

[5]Although this equation is attributed to Einstein, many scientists used this equation, including Newton, and Preston; but it was Olinto de Pretto who used it two years before Einstein's paper.

[6]Although this equation is attributed to Einstein, many scientists used this equation, including Newton, and Preston; but it was Olinto de Pretto who used it two years before Einstein's paper.

[7]S. Kaufman, W.L.Libby, Physical Review, 93, No. 6, (1954), 1337

[8]Tritium is a heavy isotope of Hydrogen, its nucleus contains two neutrons in addition to one proton.

Bibliography

[1] Campbell, N.A. *Biology*. Benjamin/Cummings Publishing Co.

[2] Giancoli, D. C. *Physics*. Prentice Hall.

[3] Alberts, B., Johnson, A., Lewis, J., Raff, M., Roberts, K., Walter, P. *Molecular Biology of the Cell*. Garland Publishing.

[4] Carey, F. A.*Organic Chemistry*. McGraw-Hill.

[5] Solomons, T. W. G.*Organic Chemistry*. Wiley.

[6] www.wikipedia.com

Index

Printed in the United States
121672LV00009B/4/P